GOD, TRUTH AND REALITY

John Hick

God, Truth and Reality

Essays in Honour of John Hick

Edited by

Arvind Sharma
Professor of Religious Studies
McGill University, Montreal, Canada

St. Martin's Press

Essay Index

First published in Great Britain 1993 by
THE MACMILLAN PRESS LTD
Houndmills, Basingstoke, Hampshire RG21 2XS
and London
Companies and representatives
throughout the world

A catalogue record for this book is available
from the British Library.

ISBN 0–333–54836–1

Printed in Great Britain by
Antony Rowe Ltd
Chippenham, Wiltshire

First published in the United States of America 1993 by
Scholarly and Reference Division,
ST. MARTIN'S PRESS, INC.,
175 Fifth Avenue,
New York, N.Y. 10010

ISBN 0–312–09109–5

Library of Congress Cataloging-in-Publication Data
God, truth and reality : essays in honour of John Hick / edited by
Arvind Sharma.
p.   cm.
ISBN 0–312–09109–5
1. Religion—Philosophy.   2. Theology.   3. Religions—Relations.
4. Hick, John.   I. Hick, John.   II. Sharma, Arvind.
BL51.G685   1993
200'.1—dc20   92–34121
                                                         CIP

Contents

v

Notes on the Contributors

Masao Abe, a leading interpreter of Buddhism, is a prominent participant in contemporary Buddhist–Christian dialogue. He is the author of numerous articles and has published extensively in both Japanese and English. His book *Zen and Western Thought* (1985) won the Book of Excellence award from the American Academy of Religion in 1987 and is being translated into German.

Marilyn McCord Adams is Professor of Philosophy at UCLA. Her publications divide between philosophy of religion and medieval philosophy and include her two-volume work *William Ockham* as well as numerous articles on Anselm and the problem of evil. She is also an Episcopal priest.

Robert Merrihew Adams is Professor of Philosophy at UCLA, where he has taught for twenty years. He formerly taught at the University of Michigan, and has been a visiting professor at Yale Divinity School. Educated in philosophy at Princeton and Cornell, and in theology at Oxford and Princeton Theological Seminary, he is the author of *The Virtue of Faith and Other Essays in Philosophical Theology*, and of many articles on metaphysics, ethics, and the history of philosophy, as well as the philosophy of religion.

William P. Alston teaches in the Department of Philosophy at the University of Syracuse. He is the editor of *Religious Belief and Philosophical Thought: Readings in the Philosophy of Religion* (1963) and co-editor of *The Problems of Philosophy: Introductory Readings* (3rd edn, 1978). His books include *Philosophy of Language* (1964); *Epistemic Justification: Essays in the Theory of Knowledge* (1989); and *Divine Nature and Human Language: Essays in Philosophical Theology* (1989).

Mohammed Arkoun, Professor of Islamic Thought at the Sorbonne (Paris III), received his Diplôme d'Etudes Supérieures from the University of Algiers in 1954 and taught Arabic language and literature in his native Algeria before receiving his doctorate in Islamic Studies from the Sorbonne in 1969. He was subsequently visiting professor at UCLA, the University of Lyon (II), the Pontifical Institute of Arab

Studies in Rome, l'Université de Louvain-la-Neuve, Princeton, and Temple University. His research and teaching have focused on Islamic philosophy, ethics, and law, both in the medieval and modern Arab context. He has lectured at universities throughout North Africa and the Middle East, as well as in Europe, Asia, and North America, and has published over twenty works in French, English, and Arabic, including *Aspects de la pensée islamique* (1963), *Al-Fikr al-'arabiyy* (1979), *L'Islam, hier, demain* (1982), *Pour une critique de la Raison islamique* (1984), *Arab Thought* (1988), *The Concept of Revelation: From Ahl al-Kitâb to the Societies of the Book* (1988), *Al-islâm: nagd wajtihâd* (1990), and *Penser l'Islam aujourd'hui* (1991). He is currently scientific director for the journal *Arabica* and is turning his attention increasingly toward the relationship between modern Islam and the West.

Paul Badham holds a personal chair, is Professor and Head of Department as well as Dean of the Faculty of Theology and Religious Studies at St David's University College, Lampster, in the University of Wales. He was a former research student of John Hick in Birmingham and is the Editor of *A John Hick Reader* (Macmillan, 1990).

John Bowker was formerly Professor of Religious Studies at the University of Lancaster, and is now a Fellow of Trinity College, Cambridge. He is also Adjunct Professor at the University of Pennsylvania, and at North Carolina State University. Among his recent books are *Licensed Insanities: Religions and Belief in God in the Contemporary World* (US title, *Is Anybody Out There?*); *The Meanings of Death* (1991: a sequel to *Problems of Suffering in Religions of the World*); and *A Year to Live* 1991). He is editor of *The Oxford Companion to Religions of the World*, which, after ten years' work, is drawing close to completion.

John B. Cobb, Jr was born in Japan of Methodist missionary parents from Georgia. He received his MA and PhD degrees from the Divinity School of the University of Chicago. He taught at Young Harris College and Emory University before going to Claremont, California, in 1958. There he taught at the school of Theology at Claremont and the Claremont Graduate School until his retirement in 1990. His publications include *A Christian Natural Theology, The Structure of Christian Existence, Christ in a Pluralistic Age, Beyond Dialogue, The*

Liberation of Life (with Charles Birch), *For the Common Good* (with Herman Daly), and *Matters of Life and Death*.

Langdon B. Gilkey has taught theology at The Divinity School of the University of Chicago and previously at Vanderbilt University. He holds a PhD from Union Theological Seminary. His works include *Naming the Whirlwind* (1969); *Religion and the Scientific Future* (1970); *Reaping the Whirlwind* (1976); *Message and Existence* (1979); *Society and the Sacred* (1981) and *Gilkey on Tillich* (1990).

Brian Hebblethwaite is Fellow and Dean of Queens' College, Cambridge, and University Lecturer in Divinity, specialising in philosophy of religion and ethics. He was educated at Magdalen College, Oxford and Magdalene College, Cambridge, before training for the ministry at Westcott House, Cambridge. He was for three years a curate in Lancashire, and returned to Cambridge in 1968. His publications include *Evil, Suffering and Religion* (1976), *The Problems of Theology* (1980), *The Adequacy of Christian Ethics* (1981), *The Christian Hope* (1984), *The Incarnation* (1987) and *The Ocean of Truth* (1988).

Anders Jeffner is Professor of Theological and Ideological Studies at Uppsala University, Sweden, since 1976. He holds degrees in philosophy, theology and psychology from Uppsala University and obtained his doctorate in philosophy of religion in Uppsala, 1966. In his research he has dealt mainly with three areas: history of ideas – especially in the borderlines between theology, philosophy and natural science; modern philosophical theology; and empirical research on worldviews and value-systems among ordinary people. His main publications in English and German: *Butler and Hume on Religion: A Comparative Analysis* (1966); *The Study of Religious Language* (1972); *Kriterien christlicher Glaubenslehre. Eine prinzipielle Untersuchung heutiger protestancher Dogmatik im deutschen Sprachbereich* (1977); *Theology and Integration* (1987); two chapters in *The World's Religions*, ed. by S. Sutherland, L. Houlden and F. Hardy (1988), and articles in English and German journals. He has also published seven books and many articles in Swedish.

Gordon D. Kaufman, Mallinckrodt Professor of Divinity in Harvard Divinity School, received his graduate training principally at Yale Divinity School (BD, 1951; PhD, 1955); before moving to Harvard (in

1963) he taught at Pomona College and at Vanderbilt Divinity School. He has concentrated his teaching and his professional work on questions of philosophical theology, theological method and philosophy of religion, and has lectured in universities in Europe, Asia and South Africa, as well as in North America. He has published a number of books, among them *Relativism, Knowledge and Faith* (1960), *Systematic Theology: a Historicist Perspective* (1968), *An Essay on Theological Method* (1975), *The Theological Imagination: Constructing the Concept of God* (1981), and *Theology for a Nuclear Age* (1985); and he is presently completing a major constructive work setting out a 'biohistorical' approach to Christian theology.

Terence Penelhum is Professor Emeritus of Religious Studies at the University of Calgary, where he was formerly Dean of Arts and Science and Director of the Calgary Institute for the Humanities. He was educated at the University of Edinburgh and Oriel College, Oxford, and has held many visiting teaching positions in Canada and the United States. His main interests are philosophy of religion and the history of modern philosophy, and his books include *Survival and Disembodied Existence, Problems of Religious Knowledge, Religion and Rationality, God and Skepticism, Butler* and *David Hume: an Introduction to his Philosophical System.*

William L. Rowe is Professor of Philosophy at Purdue University. He has taught at the University of Illinois and held visiting appointments at Wayne State University and the University of Michigan. His publications include *Religious Symbols and God, The Cosmological Argument, Philosophy of Religion, Thomas Reid on Freedom and Morality* and numerous articles. He has held a Guggenheim Fellowship, has been a fellow at the National Humanities Center, and is a past president of the Central Division of the American Philosophical Association.

Arvind Sharma is Professor in the Faculty of Religious Studies at McGill University, Montreal. He previously taught Indian philosophies, Indian religions and comparative religion in Australia and the USA. He holds an MA in economics from Syracuse University, a master's in theological studies from the Harvard Divinity School and a doctorate in Sanskrit and Indian studies from Harvard University.

Ninian Smart is J. F. Rowny Professor of Comparative Religions in the Department of Religious Studies at the University of California, Santa Barbara. He was previously founding professor of the Department of Religious Studies in the University of Lancaster, the first department of its kind in the UK. He has published a number of books of which he is chiefly proud of *Reasons and Faiths, Doctrine and Argument in Indian Philosophy, The Religious Experience, Philosophers and Religious Truth, Worldviews* and *The World's Religions*.

Rabbi Dr Norman Solomon is founder and director of the Centre for Jewish Christian Relations. Born in Cardiff, South Wales, he is a graduate of St John's College, Cambridge. He served as a pulpit Rabbi at orthodox congregations in Britain from 1961 to 1983. His book *Judaism and World Religions* was published by Macmillan, London, and St. Martin's Press, New York in 1991. He is the author of numerous monographs, and edits the journal *Christian–Jewish Relations* for the Institute of Jewish Affairs, London.

Stewart Sutherland was awarded a degree in Philosophy at the University of Aberdeen in 1963 and a degree in Philosophy of Religion at the University of Cambridge in 1965 where he was taught by John Hick during the Lent Term of 1965. He taught at the University of North Wales and the University of Stirling before being appointed to the Chair of Professor of History and Philosophy of Religion at King's College in 1977. In 1985 he was appointed Principal of King's College and since September 1990 has been Vice-Chancellor of the University of London. His major publications are *Atheism and the Rejection of God* (1977); *God, Jesus and Belief* (1984); *Faith and Ambiguity* (1984) and *The World's Religions* (ed., 1988). He was editor of *Religious Studies* from 1984 to 1990. Public appointments include Chairman of the British Academy Postgraduate Studentship Committee 1987– and Chairman of the Council of the Royal Institute of Philosophy 1988– .

Keith Ward is Regius Professor of Divinity in the University of Oxford. He is also Chairman of the World Congress of Faiths. He has taught theology and philosophy at a number of universities. Among previous appointments he has been Dean of Trinity Hall, Cambridge and Professor of the History and Philosophy of Religion at King's College, University of London. His main relevant publications are:

The Concept of God (1974); *Rational Theology and the Creativity of God* (1982); *Images of Eternity* (1987); *Divine Action* (1990); and *A Vision to Pursue* (1991).

Maurice Wiles, after reading Moral Sciences and Theology at Cambridge, taught in the University of Ibadan (1955–9). He was Dean of Clare College and University Lecturer in Divinity (1959–67) at Cambridge, and Professor of Christian Doctrine, King's College, London (1967–70), and then Regius Professor of Divinity and Canon of Christ Church, Oxford, until his retirement in 1991.

His main work has been in Patristics, with a special interest in patristic exegesis and Arianism (*The Spiritual Gospel*, 1960; *The Christian Fathers*, 1966; *The Divine Apostle*, 1967; *The Making of Christian Doctrine*, 1967) and in contemporary theological method (*The Remaking of Christian Doctrine*, 1974; *What is Theology?*, 1976; *Faith and the Mystery of God*, 1982; *God's Action in the World*, 1986).

Seiichi Yagi was born in 1932 in Yokohama, Japan. He studied philosophy at Tokyo University and completed his graduate work in Western classics at the graduate school thereof before continuing his study of the New Testament at the University of Göttingen in Germany. Presently he is Professor of Philosophy and Ethics at Toin University of Yokohama. He has also taught at the Tokyo Institute of Technology, Tokyo University, Berne University in Switzerland and Hamburg University in Germany on the Buddhist-Christian dialogue in which he has been engaged. His books include *Christ and Jesus, Contact points between Buddhism and Christianity* and *Paul/Shinran – Jesus/Zen*. His several Dialogues with Zen-Masters and Zen-philosophers have also been published.

Part I
A Biographical Sketch

The Life and Work of John Hick

PAUL BADHAM

John Hick was born in Yorkshire in 1922. He began academic studies in Law in 1941 but in the following year was required to enroll for wartime service. As a committed pacifist, Hick served with the Friends' Ambulance Service in Britain and the Middle East. In 1945 Hick returned to the University of Edinburgh, where he graduated with First Class Honours in Philosophy in 1948. He then moved to Oxford for a D.Phil. on the relation between belief and faith, and then to Cambridge for theological and pastoral studies in preparation for the Presbyterian ministry. For three years he served as a minister in Northumberland, before moving to the USA to teach Philosophy of Religion at Cornell University and Princeton Theological Seminary. In 1964 he became a Lecturer in the Philosophy of Religion at the University of Cambridge, before moving to Birmingham to be H. G. Wood Professor of Theology in 1967. After thirteen years of very active work in Birmingham, Hick was offered the Danforth Chair in the Philosophy of Religion at Claremont Graduate School in 1980 and moved wholly to California in 1982. Married in 1953, he and his wife Hazel have a daughter and three sons, one of whom is deceased.

Each stage in Hick's life has been crucial to the development of his religious understanding. An evangelical conversion experience as a young Law student convinced him of the existential reality of faith to the committed believer. Working as a philosopher in the sceptical ethos of Anglo-American Philosophy in the 1940s and 1950s he recognised the need to face the challenges posed to religious faith by the still-influential logical positivist tradition. In Birmingham, Hick took a very active role in community life as Chairman of the Religious and Cultural Panel of the Community Relations Committee and of 'All Faiths for One Race', and in the creation of a new multi-faith agreed Syllabus for Religious Education. Through these responsibilities Hick established close ties with people of many faiths and became aware of the depth of their commitment and the reality of their religious experiencing. Hick's sensitivity to people of other

3

faiths was further enhanced by experiences as a Visiting Professor in India and Sri Lanka and by more than a decade of working in the vibrant pluralism of Southern California.

John Hick established his reputation with his early books, *Faith and Knowledge* and *Evil and the God of Love*. In these works he sought to justify faith as a philosophically valid way of experiencing reality, and to show that the existence of evil did not exclude the possibility of the existence of a loving God. These works introducing the ideas of eschatological verification, experiencing-as and the 'soul-making' theodicy, have become classics, and almost all contemporary works on religious epistemology or of theodicy find it essential to engage with Hick's thought in these areas.

Many scholars who achieve early distinction devote the rest of their lives to the clarification and defence of the thinking which has made their name. Hick, however, did not rest on his laurels, but instead went on to apply the same searching spirit to other central issues of the contemporary debate such as the meaning and coherence of claims concerning the divinity of Christ, the hope of a future life, the place of Christianity among the religions of the world, and above all, the problem of religious pluralism. In each area Hick's work has been recognised as of crucial importance in that, whether they agree or disagree with his conclusions, scholars recognise the need to come to terms with his thought. *Death and Eternal Life, The Myth of God Incarnate*, and *An Interpretation of Religion* have each in their turn determined the agenda for future theological and philosophical work on these topics.

Hick's original thinking is based on a profound knowledge of the history of religious philosophy that has found expression in the production of textbooks in the philosophy of religion, which have been translated into many languages and used by students throughout the world. Hick has also sought to communicate to as wide a public as possible and his major works have been accompanied by accessible paperbacks which seek to distill the essence of his thought. In particular the book initially called *Christianity at the Centre* and later, in increasingly modified form, as *The Centre of Christianity* and then as *The Second Christianity* has been very widely read as expounding what a contemporary understanding of Christianity might be.

John Hick's work has achieved its greatness because of his readiness to learn from others and to collaborate with them. Hick has always genuinely welcomed criticism and comment on his thought and this has helped him to refine and improve its presentation. He has also acted as midwife to the work of many other scholars through his editing of Macmillan's Library of the Philosophy of Religion, through his work on the editorial boards of leading journals, and through his convening of numerous academic conferences where papers could be thoroughly discussed and evaluated before being revised for publication.

The importance of Hick's thinking can best be illustrated by inviting the reader to pick up almost any serious contemporary work in the philosophy of religion or modern theology and count the number of references to Hick in the index. But in addition to this diffused influence it is worth noting that at least 94 articles have been written by others about his work as well as some 60 book chapters, 18 doctoral dissertations and six full-length books. And these figures are almost certain to be hopelessly out of date by the time this Festschrift is published, for his latest work, *An Interpretation of Religion*, seems certain to generate more discussion than all Hick's other earlier work. It is a fitting tribute to John Hick that for this book he has been given the prestigious Grawemeyer Award in Religion for 1991. This outstanding prize is awarded by a distinguished international panel of judges for 'the most significant contribution to religious and spiritual understanding in the five years prior to the award'. It is a mark of Hick's stature that even this commendation might be thought to understate the significance of his achievement.

Part II
Appreciations

1

Professor John Hick: A Personal Appreciation

ARVIND SHARMA

I

In what follows I would like to offer a personal appreciation of Professor John Hick. I would like to offer just that – not a private nor a subjective appreciation, but indeed a personal, perhaps even a very personal, appreciation. It would not surprise me, however, if this very personal appreciation were at some point to become suddenly transformed into something so impersonal as to be universal, for such thaumaturgical transformations of thought are not entirely unknown in the philosophy of religion.

My appreciation is personal because my persona is not of the West but of the East, and not just of the East but of India, about which Kathleen Raine can still rhapsodise: 'It remains true that the Perennial philosophy is and always has been best understood in India.'[1] In a sense it is, of course, true that 'It is today something of an anachronism to speak of European or Indian civilization. Until very recently cultures were sharply divided, but now when India is but a thirty hours' journey from London [or even less] cultural divisions are beginning to disappear.'[2] Indeed, the fact that such divisions are beginning to disappear is in no small measure due to the very presence of people like Professor John Hick and to the irenic contributions they have made. However, before I pay my homage to the living, allow me, like a good Hindu (and this may be the only chance I have of being one for a long time) to pay my debts to my ancestors first.

It has been said that being a Hindu is a particular state of mind and even that it is a state of mind self-assured to the point of being smug.[3] For like many a modern Hindu I was weaned on the aphorism that *Hindu philosophy begins where Western philosophy ends* – as if philosophy can be said to have a beginning and an end. I don't think that modern Hindus quite believe this statement, for they are also told that things do not become comprehensible until they are viewed comprehensively. I also doubt whether many even like it, for they are also told to judge ideas and ideals by their fruits rather than their roots (despite the fact of some Hindus being woeful gardeners). Finally, however, I suspect that the Hindus *like* to *believe* the statement, for it excuses them from the obligation of taking Western philosophy seriously, and simultaneously also enables them to feel chauvinistically proud about doing so, which might serve to explain my juvenile delinquency in this respect, abetted by an India-oriented school curriculum.

It took me some time to discover that this oversight was not an idiosyncratic aberration on my part, the part of my family or the part of any school or university. I now incline to the view that such narcissistic neglect of Western philosophy based on a pleasant, even polite but potentially pernicious conceit may have been one of the ways the shy and in any case subjugated Hindus sustained their bruised egos through the period of intellectual colonisation by the West – to which S. Radhakrishnan's bold counter-attack was the exception which proves the rule.[4] How else is one to explain the presence of this sentiment in the writing of someone who otherwise vigorously advocated the adoption of Western learning and science and has been hailed as the maker of modern India – Raja Rammohun Roy?[5] He wrote on 23 May 1823:

> If by the 'ray of intelligence' for which the Christian says we are indebted to the English, he means the introduction of useful mechanical arts, I am ready to express my assent and also my gratitude; but with respect to *science, literature,* or *religion,* I do not acknowledge that we are placed under any obligation. For by a reference to History it may be proved that the world was indebted to *our ancestors* for the first dawn of knowledge, which sprang up in the East, and thanks to the Goddess of Wisdom, we have still a philosophical and copious language of our own which distinguishes us from other nations who cannot express scientific or abstract ideas without borrowing the language of foreigners.[6]

Today in 1992, within two centuries of what Roy has written, I am, however, prepared to endorse the sentiment that:

In the past, light came from the East; in the future it will come again. But this time it will be a rainbow ray through a prism, one face of which was made in the West.[7]

In my own life that face has been the face of Professor John Hick. Thereby hangs a tale, which I am now pleased to share.

II

The story begins in Sydney, Australia, for it was in Sydney that I gradually became less oblivious to and, I hope, also less ignorant of Western thought. Prior to that, my attempts to come to grips with it had largely ended in failure, at times in an abrupt and dramatic manner. 'What is logical positivism?' I once asked the late and deeply-lamented Professor B. K. Matilal as we headed to a seminar at All Souls College of Oxford University, during one of my few visits to Blake's other Jerusalem. 'Don't worry', he had said, 'It's dead!'

Then one day, *en route* to my office (from my studio apartment) I decided to check out a bookshop, which lay on the way and had a selection of books on religion, perhaps because of its proximity to a theological college. It was then that I cast eyes on a grey book entitled: *Philosophy of Religion*. Somewhat hesitantly I took it from the shelf and began to peruse it. To my utter astonishment I discovered that I was following the argument. My hesitation turned to eagerness and I soon faced the moment every browser comes to and is forced, as it were, to play Hamlet: to buy or not to buy? What if what I had read was but a thin silver line of comprehension on the dark thundercloud of obscurity covering the Western horizon? The book's grey cover did not help matters much in this respect. It is, however, difficult for Hindus even when the chips are down (and even if the prices are up) to refrain from buying a book on philosophy, any philosophy – as though for them the purchase is a question of investment in salvation!

So the decision was made. I bought the book and placed it on a shelf in an accessible place, from which it could be retrieved even by an absent-minded swipe of the hand. As time permitted I would dip into the book. It still made sense. A few days later, it still continued to make sense. What is more, it sent my thoughts scurrying in all directions. I could see numerous threads connecting what I was reading with what I had read in Indian philosophy. I proceeded to make appropriate marginal notations. Little did I realise that these obscure entries of cryptographic density would one day provide sufficient material for a book which would eventually have to be shortened for publication; that the threads, so bare in the beginning, would soon be enough to weave into a web on the loom of Professor Hick's celebrated text, to emerge as *A Hindu Perspective on the Philosophy of Religion*.

I think Professor Hick's *Philosophy of Religion* has achieved something unique for the philosophy of religion: it has conferred scholarly dignity on a textbook. I am not surprised that *Philosophy of Religion* has by now been translated into eleven languages (including Arabic) and has sold nearly half a million copies all over the world.

III

By now I had met the book but not the author. If I had encountered the book in Sydney I met the author in Claremont, in circumstances which even a convinced Calvinist might be compelled to consider fortuitous. I had just finished a term as Visiting Professor at McGill University, Montreal, after a stint in a similar capacity at Temple University, Philadelphia and was all set to return to my base in Sydney, Australia. On the eve of my departure, however, I was told that my travelling documents were no longer in order! The situation was not without an element of autobiographical absurdity, as I had spent close to a decade by then teaching down under in Australia, and now was not being permitted to return to resume teaching on time! The difficulties which initiated this delay prolonged it to the point where I found I had enough time on my hands to participate in a conference on Mahatma Gandhi at Claremont, which had been organised by Professor Hick. There was only one hitch: I had never met him. So I did the next best thing: called him long-distance, and wondered if there was still room on the bus. At first he said nothing. I had obviously taken him by surprise. While I waited, trying to decode the ultimate subtle verbal clue of complete but pregnant silence, the line came alive again. 'All spots are taken but we do need people to chair a few sessions. Would you be willing . . . ?' Of course Barkis was willing.

The long arm of coincidence had stretched over two continents, assisted by a punctilious and unpredictable bureaucracy, to finally bring me face-to-face with Professor Hick. In the meantime, of course, I had come to know that the person who had initially aroused my admiration as the author of a captivating textbook was a scholar of international repute.

I wondered what would make a philosopher of religion interested in Gandhi. At this conference the realisation dawned on me that philosophers, especially of religion, are in a sense intellectual saints. The work of the ones I liked best, I found was characterised not only by clarity of thought but also by a charity of outlook; for how else could one explain the fascination of such a diverse group of thinkers with Gandhi? I believe now that just as I had found something mysteriously Socratic in Gandhi, they perhaps had found something mysteriously Gandhian in Socrates. There is something tantalizing about a chalice which can now appear to contain hemlock, and now appear as holy grail, but which always contains the lethal draught of immortality. Moreover, while saints do what they can to remove pain and evil, philosophers of religion try to do the next best thing: they try to explain and understand it and, thereby, in some sure if obscure way, also help relieve it.

IV

Though I had met Professor Hick at Claremont, California, it was in Brighton, England, that I came to know him. It was at the World Philosophy Congress, 21–27 August 1988.

As we settled down at the dinner table, the pleasantries out of the way, one of the first questions Professor Hick asked me was:

'Arvind, tell me, do you believe in rebirth?'

A long pause followed. It was followed by a still longer pause. I had to be careful. This was no small talk. I was talking to perhaps the foremost philosopher of religion of our time.

'I do not disbelieve in it', I finally said. 'I am happy to accept it as a part of my cultural heritage but were it ever scientifically established that it does not occur, it would not shatter my worldview.'

'How very interesting', he said, taking his eyes off the menu to which my initial silence must have driven him. 'If I were asked the same question I would say: I don't believe in it but it would not shatter my worldview if it were established to be a scientific fact.'

You can imagine the kind of intellectual repast the rest of the dinner was. I have no recollection of what we ate but I recall in vivid detail our discussion about why reality should be one rather than many and why should religions be many if reality is one.

It is difficult for me to convey the ambience of our discussion because it was what I always thought a philosophical conversation should be. Hardly any philosophers were referred to or schools of philosophy, for that matter, by name. Each argument was met only by a counter-argument. We called them as we saw them, as baseball umpires are supposed to – where the standing of the players makes no difference. We conversed as wise men and not as kings. Not that I am wise, for modesty would prevent one from asserting that even if it were true, and humility would prevent Professor Hick from admitting it even though it is true. I say we conversed as wise men and not as kings because I have a particular allusion in mind. The Greek king Menander (Pali: Milinda) once approached the Buddhist monk Nāgasena for an interview. I now cite what happened as a result from *The Questions of King Milinda (Milindapañha)*:

> Said the king, 'Bhante Nāgasena, will you converse with me?'
> 'Your majesty, if you will converse with me as the wise converse, I will; but if you converse with me as kings converse, I will not.'
> 'Bhante Nāgasena, how do the wise converse?'
> 'Your majesty, when the wise converse, whether they become entangled by their opponents' arguments or extricate themselves, whether they or their opponents are convicted of error, whether their own superiority or that of their opponents is established, nothing in all this can make them angry. Thus, your majesty, do the wise converse.'
> 'And how, bhante, do kings converse?'
> 'Your majesty, when kings converse, they advance a proposition, and whoever opposes it, they order his punishment, saying, "Punish this fellow!" Thus, your majesty, do kings converse.'
> 'Bhante, I will converse as the wise converse, not as kings do. Let your worship converse in all confidence. Let your worship converse as unrestrainedly as if with a priest or a novice or a lay disciple or a keeper of the monastery grounds. Be not afraid!'
> 'Very well, your majesty', said the elder in assent.[8]

In the spirit of ecumenism, which Professor Hick has himself done so much to foster, I should also add that after that memorable dinner I realised why some of the Upaniṣadic dialogues conclude with such comments as: 'And it was Reality they talked about. And it was Reality they praised.'

V

Professor John Hick arrived a few days in advance of the Birks lectures he had been invited to deliver at McGill University in 1989. When I checked at the hotel to confirm his reservation I was told that he had already arrived the previous day – in an Einsteinian sort of way – and here I was Kafkaesquely afraid that his reservation may have been bungled! I met him in the hotel lounge. They took so long to serve tea that we had to make do with philosophy. I remember both of us sharing a sense of impasse on the issue of natural evil, for neither Irenaean theodicy nor Karma quite seemed to justify the extent of it. Of course nature need not be any less economical with its fungi than with its flowers but the fecundity of evil continues to challenge the rationality of human minds.

During his lecture Professor Hick chose to speak on Christianity and developed the thesis that Jesus probably considered himself a prophet, an eschatological prophet maybe but not the Son of God – though joined to him in special filial devotion. All this was very interesting to me as a non-Christian, but I think it was the conclusion Professor Hick drew from all this which my Christian friends found more sensational than the facts themselves. He suggested that if the Christians shared Jesus's self-perception rather than the early Church's perception of Jesus – especially the trinitarian identification with God – one of the main theological obstacles to Christian concord with Jews and Muslims would be removed, for then all the three religious communities would be able to accept Jesus as a prophet in common. Moreover, if Jesus was God then his words and actions possessed finality; as a prophet they would possess only divine liminality, and in this sublime ambiguity of his status the brotherhood of religions would be fostered.

As a Hindu, of course, I was delighted by the ecumenical prospect thus opened up. In the last lecture Professor Hick turned to sainthood as the test of faith and it seemed he had come full circle back to theology after an excursion into philosophy. The fact that some forms of reasoning may be circular does not make them false – in fact it may make them roll.

At the time I thought that I was so affected by Professor Hick's lectures because as a non-Christian my ecumenical appreciation of them was untrammelled by any awareness of textual uncertainties or theological complexities. They just made eminent sense. Hindsight allows me to recognise and remedy the shallowness of my view. At that time because Professor Hick seemed so non-Western to me, he as a Westerner seemed so persuasive; I now venture the opinion, reversing my earlier judgement, that it was because he was so quintessentially Western that he was so appealing. Western civilisation is indebted in equal measure to Greece and to Palestine.[9] From the former it has derived its love of wisdom, from the latter its wisdom of love. In the course of its development to modernity it may have become historically endowed with the two qualities with which Buddhism was inceptionally endowed – compassion (*karuṇā*) and wisdom (*prajñā*).[10] Could it not be that the talks given by Professor Hick warmed our hearts even as they quickened our imagination because, in what he was saying, these two rays of Western civilisation were intersecting illuminatingly to generate luminous patterns of enlightened understanding?

Dean Donna Runnalls conferred on me the rare dignity of thanking Professor Hick on behalf of the Faculty at the conclusion of the series of lectures. Sometimes it is given to a person to speak only for himself and sometimes it is given to a person to speak for all. When I rose to thank Professor Hick it was one of those rare occasions when I could speak both for myself and for all when I expressed gratitude to him for having visited us. That I was not alone in feeling the way I did was demonstrated when the audience responded: not with the sound of one hand clapping (that would be carrying ecumenism too far) but with a standing ovation reinforced by the sound of many hands clapping.

Notes

1.   Kathleen Raine, 'Passage to India', *Temenos* 9:298.
2.   A. L. Basham, *The Wonder that was India* (London: Sidgwick & Jackson, 1954), p. 487.
3.   Ainslie T. Embree (ed.), *Alberuni's India: Translated by Edward C. Sachau* (New York: W. W. Norton, 1971), pp. 22–3.
4.   Sarvepalli Radhakrishnan, *Radhakrishnan: A Biography* (Delhi: Oxford University Press, 1989), Chapters 4 and 5.

5. V. S. Naravane, *Modern Indian Thought* (New York: Asia Publishing House, 1964), p. 23.
6. William Theodore de Bary *et al.*, *Sources of Indian Tradition* (New York: Columbia University Press, 1958), p. 580.
7. Percival Spear, *India: A Modern History* (Ann Arbor: University of Michigan Press, 1961), p. 455.
8. Henry Clarke Warren, tr., *Buddhism in Translations* (Cambridge, Mass.: Harvard University Press, 1915), pp. 128–9.
9. Arvind Sharma, *A Hindu Perspective on the Philosophy of Religion* (London: Macmillan, 1990), p. ix.
10. Walpola Sri Rahula, *What the Buddha Taught* (New York: Grove Press, 1974), p. 46.

2

John Hick's Contribution to the Philosophy of Religion
WILLIAM L. ROWE

It is with considerable pleasure that I write this brief appraisal of some of John Hick's contributions to the philosophy of religion. I write with pleasure because I have long admired him and his work. I write only of some of his contributions because they are so extensive and far-reaching that any significant appraisal of his many important contributions is, I believe, beyond the competence of any single scholar.

The aspects of Hick's scholarly work that I find most interesting are (1) his thesis that the world is religiously ambiguous, permitting both a rational belief in the reality of the divine and a rational belief that the natural universe is exhaustive of reality, (2) his efforts to show that his soul-making theodicy can reconcile the existence of the evils in our world with the existence of a God who is unlimited both in goodness and power, and (3) his more recent efforts to develop a comprehensive theory of religion based on the theme of religious pluralism.

Early in his career Hick adapted Wittgenstein's idea of 'seeing as' as a conceptual tool for understanding all of our experience of the world and the things making it up. Given different concepts and/or different backgrounds, two individuals may encounter the same reality, the one experiencing it as one thing, the other experiencing it as something else. Of course, if two people have the concept of red and have normal vision and are similarly placed, they cannot help but see something as red. But even in ordinary visual experience, one person may see a complicated series of dots on paper as a picture of a human face, while another may see it only as a series of dots. Hick argues that the world and events in it may be experienced merely as natural phenomena and also may be experienced religiously. But if there is a God, why should he not make his presence evident to us in a compelling way? Why does God hide himself

18

among the series of dots, rather than confronting us unambiguously like the redness of a brilliant sunset? Hick's answer is that if God's acts were overwhelmingly manifest and unmistakable, then we would have no *cognitive freedom* in relation to our maker. What is most valuable is the state in which a person comes *freely* to develop spiritually into a child of God. All this sounds reasonable if the ultimate reality is a personal being. For a personal deity might very well value creatures responding to him freely. Whether this fits harmoniously with Hick's later views of the Real is another matter.

Hick's response to the perennial challenge of the problem of evil is to develop and defend a theodicy stemming from Irenaeus, a theodicy in which the divine purpose is to create imperfect creatures within an environment in which they can freely develop themselves into moral and spiritual beings and eventually enter into an eternal life of love and fellowship with God. In support of Hick's soul-making theodicy, I do think (a) that if we believe there is an omnipotent, perfectly good being, it would not be unreasonable for us to believe that this being might have such a purpose for us, and (b) that given this purpose it is understandable why such a being would permit the existence of moral and natural evil in the world. For unless there are real obstacles in nature to overcome, and unless human beings are capable of doing real harm to one another, freely attained moral and spiritual growth would be practically, if not theoretically, impossible.

Although Hick's soul-making theodicy can explain why the world contains both moral and natural evil, it initially seems incapable of accounting for the apparently excessive amount of evil in our world and the fact that much of this evil seems quite unrelated to moral and spiritual development. Hick is aware of this major difficulty for his theodicy. Indeed, what seems obvious to Hick and to us is (1) that the amount and intensity of evil in our world far exceeds what is needed for soul-making, and (2) that the evils in our world are distributed in a haphazard fashion, apparently unrelated to anyone's stage of development in soul-making. In light of this, how can anyone seriously propose the good of soul-making as the reason for God's permission of all the pain and suffering in our world?

Hick's persistent answer is to employ what he calls the method of 'counterfactual hypothesis' and to emphasise the importance of mystery in soul-making. Let's see how the argument goes with respect to the fact that the amount and intensity of evil in our world appears to far exceed what could be rationally intended for soul-making. In response, Hick asks us to consider a world in which no evil occurs in an amount beyond what is needed to play a role in significant soul-making. Moreover, he asks us to suppose that we all *know* that this is so. He then argues that the result would be that we would make no significant efforts to overcome evil. But it is precisely such efforts (or the need for them) that lead to significant moral growth and development. A similar line of argument is developed for the haphazard, random distribution of evil. In a world in which suffering by a person is permitted only if it is merited or needed for soul-making, then if we further suppose that we all *know* this to be so, no one would make efforts to relieve the suffering of others. Paradoxically, then, soul-making would be considerably limited in a world in which we all knew or rationally believed that suffering is permitted only as it is required for soul-making.

The point of Hick's argument seems to be this. Significant soul-making requires not only the existence of evils; it also requires that it be *rational for us to believe* that excess evils exist; it must be rational for us to believe that evils occur that omnipotence could have prevented without loss of significant soul-making. For if we were to believe that each evil that occurs is one that even an omnipotent being could not prevent without loss of soul-making, we would make no significant efforts to overcome evils. And, as we've noted, it is precisely such efforts that are crucial to significant moral growth and development. Significant soul-making, then, has two requirements: First it has a *factual requirement*: there must be real evils to be overcome. Second, it has an *epistemic requirement*: it must be rational for us to believe that excess evils occur in our world. This second requirement has the air of paradox. It seems to say that evils not needed for soul-making are, after all, needed for soul-making. But it doesn't say this. What Hick's paradox says (roughly) is that rationally believing that there are evils not needed for soul-making is, after all, needed for soul-making. And, although paradoxical, such a claim is not incoherent. (An analogy to Hick's paradox might be the following. Suppose a marathon runner is such that if he believes that he will win, he won't train and, therefore, won't win. But if he has grounds for believing that he will lose, he will train to the utmost so as to come as close to winning as he can. Of such a person it might be correct, although paradoxical, to say: 'rationally believing that he won't win is, after all, required if he is to win'.)

How does Hick's argument strengthen his theodicy? Well, having noted that soul-making requires real evils to be overcome, the problem was that it seems obvious to us that the amount and intensity of evil is far in excess of what an omnipotent being would have to permit for significant soul-making to occur. Hick's ingenious response is that if it were not rational for us to believe that excess evil occurs, soul-making would be significantly diminished. Some might reject his claim. I am inclined to accept it. And what this implies is that the amount, intensity and distribution of evil in our world must be such as to create and sustain our belief that evils occur in excess of what an omnipotent being would need to permit for our moral and spiritual growth.

Suppose we grant the force of Hick's argument. My objection to it is that it doesn't really solve the problem of the amount and intensity of evil in our world. For it not only seems obvious to us that evil occurs far in excess of what an omnipotent being would have to permit for soul-making, it also seems obvious to us that evil occurs far in excess of what an omnipotent being would have to permit for us to be rational in believing that excess evil occurs. Clearly, if there is an omnipotent being, such a being could have prevented a good deal of evil in our world without in the least altering the fact that the amount and intensity of evil makes it rational for us to believe that evils occur in excess of what an omnipotent being would need to permit for our moral and spiritual growth. Who would say that if only five million had been permitted by omnipotence to perish in the holocaust it would *not* have been rational to believe that evils occur that omnipotence could have prevented without loss of our moral and spiritual growth? Hick's argument does show that our world must have enough evil to support the belief that there are excess evils. But since it is clear that evil occurs far in excess of what is necessary to support such a belief, Hick's argument, in my opinion, doesn't solve the problem of the amount, intensity and distribution of evil in our world.[1]

In the last decade or so, Hick has been developing a comprehensive theory of religion based on the theme of religious pluralism. In Hick's mind, religious pluralism is the major alternative both to religious scepticism (all religious experience is basically delusive) and religious dogmatism (only the religious experience of one's own tradition is veridical). According to religious pluralism, all the major religious faiths 'constitute different ways of experiencing, conceiving and living in relation to an ultimate divine Reality which transcends all our varied visions of it'.[2]

Of course, since the non-theistic varieties of Buddhism and Hinduism fall within the scope of the thesis of religious pluralism, the ultimate divine Reality cannot be a personal being. Hick adopts the Kantian distinction between reality as it is in itself (the noumenally real) and reality as it appears to us (the phenomenally real). Ultimate Reality (The Real) as it is in itself has no substantive properties, being neither personal nor impersonal, good nor evil, etc. But the Real appears to us as (is experienced as) personal deities or impersonal absolutes.

What, then, is the ontological status of the various personal deities (the God of Israel, the Holy Trinity, Shiva, Allah, Vishnu, etc.) and impersonal absolutes (Brahman, Nirvāṇa, Śūnyatā, etc.) that are the experienced ultimates of the various religions? It is exceedingly difficult to think that they are existing realities in the universe with the same ontological status as trees and stones. Although Hick does not commit himself, I suspect that he thinks of them as analogous to 'veridical hallucinations' – no such entities really exist, but these 'appearances' are occasions of a salvation/liberation process in which human beings are transformed from self-centred to reality-centred beings.

Hick's theory has the virtue of attributing a degree of validity to each of the world's great religious traditions. I will mention only two points that strike me as possible difficulties. Since the Real in itself is not personal, it would seem that those forms of Hinduism and Buddhism that hold that the religious ultimate is not a personal being enjoy a degree of intellectual superiority over the theistic religions: Judaism, Christianity, and Islam. Second, Hick's insistence that the world be religiously ambiguous makes sense in those religions in which the ultimate is a personal being who might well value humans coming *freely* to love him. But it is difficult to see this as the reason for the world being religiously ambiguous in those religious traditions that hold the religious ultimate to lack the qualities essential to personhood.

Hick's writings in philosophy of religion constitute a major intellectual achievement. His work on the problem of evil, *Evil and the God of Love*, contains the most plausible theodicy to be developed in this century. And his recently expanded Gifford Lectures, *An Interpretation of Religion*, is clearly the most sustained and powerful argument for the philosophy of religious pluralism we have. The intellectual impact of his work on philosophy, theology, religious studies, and related disciplines will be felt for many years to come.

Notes

1. Portions of the above are taken from my essay, 'Paradox and Promise: John Hick's Solution to the Problem of Evil', in *Problems in the Philosophy of Religion: Critical Studies of the Work of John Hick*, ed. Harold Hewitt, Jr (London: Macmillan, 1991).
2. John Hick, *An Interpretation of Religion* (London: Macmillan, 1989), pp. 235–6.

3
John Hick: *Faith and Knowledge*
WILLIAM P. ALSTON

I am delighted to have this opportunity to express appreciation to John Hick for what I have received from his writings, from his example, from his encouragement, and from his assistance. Before I get embroiled in all that, let me also express appreciation for the privilege of enjoying his friendship for the last four decades and more.

I first met John at a summer Philosophy of Religion conference organised by Paul Holmer and held at the University of Minnesota in the late 1950s. John was then on the faculty of the Department of Philosophy at Cornell University, and I held a similar position at the University of Michigan. This was shortly after the publication of the first edition of *Faith and Knowledge*, of which more below. I was slightly ahead of John at that time on the academic ladder, but that book made it abundantly clear that he was light years ahead of me in thinking about philosophical theology.

In John's next incarnation, as Stuart Professor of Christian Philosophy at Princeton Theological Seminary, I was privileged to take part in a notable conference there which he organised, the proceedings of which appeared as *Faith and the Philosophers*.[1] Then in the mid-1960s John moved back to England, to Cambridge and then to Birmingham, and as a result our contact was restricted to occasional correspondence. But with his return to the US at Claremont in the late 1970s there was the opportunity for additional contact, especially at various conferences, and I have been able to have a number of discussions with him in that connection. Finally, as editor of *Faith and Philosophy*, the journal of the Society of Christian Philosophers, I succeeded in inducing him to be the Guest Editor of a special issue on Religious Pluralism, a slot for which he is uniquely qualified.

I go through this bit of history to indicate that I do not write as one who has enjoyed daily contact with John, as I would have as a colleague. Our face-to-face contact, though always cordial and more than superficial, has been restricted to widely separated, relatively brief occasions. I say this to put the following remarks in context. Despite the relative paucity of personal interaction, John's influence on me has been a major one, as I shall proceed to indicate. But one further point before getting into details of content. One characteristic that has always struck me about John is the unfailingly sympathetic consideration he is prepared to give views from all quarters, including those most strongly opposed to his own. The combination of (1) many well-developed, detailed, and strongly defended views of one's own, and (2) a disposition to give careful and sympathetic attention to contrasting views of others, is by no means a common one. By exemplifying it John has been all the more a valuable resource to his fellow thinkers.

Now back to *Faith and Knowledge*, which will be my main illustration of John's influence on my own thought. From the first edition, the book made a profound impression on me, primarily for its insistence on the point that theistic faith, when live and fully-formed, rests on the experience of the presence and activity of God in our lives.

We become conscious of the existence of other objects in the universe, whether things or persons, either by experiencing them for ourselves or by inferring their existence from evidences within our experience. The awareness of God reported by the ordinary religious believer is of the former kind. He professes, not to have inferred that there is a God, but that God as a living being has entered into his own experience. He claims to enjoy something which he describes as an experience of God.[2]

Moreover, John insisted that this experience of God exhibits basically the same structure as our experience of the physical and (human) social environment. This is not to say there are not important differences between these modes of experience, for example the degree to which they impose themselves on us willy-nilly, as opposed to our having a choice in the matter. On the contrary, John has provided an illuminating discussion of such differences. But, according to his story, behind these differences is a fundamental commonality in structure. This means that it will be difficult for one to deny that we, or some people at least, experience the presence of God in our lives while accepting the common conviction that we do genuinely experience physical objects and other human beings.

These ideas resonated with convictions (or semi-convictions) I had had for some time in a more inchoate form, and this book provided invaluable inspiration and nourishment for my thinking about the matter. And, as is typically the case in philosophy, it provided material not only to assimilate but also to react against. The experience of God on which John was focusing was a 'mediated' experience. The passage quoted last continues as follows.

The ordinary believer does not, however, report an awareness of God as existing in isolation from all other objects of experience. His consciousness of the divine does not involve a cessation of his consciousness of a material and social environment. It is not a vision of God in solitary glory, filling the believer's entire mind and blotting out his normal field of perception. . . . He claims instead an apprehension of God meeting him in and through his material and social environments. He finds that in his dealings with the world of men and things he is somehow having to do with God, and God with him. The moments of ordinary life possess, or may possess, for him in varying degrees a religious significance. (pp. 95–6)

Thus the normal experience of God comes to us 'through' our experience of nature and society. We are aware of God as manifested in those realms. As such, it is an experience of a certain kind of 'significance' possessed by the physical and social environments, a significance that is apprehended by what John called an act of 'interpretation'.

The monotheist's faith-apprehension of God as the unseen Person dealing with him in and through his experience of the world is from the point of view of epistemology . . . an interpretation of the world as a whole as mediating a divine presence and purpose. . . . Behind the world – to use an almost inevitable spatial metaphor – there is apprehended to be an omnipotent, personal Will whose purpose toward mankind guarantees men's highest good and blessedness. The believer finds that he is at all times in the presence of this holy Will. (pp. 144–5)

But if the so-called 'experience of God' is a matter of the believer's *interpreting* her experience in a certain way, does it provide the believer with the epistemological leg-up it seemed to promise? The atheistic critic could claim that unless the believer has sufficient independent warrant for the scheme that is used in this 'interpretation', that scheme is arbitrarily read into the experience. But that means that claim to 'experience God' is doing nothing for the epistemic status of theistic belief. That status hangs solely on the extra-experiential warrant we have for the scheme that forms the content of the interpretation we impose to constitute the experience. Whatever other religious values the experience of God provides, it is doing nothing for us epistemologically.

It is at this point that John plays his 'commonality of structure' trump card. On his view the interdependent factors of interpretation and significance are essential for any form of experience of the world, even relatively uncontroversial ones like our experience of the physical and social realms.

> I shall try to show, in various fields, that 'mediated' knowledge, such as is postulated by this religious claim, is . . . a common and accepted feature of our cognitive experience. To this end we must study a basic characteristic of human experience, which I shall call 'significance', together with the correlative mental activity by which it is apprehended, which I shall call 'interpretation'. We shall find that interpretation takes place in relation to each of the three main types of existence, or orders of significance, recognized by human thought – the natural, the human, and the divine; and that in order to relate ourselves appropriately to each, a primary and unevidenceable act of interpretation is required which, when directed toward God, has traditionally been termed 'faith'. Thus I shall try to show that while the object of religious knowledge is unique, its basic epistemological pattern is that of all our knowing. (96–7)

> Our inventory, then, shows, three main orders of situational significance, corresponding to the threefold division of the universe, long entertained by human thought, into nature, man, and God. The significance for us of the physical world, nature, is that of an objective environment whose character and 'laws' we must learn, and toward which we have continually to relate ourselves aright if we are to survive. The significance for us of the human world, man, is that of a realm of relationships in which we are respons-

ible agents, subject to moral obligation. This world of moral significance is, so to speak, superimposed upon the natural world, so
that relating ourselves to the moral world is not distinct from the
business of relating ourselves to the natural world but is rather a
particular manner of so doing. And likewise the more ultimately
fateful and momentous matter of relating ourselves to the divine,
to God, is not distinct from the task of directing ourselves within
the natural and ethical spheres; on the contrary, it entails (without
being reducible to) a way of so directing ourselves. (p. 107)

On this quasi-Kantian view all experience of objects, of the world,
involves *interpreting* experience by the use of a certain conceptual
scheme. There is no more direct way of experiencing X, in which X
simply presents itself to us independent of all conceptualisation. As
John came to put it later, all experiencing is 'experiencing-as'. And in
none of these cases can we find any independent warrant for the
scheme used in the basic interpretations involved. As the passage
quoted from pp. 96–7 put it, the act of interpretation is
'unevidenceable'. Hence the above criticism collapses. One cannot
demand an independent warrant for the interpretative scheme of
religious experience without, in parity, making such a demand for
the other areas of experience as well. And since the demand cannot
be met anywhere, the logic of the criticism would lead us to reject the
epistemic credentials of all experience.

This is a powerful defence of the (epistemic) autonomy of religious experience, as a basis for religious belief. To be sure, the
atheistic critic might still contend that the interpretative schemes for
our experience of the natural and social worlds are more acceptable
than that for our experience of God, and those contentions would
have to be considered. But the condemnation of any empirical support of theistic belief on the grounds that it involves the use of an
unwarranted interpretative scheme would have been discredited.

My own thinking on this matter has been enriched by finding
something here to rub against, as well as something to embrace. I am
not at all convinced that anything properly called 'interpretation' is
essential to the experience of objects. More specifically, I am not
convinced that experiencing something as a tree, a computer, a
colleague, or the divine creator just is *taking* what I experience to be
a tree, a computer, a colleague, or the divine creator. I don't even see
sufficient reason to suppose that it amounts to applying the concept

of a tree . . . to what I experience. I can't really go into the matter here, but I am convinced that something's looking to me like a tree, computer . . . is, in principle, independent of any concept-deployment, judgement or belief on my part, however frequently the latter occurs along with the former. For something to look like a tree to me is simply for the object to be presented to my awareness as bearing certain features. (Of course, I couldn't realise that it looks like a tree without applying to it the concept of looking like a tree, but that is another matter.) In any event, now that my own thought on the experiential basis of theistic belief is, in the fullness of time, reaching fruition in book form,[3] it involves the view of the matter just hinted at. I hang on to the point that the generic structure of the experience of objects ('perception', as I put it) is the same across the board, for sense-perception of the physical and social environment and for the 'perception' of God, but my depiction of that commonality is in direct realist rather than in more Kantian terms.

Another point at which I deviate from *Faith and Knowledge* has to do with the thesis that all experience of God is *mediated* by sense experience of the physical and social world. I do not doubt that there is such mediate experience of God and that it plays a large role in religion. But I am also convinced that there is direct non-sensory experience of God, and that it is both widespread and even more important for the epistemology of religious belief. I note that in his recent magnum opus, *An Interpretation of Religion*, John gives a place to such direct awareness of God, though not nearly so prominent a place as I do.

I have gone into these issues concerning religious experience because I know no better way of recording my indebtedness to John than to illustrate his impact on my thought; and the topic of religious experience is where that impact is most noticeable. But it would be highly misleading to suggest that I have not learned much from him in other areas as well. Like most of the rest of those who are concerned with religious issues, I think of his treatment of the problem of evil in *Evil and the God of Love* as the definitive statement of the 'soul-making theodicy'. And for many of us the book is the major source for the history of the discussion as well. As for problems posed by religious pluralism, John is, of course, the thinker (at least within the Christian tradition: I cannot speak of others) who has done the most to advance the discussion of this perennially thorny problem. His quasi-Kantian position is *the* view that no one grappling with the issue can ignore, a point borne out by the fact that no one discussing the problem nowadays does ignore it, including the present writer.

I hope and trust that we can look forward to a continued intellectual and spiritual nourishment and stimulation from John's future publications and personal presence. Meanwhile, thanks again, John, for all that you have given us in the past.

Notes

1. John Hick, *Faith and the Philosophers* (New York: St. Martin's Press, 1964).
2. John Hick, *Faith and Knowledge* (second edition) (Ithaca, New York: Cornell University Press, 1957), p. 95. All quotations from this work will be from the second edition.
3. John Hick, *Perceiving God* (Ithaca, New York: Cornell University Press, 1991).

Part III
Essays in Honour of
John Hick

4

God and Absolute Nothingness

MASAO ABE

I

In this chapter[1], by the term God I indicate the Christian notion of God who is Yahweh and Father of Jesus Christ. By the term absolute nothingness I denote the Buddhist notion of *śūnyatā* as the Buddhist ultimate Reality. To speak of 'absolute nothingness' I make a distinction between relative nothingness and absolute nothingness. Relative nothingness is a counterpart of 'somethingness'. It is an absence or negation of somethingness. So it is a negative and nihilistic concept. Unlike relative nothingness, however, absolute nothingness is not negative nor nihilistic, but positive and dynamic. It is neither somethingness nor nothingness in the relative sense. Therefore it is beyond the duality of somethingness and nothingness, and thereby includes both somethingness and nothingness. Being freed from the duality of somethingness and nothingness, absolute nothingness is the creative source for both somethingness and nothingness, being and non-being.

When one uses the expression 'God *and* absolute nothingness' one usually implies that the Christian notion of God is *not* absolute nothingness and that absolute nothingness is fundamentally *different from* the notion of God. Against such a usual implication, under the title 'God and Absolute Nothingness', I would like to suggest that both the Christian notion of *God* and the Buddhist notion of *śūnyatā* can be (or should be) understood equally to be absolute nothingness. By saying this I do not insist that the Christian notion of God and the Buddhist notion of *śūnyatā* are the same.

On the contrary, I am suggesting that there are two sorts of absolute nothingness which are significantly different from one another; that is, absolute nothingness as the Christian notion of God and absolute nothingness as the Buddhist notion of *śūnyatā*. And the

33

former (that is, absolute nothingness as the Christian notion of God), may be compared to an infinitely large *circle*, whereas the latter (that is, absolute nothingness as the Buddhist notion of *śūnyatā*) may be likened to an infinitely large *sphere*. In what follows, I offer a more detailed explanation of what I mean.

II

In the history of Christianity, God has often been interpreted as 'Being'. For in Christianity God is believed to be eternal, immutable and omnipresent. This interpretation is probably based on Yahweh's self-declaration to Moses at Mount Sinai, 'I am that I am' (Exodus 3:14). While this expression had originally a very active sense, it came to be interpreted as static immutable being. Philo's name for God is *'ho ōn'*, 'the Being' or 'He who is'.[2] In our century, emphasising an essential qualitative difference between Being with a capital B and any kind of being with a small 'b', including supreme being, Paul Tillich defined God as the ground of Being or the power of Being which is the root and source of all beings in the universe.[3]

As theologians like Dr T. Boman[4] and my Japanese teacher of Christianity, Dr Tetsutaro Ariga,[5] have said, however, the original Hebrew of the above statement, "ehyeh 'asher 'ehyeh' has a different connotation because the Hebrew word *hāyāh*, which is the root of *'ehyeh* (I am), does not simply mean to *be*, but to *become*, to *work*, and to *happen* at one and the same time.

Accordingly, Yahweh's original Hebrew statement may be more correctly translated as 'I am becoming that I am becoming', or 'I am happening that I am happening'. This is the reason that, criticising the Greek-oriented ontological interpretation of Christianity, Dr Ariga advanced 'hayatology'[6] rather than ontology as a more appropriate approach for theology. In an hayatological interpretation of Christianity, God as 'Becoming' or 'Happening' is understood more dynamically than as 'Being', and thereby expresses the Christian notion of God much more deeply and appropriately.

In a similar vein, Process Theologians represented by John Cobb, Shubert Ogden and others are trying to interpret God as an actual entity involved in the process of the world and history. God is not Being or Substance – simply beyond time and space – but is of dipolar nature; the primordial nature is trans-temporal and the consequent nature is temporal. In Process Theology the ultimate Reality is not God but creativity.[7] God as well as the world are outcomes of the basic principle of creativity. In short, God is not Being but Becoming in Process Theology.

I am not, however, satisfied with an interpretation of God as Becoming. 'God is love' (1 John 4:8) is the most fundamental definition of the Christian notion of God. The God who is love is not merely 'becoming' a human, but rather is 'emptying himself' to save suffering humanity. This is clearly described in Paul's Christological hymn in Philippians 2:5–8:

> Have this mind among yourselves which is yours in Christ Jesus, who though he was in the form of God, did not count equality with God a thing to be grasped, but emptied himself, taking the form of a servant, being born in the likeness of a human being. And being found in human form he humbled himself and became obedient unto death, even death on a cross.

To me, this is one of the most impressive and touching passages in the Bible. *Kenosis*, self-emptying, is the key term of this hymn. Through the kenosis, death and resurrection of the Son of God, God the Father reveals Godself in terms of the unconditional love beyond discriminatory justice. The unfathomable depth of God's love is clearly realised when we come to know and believe that Christ as the Son of God emptied himself and became obedient to the point of death, even death on the cross.

Christ did not merely disguise himself as a servant, as Docetism suggests, but in fact became a servant. Since the term 'form' (*morphē*) in the above passage signifies not mere shape or appearance, but substance or reality, we can say that in Paul's understanding the Son of God abandoned his divine substance and took on human substance to the extreme point of becoming a servant crucified on the cross. Accordingly, Christ's kenosis signifies a transformation not only in appearance but in substance, and implies a radical and total self-negation of the Son of God.

We should not, however, overlook that in the kenosis of Christ the humiliation of Christ is inseparably related to the exaltation of Christ. Immediately after the above quotation from the Epistle to the Philippians (2:9–11), the following passage occurs:

Wherefore also God highly exalted him, and gave unto him the name which is above every name; that in the name of Jesus every knee should bow, to things in heaven and things on earth and things under the earth, and that every tongue should confess that Jesus Christ is Lord, to the glory of the Father.

The state of humiliation and the state of exaltation are, however, inseparable – not immediately, but paradoxically through the complete abnegation of the Son of God. Thus I would like to formulate the doctrine of Christ's kenosis as follows:

The Son of God is not the Son of God (for he is essentially self-emptying). Precisely because he is not the Son of God, he is truly the Son of God (for through self-emptying he completely identifies himself with humanity).[8]

Now, if Christ, the Son of God, empties himself, should we not consider the self-emptying of God – the kenosis of the very God? We must now ask together with Jürgen Moltmann, 'What does the cross of Jesus mean for God himself?'[9]

Christian theology generally states that the Son of God became a human without God ceasing to be God. My question, however, is, 'Does not the kenosis of Christ have its origin in God the Father; that is, in the kenosis of God?' For without the self-emptying of God the Father, the self-emptying of the Son of God is inconceivable. In the case of Christ, kenosis originated in the will of God, but in the case of God, kenosis is implied in the original nature of God, that is, love. In his book *Foundations of the Christian Faith*, Karl Rahner states:

The primary phenomenon given by faith is precisely the self-emptying of God, his becoming, the kenosis and genesis of God himself. . . . Insofar as in his abiding and infinite fullness he empties himself, the other comes to be as God's very own reality.[10]

If this is the case, God's self-emptying must be understood not as partial but as total to the extent that God's self-emptying is dynamically identical with God's abiding and infinite fullness. Although this kind of *total* self-emptying of God is not clear enough in Rahner's interpretation, I believe that if God is really unconditional love, then self-emptying must be total, not partial.

Only through this total kenosis and God's self-sacrificial union with everything in the world is God truly God. Here we fully realise the reality and actuality of God which is entirely beyond conception and objectification. The *kenosis* of God is the *pleroma* (fullness) of God (Col. 1:18). This kenotic God is the ground of the kenotic Christ. The God who does not cease to be God even in the self-emptying of the Son of God, that is, the kenosis of Christ, is not the true God. Accordingly, concerning faith in God it must be said:

God is not God (for God is love and completely self-emptying). Precisely because God is not a self-affirming God, God is truly a God of love (for through complete self-abnegation God is totally identical with everything including sinful humanity).[11]

This means that kenosis or emptying is not an attribute (however important it may be) of God, but the fundamental nature of God. God is God, not because God had the Son of God take a human form and be sacrificed while God remained God, but because God is a suffering God, a self-sacrificing God through total kenosis. The kenotic God who totally empties Godself and totally sacrifices Godself is, in my view, the true God.

The notion of kenotic God opens up for Christianity a common ground with Buddhism by overcoming Christianity's monotheistic character, the absolute oneness of God, and by sharing with Buddhism the realisation of absolute nothingness as the essential basis for the ultimate. This can be accomplished through the notion of the kenotic God – not through losing Christianity's self-identity, but rather through deepening its spirituality.

III

In the above I have tried to show that the Christian notion of God should not be interpreted to be 'Being' or 'Becoming' but rather 'absolute nothingness' in terms of God's total self-emptying; that is, the total kenosis of God. The basic statement of Christianity, 'God is love', is most profoundly and fully realised precisely in this way. And with this understanding we can find a point of close contact between Christianity and Buddhism.

To repeat, both the Christian notion of God and the Buddhist notion of *śūnyatā* may be equally understood to be 'absolute nothingness'. This, however, does not indicate that they are exactly the same sort of absolute nothingness. Rather, it implies that the absolute nothingness as God and the absolute nothingness as *śūnyatā* are subtly and significantly different from one another. How are they different? In order to clarify the similarity and difference between them, both of which may be equally understood as absolute nothingness, we must try to discuss the meanings of the two key notions.

Now I would like to discuss the Christian notion of God as represented by Hans Küng and offer a Buddhist interpretation of God. In his book *Does God Exist?*, Hans Küng says: 'God in the Bible is subject and not predicate: it is not that love is God, but that God is love. God is one who faces me, whom I can address.'[12] My question to this statement is as follows: Can I not address God, however, not from outside God, but within God? Again, is it not that God faces me within God, even if I turn my back on God? God who faces me and whom I address is God as subject. However, God within whom I address God and within whom God meets me is not God as subject but rather God as predicate. Or, more strictly speaking, that God is neither God as subject nor God as predicate, but God as *Nichts*,[13] as absolute nothingness.

In God as *Nichts*, God as subject meets me even if I turn my back on that God and I can truly address the God as Thou. The very I–Thou relationship between the self and God takes place precisely in God as *Nichts*. Since God as *Nichts* is the '*ungrund*'[14] ground of the I–Thou relationship between the self and God, God as *Nichts* is neither subject nor predicate but a 'copula'[15] which acts as a connecting or intermediary link between the subject and the predicate. This entails that God as *Nichts* is *Nichts* as God: God is *Nichts* and *Nichts* is God. And on this basis we may say that God is love and love is God because *Nichts* is unconditional, self-negating love. This is the absolute interior of God's mystery which is its absolute exterior at one and the same time. We may thus say,

God is love because God is *Nichts*:
Nichts is God because *Nichts* is love.[16]

Here, both human longing for salvation and the deepest mystery of God are thoroughly fulfilled.

To speak figuratively, this notion of God as *Nichts* may be compared to an infinitely large circle. Unlike a finite circle, which consists of a fixed centre and a fixed circumference, in an infinitely large circle there is neither a fixed centre nor a fixed circumference. It is entirely open, limitless and boundless. To speak of centre, every point in an infinitely large circle can be a centre: to speak of circumference, everywhere in an infinitely large circle can be a circumference. Here there is no rigid distinction between centre and circumference. In an infinitely large circle as a metaphor of 'God as *Nichts*', centre represents God, while each point of circumference indicates a human self.

And here in this infinitely large circle God as the centre and human individual selves, each a point on the circumference, are completely interpenetrating and dynamically united. This symbolises the all-loving God who is *Nichts*. And an infinitely large circle itself, which consists of a complete interpenetration between God and the individual self, is *Nichts* or unconditional love which is God. Right here, God is love and love is God: God is *Nichts* and *Nichts* is God.

When Hans Küng says, 'God in the Bible is subject and not predicate: it is not that love is God but that God is love', his notion of God cannot be compared to an infinitely large circle but to a finite circle. God as subject is a fixed centre and human selves form the circumference. Even though Küng emphasises that God is love, he denies that love is God. In this interpretation of God a complete interpenetration between God and human selves is lacking. The otherness of God is definitely clear. Does this interpretation represent the most authentic understanding of the Christian notion of God? Can the human self with its distinctiveness be completely redeemed in this interpretation?

Although I am emphasising a complete interpenetration between God and human selves realised in an infinitely large circle, I am not suggesting a pantheistic interpretation of God, which is foreign to Christianity. Rather I am trying to deepen Christian spirituality as much as possible.

My suggestion is that God is neither subject nor predicate but a 'copula' which, being *Nichts* or absolute nothingness, acts as an intermediating and interpenetrating link between subject and predicate. This dynamic notion of God cannot be compared to a finite circle with a fixed centre and circumference, but to an infinitely large

circle in which centre and circumference are completely interpenetrating.

Here God is not a fixed substantial centre and God's otherness
and transcendence are non-substantial. When God is likened to an
infinitely large circle, God is understood to be a sort of absolute
nothingness, completely open, boundless, and limitless. But insofar
as it is understood to be an infinitely large *circle* there must be a sort
of centre and circumference, both being completely non-substantial
and intangible. For even though it is infinitely large, the circle has a
two-dimensional spatiality.

Christianity is fundamentally a theocentric theism, based on one
absolute God, Yahweh, to whom a personal I–Thou relation is
crucial. This one God, however, should not be compared to a fixed
and substantial centre of a finite circle but to a completely non-
substantial and non-objectifiable centre of an infinitely large circle.
Likewise, each human self should not be likened to a particular point
of a fixed and substantial circumference of a finite circle which must
converge into a fixed centre, God. Rather it should be compared to a
particular non-substantial point of the circumference of an infinitely
large circle because in one's faith in God, one's ego-self must completely die with Christ and resurrect with Christ day by day. When
Paul confesses, 'It is no longer I who live, but Christ who lives in me'
(Galatians 2:20) Christ is not a substantial subject facing Paul, whom
Paul can address, rather Christ is the root and source of Paul's
resurrected true self. In his faith in Christ the substantial otherness
of God is completely overcome and he now lives the life of Christ.
Just as the non-substantial and unobjectifiable centre and the particular point of the non-substantial and unobjectifiable circumference in an infinitely large circle are interpenetrating, God and Paul
are interpenetrating in his faith.

This, however, does not indicate pantheism or a naturalistic mysticism. For in Paul's case the interpenetration between God and
himself contains an irreversibility with God as superior. Accordingly, even in his confession quoted above and in the following
words in which Paul talks about the faith which is in 'the Son of God,
who loved me and gave himself up for me' (Galatians 2:20) Paul
seems to recognise a sort of otherness or transcendence of the Son of
God. God is the Lord of Grace and Paul is a receiver of divine grace.
It is, however, not a substantial otherness compared to the fixed
centre of a finite circle, but a non-substantial, unobjectifiable otherness
well-likened to a non-substantial centre of the infinitely large circle.

Christianity is fundamentally theocentric, but the central God who is all-loving and self-emptying is not Being or Becoming but non-substantial absolute nothingness. God is unobjectifiable and non-substantial absolute nothingness, but as such God is a centre into which all individual selves must converge through faith. This is the reason I have compared the Christian notion of God to the infinitely large circle.

IV

The Buddhist notion of *śūnyatā* properly indicates absolute nothingness but in a subtly and significantly different sense from the case of the Christian notion of God. In order to show the affinity and difference between the Christian notion of God and the Buddhist notion of *śūnyatā* I would now like to compare the latter to an infinitely large *sphere* in contrast to the previous image of an infinitely large *circle*.

Gautama Buddha did not accept the age-old Vedantic notion of the Brahman as the sole and enduring reality underlying the universe. Instead, he advocated the law of dependent co-origination as the basic principle of Buddhism. This law emphasises that everything in the universe co-arises and co-ceases with everything else. Nothing exists by itself. This complete interdependency is possible because everything has no fixed, enduring selfhood but is ultimately non-substantial. Nagarjuna later elucidated this point in terms of *śūnyatā* and emphasised it as the ultimate reality in Buddhism.

Śūnyatā literally means emptiness or voidness, indicating the absence of enduring self-being or the non-substantiality of everything in the universe. It is beyond all dualities and yet includes them. In the realisation of *śūnyatā*, not only sentient beings but also the Buddha, not only *samsāra* but also *nirvāna*, are without substance and are empty. Accordingly, neither Buddha nor *nirvāna*, but the realisation of the non-substantiality of everything – that is, the realisation of *śūnyatā* – is ultimate. This is the reason Buddhism does not accept the notion of one absolute God such as the creator or ruler of the universe. This rejection of absolute oneness is especially clear in Zen.

Zen raises a question, 'When everything returns to Oneness, to where does that Oneness return?' Yet even this question is not the final one for Zen. Rather Zen starts with that question. It also emphasises, 'On meeting a buddha slay the buddha, on meeting a patriarch slay the patriarch. . . . Only then you attain emancipation.

By not cleaving to things, you freely pass through.'[17] It is by breaking through the absolute Oneness that *śūnyatā* can be legitimately grasped.

Accordingly, *śūnyatā* as the Buddhist Reality should be compared not to an infinitely large circle but to an infinitely large sphere. For as I stated before, an infinitely large circle still has a spatiality, though non-substantial – thereby it has a non-substantial centre and circumference which are to be distinguished. By contrast, an infinitely large sphere is free even from two-dimensional spatiality and opens three-dimensionally in all directions.

Buddhism is not a theocentric religion, to say nothing of an anthropocentric, egocentric, or cosmocentric religion. It is not orientated by any kind of centrism. This is precisely an implication of *śūnyatā*. When *śūnyatā* is likened to an infinitely large sphere, one can say more strongly than before that every point can equally be a centre and a circumference at one and the same time: each point is completely interpenetrating with every other point. There is no irreversibility between centre and circumference, in fact a complete reversibility is fully realised. This is a realisation of the law of dependent co-origination and herein everything is realised in its distinctive uniqueness while being interdependent and interpenetrating each other.

V

If the above discussion comparing the Christian notion of God to an infinitely large circle and the Buddhist notion of *śūnyatā* to an infinitely large sphere is acceptable, we may make the following five points.

First, in the Christian notion of God which is likened to the infinitely large circle, the substantial otherness is completely overcome and God and the self, transcendence and immanence, are interpenetrating. Yet the interpenetration between God and the self is irreversible with God as the Lord of Grace. As we can see, from a special distinction between non-substantial centre and the non-substantial circumference in an infinitely large circle, the otherness of the central God (though not substantial) remains in its relation to the human self.

The human self is not completely identical with the central God, but is situated on a non-substantial circumference. In this special sense, transcendence and immanence, God and creatures are not fully identified. In order to fully realise the dynamic identification between transcendence and immanence, God and the self, then even God as the non-substantial centre must be broken through as in Meister Eckhart's *Durchbrechen*. This means that an infinitely large circle must be transformed into an infinitely large sphere. God as absolute nothingness must be transformed into *śūnyatā* as absolute nothingness.

Second, in the Buddhist notion of *śūnyatā* likened to an infinitely large sphere there is no centre at all, whether substantial or non-substantial. It is completely open and boundless in all directions. Accordingly, the realisation of *śūnyatā* tends to lack the criterion for value-judgement and directionality in history. In order to overcome this negative tendency and to clearly establish the criterion for value-judgement and directionality in history, *śūnyatā* must be completely negated and emptied. Emptiness must be emptied. This means that an infinitely large sphere must be transformed into an infinitely large circle. *Śūnyatā* as absolute nothingness must be transformed into a personal God as absolute nothingness. In Buddhist tradition that is exemplified by Vairocana Buddha and Amida Buddha.

Third, an infinitely large sphere can embrace an infinitely large circle, but not vice versa. Likewise, *śūnyatā* can embrace God, but not vice versa. Even so, there is no immediate, continuous path from an infinitely large sphere to an infinitely large circle, from *śūnyatā* to God. In order for an infinitely large sphere really to embrace an infinitely large circle in its uniqueness, it must break and negate itself and transform itself into an infinitely large circle. In other words, *śūnyatā* must self-consciously empty itself and transform itself into a personal God. If *śūnyatā* understands that it can immediately or directly become a personal God without self-emptying it will then appear demonic because the personal God thus realised is a personification of self-affirming *śūnyatā*.

Fourth, an infinitely large circle cannot embrace an infinitely large sphere. Likewise, God cannot embrace *śūnyatā*. There is a discontinuity from the former to the latter. In order for the former to turn into the latter the former must negate itself. It means that the irreversibility implied in the interpenetration between God and the self – that is, even the non-substantial otherness of God in Christian faith – must be overcome and a complete interpenetration and reversibility between God and the self must be fully realised. Otherwise the otherness of God still remains in our faith and we are not completely free of the problem of the demonic. For as Augustine says, on the one hand we belong in *civitas dei* and, on the other, we belong in *civitas diaboli*. By believing in an absolute God we touch the devil as well as God.

Fifth, the realisation of *śūnyatā* must negate itself and thus overcome its demonic character. Only then can it provide a proper foundation for a personal God. When the complete reversibility realised in *śūnyatā* is self-negated and turns into an irreversibility, then faith in the otherness of God will be established anew without the problem of the demonic. Likewise, the personal God must completely negate God's otherness and transcendence if it is to avoid its possible affiliation with the demonic. Then faith in God returns to its deepest source and awakens to *śūnyatā*, which is neither God nor the devil.

Speaking from both sides – that is, from the side of a personal God compared to an infinitely large circle and the side of *śūnyatā* symbolised by an infinitely large sphere – *self-negation* is necessary in order to be transformed into the other side and to realise the most profound and most real common ground for both. That common ground is the realisation of absolute nothingness, which is neither God nor *śūnyatā*, to be realised by breaking through the identity of God and the devil.

Notes

1. This paper was originally presented at the International Conference on Buddhism and Christianity, at De Tiltenberg, Nederland, 2–4 June 1990. Some portions of this paper have been taken from my article, 'Kenotic God and Dynamic Sunyata' in John Cobb and Christopher Ives (eds), *The Emptying God: A Buddhist–Jewish–Christian Conversation* (Maryknoll, New York: Orbis Books, 1990), pp. 9–17, 25–6. The author is grateful for the suggestions and assistance of the Rev. James Ishmael Ford at the final stage of this paper.

2. Alan Richardson and John S. Bowden (eds), *Westminster Dictionary of Christian Theology* (Philadelphia: Westminster Press, 1983), p. 63.

3. Paul Tillich, *Systematic Theology*, Vol. II (Chicago: University of Chicago Press, 1951–63), pp. 10, 87, 125, 126.

4. Thorlief Boman, *Das hebräische Denken im Vergleich mit dem Griechischen* (Gottingen: Vadenhoeck & Ruprecht, 1954), especially 1, Teil I-III.

5. Tetsutaro Ariga, 'Kirisutokyo-shiso niokeru Sonzairon no Mondia' (The Problem of Ontology in Christian Thought), *The Collected Works of Tetsutaro Ariga*, Vol. IV, p. 184.

6. Ibid., pp. 177–200.

7. John Cobb and David Griffin, *Process Theology: An Introductory Exposition* (Philadelphia: Westminster Press, 1976), p. 141.

8. John Cobb and Christopher Ives (eds), *The Emptying God*, p. 11.

9. Jürgen Moltmann, *The Crucified God* (London: SCM, 1973), p. 201.

10. Karl Rahner, *Foundations of Christian Faith: An Introduction to the Idea of Christianity* (New York: Seabury Press, 1978), p. 222.

11. *The Emptying God*, p. 16.

12. Hans Küng, *Does God Exist?* (Garden City, New York: Doubleday, 1980), p. 64.

13. From the German, meaning 'nothing' or 'nothingness', and used in various ways by such philosophers and theologians as Hegel, Heidegger, and particularly Meister Eckhart and Jacob Boehme. Here, however, the term *Nichts* indicates 'absolute nothingness', as discussed earlier.

14. A term first used by Jacob Boehme, and meaning 'groundless'.

15. From the Latin, 'to bind together'.

16. *The Emptying God*, p. 26.

17. Ruth Fuller Sasaki, *The Record of Lin-chi*, p. 25 (adapted).

5

Aesthetic Goodness as a Solution to the Problem of Evil[1]

MARILYN McCORD ADAMS

1 INTRODUCTION

There is a widespread (if often implicit) view that within the field of values, morality takes pride of place. If not sharply distinguished from the political, moral value is taken to be as different in kind from those treated by aesthetics as from those codified in rules of etiquette! On this picture, no matter what aesthetic considerations may be advanced, they can always be trumped by appeals to human happiness, welfare, and equality. Conversely, those who embrace art for art's sake are forced into the posture of 'thumbing their noses' at morality.

Influential as this compartmentalisation of moral and aesthetic has been both in moral philosophy and Christian piety, it is unsurprising if it has left its mark on contemporary discussions of the problem of evil as well. Confronted with the question, whether

(1) God exists, and is omnipotent, omniscient, and perfectly good

is logically compossible with

(2) Evil exists,

it is typical to insist that 'perfectly good' (in (1)) be construed in terms of *moral* goodness. Likewise, attempts by Nelson Pike[2] and Roderick Chisholm,[3] in effect, to reintroduce aesthetic considerations into the discussion, have encountered significant resistance. Both philosophers attempt to shift the burden of proof regarding the logical compossibility of (1) and (2) from the believer to the atheist by appeal to the aesthetic relation of organic unity. Drawing on themes from Leibniz's Best of All Possible Worlds theodicy, Pike argues that for all we know the best of all possible worlds contains instances of evils (which bear a relation of organic unity to the whole); and that if this were the case, (1) would be logically consistent with (2). Likewise, Chisholm distinguishes the merely additive relation of 'balancing off' (which occurs when opposing values of *mutually exclusive* parts of a whole partially or totally cancel each other out) from that of 'defeating' (which cannot occur by the mere addition to the whole of a new part of opposing value, but involves some organic unity among the values of parts and wholes). His suggestion is that since evils can bear relations of organic unity to larger positively-valued wholes, the theist is entitled to claim that it is logically possible for such evils as we observe to be thereby defeated.

Terence Penelhum renders a Scottish verdict of 'not proven' on their reflections. For he rightly insists that arguments from evil against the rationality of religious belief must understand 'perfectly good' (in (1)) and 'evil' (in (2)) the way the religious tradition in question does. He warns that religious values are bound to be at some variance from secular values, and to restrict both the range of telling objections and the variety of available theodicies. For example, that our world could not be the product of an omniscient, omnipotent pleasure-maximiser, does no damage to Biblical religion, which does not construe 'good' and 'evil' hedonistically anyway. By the same token, since Christianity exalts the values of personal welfare, character, and loving relationships,[4] it could not consistently regard the delicate pink flush produced in the cheeks of the tubercular patient as God's principal reason for permitting the disease.[5] Turning to Pike and Chisholm, Penelhum wonders whether the permission of evils *aesthetically* related to greater goods in the way they suggest, is really consistent with Divine goodness as the believer conceives of it. What if some evils were to be found, that the believer's values would not allow to be defeated by their relation of organic unity to the cosmic whole?[6]

Penelhum closes with the question; for others, its answer is ready to hand. Ivan Karamazov contends that his examples of torture and child abuse cannot be rendered compossible with the moral value of *justice* by appeal to a higher cosmic harmony. Likewise, Eleanore Stump deems such aesthetic considerations at best supplementary, insisting that every instance of suffering must be necessary for the salvation of the victim, if Divine *goodness to created persons* is to be guaranteed.[7] Philip Quinn goes further, maintaining that aesthetic considerations of simplicity and variety are 'utterly irrelevant' in

assessing which possible world an omniscient, omnipotent, and perfectly good creator could make.[8] Aesthetic goods would be central to
a solution to 'the problem of ugliness': viz., of how

    (3) God exists, and is omnipotent, omniscient, and a person of
        supremely good taste.

could be logically compossible with

    (4) The world that exists contains some negative aesthetic values.

But the traditional problem of evil focuses on Divine morals, not
taste!

These authors illustrate the tendency within analytic philosophy
of religion, where defeaters of evil compossible with Divine goodness are concerned, to move from

    (T$_1$) Some sorts of aesthetic goodness are *insufficient* to defeat the
        evil of some sorts of personal suffering

(e.g. the delicate-pink flushed cheeks are insufficient to defeat the ills
of tuberculosis; maximum-variety-with-maximum-simplicity in the
cosmic order, to defeat the evil of child torture) to

    (T$_2$) Some sorts of aesthetic goodness are *at most supplementary* to
        the defeat of the evils of (some sorts of) personal suffering to

    (T$_3$) Aesthetic goods are *utterly irrelevant* to the defeat of evils
        in the amounts and of the kinds found in this world.

Beneath the surface is the parallel slide from the observation that
aesthetic and moral goodness sometimes break apart (in that some
instances of the former do not exemplify the latter) through over-
generalisation to a full-scale compartmentalisation of aesthetic from
moral value and goodness to persons.

In my judgement, such compartmentalisation of moral and aesthetic values is bogus. Not only is it untraditional – e.g. in wrestling
with the problem of evil, St Augustine appeals to beauty, both of the
cosmic order[9] and of God;[10] Leibniz leads with the aesthetic when he
commends maximum variety with maximum simplicity as criteria
for the *best* of all possible worlds; and Jonathan Edwards contends
that beauty is the principal attribute, not only of God, but of being
generally[11] – it is contrary to common sense. We have assumed
otherwise because we have failed to appreciate the variety of aesthetic goods and the range of ways they benefit created persons.
Once we refresh our memories, we will see not only how aesthetic
goods are *relevant* to, but also how they could be *sufficient* for theodicy.

2 PRELIMINARIES

First, some preliminaries are in order.

2.1 Aesthetic Assumptions

As to the metaphysics, (i) I am an unabashed realist about aesthetic value. This position coheres with my general theological Platonism, which I make no attempt to defend here. Otherwise, my case involves no more than elementary (if not uncontroversial) aesthetics.[12] (ii) I help myself to the distinction between *the sensuous values* of something (e.g. delightful colour, texture, or tone) and *its formal values* (e.g. the arrangement of the aforementioned values in a painting, sculpture, symphony, etc.). Likewise, if (as I believe) there are non-physical spiritual realities, I assume an analogous contrast between 'sensuous' and formal aesthetic values applies to them. Again, (iii) aesthetic goods, both sensuous and formal, may be related to other goods either as constituents or instrumentally as means. But (iv) I take for granted that there is an aesthetic way of looking at things that involves paying attention to something for its own sake, as opposed to seeing it as a means to some further end, and which focuses on the object or feature itself as opposed to one's own relation to it. Finally, I hold that both (v) aesthetic goods are intrinsically valuable; and if (iv) the aesthetic point of view appreciates them for their own sake, (vi) the aesthetic contemplation of aesthetic goods is itself intrinsically valuable.

2.2 Scope Restriction

Moreover, to keep this discussion within limits, I shall focus on exhibiting the centrality of aesthetic values within my own solution to the problem of evil, and leave the reader to transfer my points to the one s/he prefers. Briefly, in other papers[13] I have agreed that God's *goodness to created persons* is the central issue in theodicy, and the existence of horrendous evils – i.e., evils *e* the participation in which (as either victim or perpetrator) by a person *p* gives everyone *prima facie* reason to believe that *p*'s life cannot, given its inclusion of *e*, be a great good to *p* on the whole – is the principal challenge to it. Moreover, I have contended, God is good to a person *p* only if God ensures that *p*'s life is a great good to *p* on the whole, and that any horrendous evils *p* participates in are made meaningful by being defeated, not merely within the context of the world as a whole, but within the scope of *p*'s individual life.[14] I deny that any package of merely created goods could defeat horrendous evils, but maintain that God is an incommensurate good, personal intimacy with Whom is an incommensurate good for a created person. Consequently, *postmortem* beatific intimacy with God would not merely 'balance off' but engulf participation in horrendous evils, and would ensure any person who had it a life that was a great good to him/her on the whole. Moreover, horrors could also be defeated by being made meaningful through integration into that person's, on the whole overwhelmingly felicitous, relationship with God. And I have drawn on the mystical literature for possible modes of integration.

I turn now to show how such a solution – focusing as it does on Divine goodness to persons – is riddled with aesthetic values.

3   AESTHETIC GOODS AS NECESSARY: COSMIC ORDER, SURVIVAL, AND SANITY

So far, we have already called to mind one aesthetic property: viz., that of the order of the world as a whole. Of course, Pierce has taught us that 'cosmic order' is a slippery because trivial notion: given any batch of things however situated, some (mathematical) order or other obtains between them. Thus, he insists, any distinction of order from chaos involves a necessary reference to the interests, aims and tastes of persons. Leibniz himself anticipated this point, but thought to rest his theodicy on a non-trivial cosmic ordering, the maximum variety with maximum simplicity that allegedly characterises the best of all possible worlds.[15] At any rate, so long as we include God among the persons whose purposes and tastes are at issue, I have no need to debate this point. My argument rests on the twin observations that even trivial orderings are aesthetic properties, and that in any event the cosmos exhibits order of a sort beneficial to human kind. For evidence, I turn to the common place.

Evolutionists tell us that human survival depends on some sort of commensuration (they would say 'adaptation') between human capacities and the environments in which we live. In particular, human survival depends on our having a picture of the way the world is that is informative enough to enable us to cope with it. This 'match' does not require that the 'objective' world really be ordered by regularities simple and stable enough for human beings to grasp and use to predict and gain some measure of control over it. It is not even necessary that humans be able to work up to an accurate picture of the 'objective' structure of things by successive approximations. Rather, a 'phenomenalist' understanding of the correspondence will do. Human survival *instrumentally* requires a world whose structural properties and regularities can be modelled well enough by human cognitive capacities to enable human beings to make reliable predictions; conversely, it depends upon human beings having a taste for theories that thus model the world.

Besides the collective human capacity for folk- and academic science, developmental psychologists insist that human personality and sanity depend on the individual psyche's functioning as an effective theory-maker in relation to the data of its psychic field. They imagine that the infant starts with a booming, buzzing confusion and (unconsciously) gropes with all of its powers to find some organising principle that will reduce the variety of its data to a manageable simplicity. The earliest of these begin the differentiation of the self from the 'subjective' world. Because the child's capacities are meagre, its first theories are easily overthrown; as its powers increase, its models become more durable, as they approach an adult conception by successive approximations. Experiencing the world as ordered in a way that is congruent enough with reality, is *constitutive* of human sanity. Experiencing the world as chaotic, or losing one's taste for orderings that 'match up' with the 'objective' world, is part of what it is to be insane.

Returning to the problem of evil, my point is that such structural properties as the world really has are *aesthetic* properties. Moreover, if developmental psychologists are right to posit a bias in the human psyche towards managing variety with simplicity, and if (as has been traditionally assumed) the latter is a positive aesthetic value, human beings have a taste for modelling the world with aesthetic goods. Consequently, God's producing a world whose 'objective' aesthetic properties can be fruitfully modelled by human beings in terms of aesthetic goods, is one way God has of benefiting and hence of being *good to* human beings. For by doing so, God supplies conditions *instrumentally* necessary for human survival, conditions partially *constitutive* of human personality and sanity.

As for Penelhum's caution that the materials of theodicy must accord with religious values, it is worth noting how the Hebrew Bible represents God establishing order out of chaos relative to His own purposes – an order which, though partly inscrutable, benefits human beings. Thus, the *P*-creation narrative modifies a Babylonian story in which the hero-god conquers a watery-chaos monster, and divides its body to construct the world. Similarly, in Genesis 1, God creates by separating the light from the darkness (Gen. 1:4), the day from the night (Gen. 1:14–19), the waters from the sky (Gen. 1:7–8) and the dry land (Gen. 1:9–11); by differentiating plant and animal kinds and assigning the boundaries of their habitations and seasons (Gen. 1:11–13, 20–5). And then God hands it over to human beings to govern and to use (Gen 1:26–31). Likewise, Biblical interest in the Act–Consequence principle ('good for good , evil for evil') should, in the first instance, be seen, not as part of an argument about whether retributive justice or mercy is the more perfect Divine attribute, but as a hedge against moral chaos in the world, as assurance to human beings that there is something we can do (i.e. be virtuous) to avoid the worst. Thus, in contrast to non-Biblical versions of the Flood Story, Genesis 6–9 explains this near-abandonment of creation to chaos, not as an expression of divine caprice, but rather of God's moral order in the face of human wickedness (Gen. 6:5–8, 11ff.). Likewise, the Law and ritual define and structure Divine–human relations, so as to make contact with God safe and predictable for human kind.

4   AESTHETIC GOODS AS INGREDIENTS IN A GOOD LIFE

I have insisted that God's *goodness to* created persons involves His guaranteeing to each a life that is a great good to him/her on the whole. But what makes for a good life? Once more, I turn to the commonplace.

4.1   'The Good Things of Life'

First, and most obviously, a good life includes satisfying relations to at least some of 'the good things of life'. Many would include (i) *sensory pleasures* in their number: delight in pleasant colours, sounds, and flavours; the comfort or excitement of textures and feels. Most would count (ii) *the exercise of creative capacities* – to paint, sing, dance; to understand and nurture people; to make intellectual breakthroughs – among the intrinsically worthwhile. Again, almost everyone values (although perhaps too few enjoy) (iii) *intimate personal rela-*

tionships, characterised by mutual love, support, and appreciation. Importantly for our purposes, (iv) *aesthetic enjoyments* not only make the list, but are integrated into its other members as well. For example, (iv.i) the enjoyment of sensuous values is often aesthetic in its appreciation of the intensity of a colour, the gracefulness and balance of a shape or contour, the delicacy of a rose, the subtle balance and blending of flavours in a dish. (iv.ii) Likewise, aesthetic appreciation of the formal structure and arrangement of complex wholes – whether in nature, paintings, symphonies, or mathematical proofs – makes a positive contribution to life experiences. (iv.iii) Less often remarked nowadays (but cf. Plato, *Symposium*) is the fact that the joy of personal relationships also has its aesthetic dimensions, and that not only in the aesthetic contemplation of bodily beauty. There is also the 'sensuous' sweetness and tenderness of personal presence; the beauty of personality found in grace, elegance, gentle simplicity, wit and charm. Moral virtue also enhances the soul's beauty, involving as it does a two-tiered aesthetic skill: to balance and harmonise its own competing drives, interests, and functions within; and to produce acts that are not only generically good (e.g. alms-giving in place of theft) but fit the circumstances (i.e. at an appropriate time, place, in relation to suitable persons and ends). Likewise, the history of a personal relationship is a story with its own formal aesthetic properties; which ones they are greatly affects the value the relationship contributes to the lives of the persons involved (see 4.4 below).

Cast in the language of some philosophers, satisfying relationships to intrinsic goods are themselves intrinsically good; and in many ordinary cases, the aesthetic contemplation of aesthetic value numbers among their constituents.

4.2 The 'Meaning' and 'Purpose' of Life

Sometimes, a quite temporary but satisfying relationship to some great enough good (as in doing a dramatic heroic act or composing a great symphony) will be enough to make a person feel (and others agree) that his/her otherwise miserable, unproductive, and shapeless life was worth living. But usually it makes a difference how the bitter and the sweet are distributed and balanced over the whole course of a life. Moreover, a good life is expected to be one that has 'meaning' and 'purpose'. This fact reflects the interaction of two common human instincts. First, *our generalised psychological drive to impose a simplifying order on data* has an instance in the urge to find some simplifying generalisations or patterns structuring the experiences of our own or other persons' lives. In addition, we human beings commonly exhibit *a drive to self-transcendence*, to relate ourselves to something beyond ourselves, typically to something larger or in some sense more valuable or more permanent. Our life experiences can become organically related, our lives as wholes organised around some goal or ideal at which we ourselves aim. This may be conscious (as when one offers one's life in service of one's country, or bends one's energies to the cause of social justice or the ideal of world peace, or devotes oneself to the conquest of disease, to advancing the frontiers of science, to art, to the family, or even to solving the Liar Paradox). Or it may be unconscious (as when one repeatedly contrives to become just like or exactly opposite to daddy). Alternatively, our lives may be moulded and expended by the individual or collective schemes of others, once again, consciously (as with the soldier in the dictator's army, or the salesman of a large company) or unconsciously (as when we come to exemplify a certain culture). When all else fails, many find comfort in relating themselves to nature, in recognising themselves as instances of a natural kind of longstanding, their disease and death as causal products of natural regularities.

4.3   Internal vs External Points of View

The value of a person's life may be assessed *from the inside* (in relation to that person's own goals, ideals, and choices) and *from the outside* (in relation to the aims, tastes, values, and preferences of others). Not surprisingly, such assessments may disagree. Hitler may have seen positive value in the lives of his soldiers, who expended their energies and died as cogs in the war-machines of the Führer's mythological designs. Doubtless many of them put a higher premium on the civilian goals of home, family, and non-military career; others felt their lives contaminated beyond cleansing by their participation in the Holocaust. Conversely, the hermit or monk who abandons the world in search of God, and the 'yuppy' pressing his limits towards his first million or the starlet thirsting for fame, may view each other's lifestyles as foolish wastes.

My notion is that for a person's life to be a great good *to him/her* on the whole, the external point of view (even if it is God's) is not sufficient. Rather the person him/herself must value and actually enjoy his/her relations to enough and great enough goods. A lifetime supply of chocolate will not benefit the choc-allergic, nor regular concert attendance the deaf. (This is not to say that the person must agree to the judgement that his/her life has been a great good to him/her on the whole. The life of a curmudgeon might be filled with his/her enjoyment of good things; and yet, since s/he enjoys being a curmudgeon, s/he might not admit it.) Likewise, if a person's life is to have positive meaning *for him/her*, that person must not forever see his/her life as expended only or principally for ends or ideals to which s/he is at best indifferent and at worst despises. Presumably, no human person will ever recognise, much less consciously value, all of the over-arching patterns under which his/her life experiences are subsumed. But a person's life will have positive value for him/her, only if s/he eventually recognises some patterns organising some chunks of his/her experiences around goals, ideals, relationships that s/he stabilises in valuing.

4.4 Form and Structure as Ingredients of a Good Life

Returning to our theme, the structure and arrangement of experiences in a life, the patterns of distributions of goods or ills, the relations of those experiences to self-transcendent goals or ideals, are alike aesthetic properties. Which formal aesthetic properties are partially constitutive of a person's life makes a dramatic difference to how good or meaningful that person's life is. (i) Contrast, for example, a life with an idyllic childhood and a miserable adulthood, with one in which moderate goods and ills are sprinkled through the whole. Again, isolated evils (such as the loss of property in an earthquake) can be far more tolerable than others organically related to important aspects of one's life (e.g. parental abuse of children). On the other hand, a mere Chisholmian balancing-off of evils with good (the pain of a stubbed toe with the pleasure of a beautiful sunset) cannot endow the evils with the meaning of making a positive contribution to any great enough goods. (ii) Further, insofar as unity, integrity, harmony, and relevance are valuable aesthetic properties in a life, they will differentially value similar acts, experiences, character traits, etc., depending on the life context. For example, sensory enjoyments (good, considered in themselves) obstruct the desert father's quest for purity of heart that wills one thing, while the latter's ascetic renunciations sound a dissonant chord within a life that aims at the Golden Mean. Exchanging Harris tweed for Indian peasant garb would (almost always) be irrelevant to vicarage life in rural England; but for Gandhi it was an act of integrity and solidarity. The cultivation of intellectual sophistication and managerial skills would have spoiled the simplicity and charisma of St Francis, but were fitting in St Bonaventure who found his vocation in organising the Franciscan order and integrating its work into university life.

For a more theological illustration of the difference aesthetic organisation can make to the value of a person's life (as to the world as a whole), consider the contrasting soteriological plot-lines of apocalyptic theology and the passion narratives of the Synoptic Gospels.

4.4.1 Apocalyptic Soteriology

Apocalyptic theology offers us two, one-dimensional collective characters: the righteous and the wicked. Likewise, its plot recognises two opposite conditions – one all good (powerful, flourishing, enjoying a monopoly on the goods) and the other all bad (powerless, horrendous suffering verging on destruction) – and two ages. Its plot-line moves from one age to the other via the intervention of a heavenly rescuer who effects a simple reversal. First, in this present evil age, the wicked prosper and the righteous suffer. This will continue until the powers of darkness have done their worst, which includes the very undoing of creation. Then, the Son of Man will come with His angels, who usher the righteous into heavenly bliss and consign the wicked to torture chambers either eternally or until they wither away. According to this scenario, evil is not defeated, but balanced off in a retributive ordering: the sufferings of the righteous are cancelled (without being seen to have contributed to any good) by heavenly joys, while the crimes of the wicked are balanced off by their torment in hell and/or subsequent annihilation. The two collective actors swap positions, but do not change character. The wicked are not redeemed, nor does suffering come to an end. Sharing as it does all the aesthetic defects of a grade-B Western,[16] apocalyptic theology pays the price of limited plot-resolution.

4.4.2 Lucan Passion Narratives

There is an element of the one-dimensional in Luke's passion narrative, as well. For the evangelist represents the crucifixion as the decisive battle between two one-dimensional characters: God and Satan (cf. Lk 4:1–13; 22:3, 53); Jesus is God's righteous chosen one (Lk 3:22, 9:35, 23:47); Judas (22:3), the Pharisees, chief priests, and scribes (22:53) have become (temporarily) instruments of Satan. Nevertheless, the plot drips with tragi-comic irony, as every step the enemies of Jesus take to bring His ministry to a definitive end (cf. Lk 6:11, 11:53–4, 19:47–8, 22:2, 4–6) actually occurs according to the definite plan and foreknowledge of God (Acts 2:23) and forwards the plot, enabling Jesus to fulfil His vocation (Lk 9:22, 30–1, 44; 19:31–3; 24:6–7, 25–7, 44–7). Judas's action of betraying Jesus into woe (Lk 22:3–5) in fact brings woe on Judas by whom the Son of Man is betrayed (Lk 22:22; Acts 1:16–20). The chief priests and scribes who hope to destroy His ministry by having Him killed among the criminals, fulfil the prophecy that He should be numbered among the transgressors (Is 53:12; Lk 22:37; 23:32). They who denounce the kingship of Jesus before Pilate and accuse him of perverting the nation (Lk 23:2) themselves pervert the nation by persuading the people of God to reject their kind (Lk 23:13–25). They who condemn Jesus as a blasphemer (Lk 22:66–71; cf. 5:21, 11:15) themselves blaspheme, echoing the devil's taunts (Lk 4:3, 9) ironically twisting God's own testimony concerning Jesus (Lk 3:22, 9:35, 23:35). The Jewish leaders would mock the kingship of *Jesus* by crucifying Him, but Pilate mocks *Jewish* kingship by crucifying Jesus as King of the Jews (Lk 23:38). Consistently, Jesus's enemies, in mocking, advertise the truths they reject: His captors' taunting 'Prophesy!' (Lk 22:63–5), fulfils the most detailed of Jesus's passion predictions (Lk 19:32–3). The rulers of the people ironically mouth the truth that 'he is the Christ of God, His Chosen One' (Lk 23:35). Pilate proclaims to all who pass by that Jesus is King of the Jews (23:38), and Jesus makes The Skull his royal court. Mounting the cross, His throne of judgement, Jesus continues to expose the thoughts of the hearts of many in Israel by evoking their reactions to Him (Lk 2:34–5), to exercise His authority to forgive sins (Lk 23:34, 39–43; cf. 5:20–4, 7:48), His royal prerogative to open the gates of Paradise (Lk 23:43). And, of course, these regal acts receive the Divine seal of approval, in Jesus's resurrection and exaltation (Lk 24; Acts 2:22–4, 32–6; 3:26; 4:10–13; 13:30, 33). Yet, this plot does not rest content with a simple reversal of fates. The human enemies of God are not left one-dimensional: for the worst they do in the Passion narrative in their role as instruments of the devil, is turned by God into a fresh opportunity for them to step out of this role, through repentance, a change of heart (Acts 2:23, 36–42; 3:17–26; 13:26–32)! On this, more subtle because highly ironic scenario, not only can the disciples who follow Jesus to martyrdom look forward to the promised Divine vindication (Lk 9:23–6; 22:28–30). Those who consented to the death of Jesus and repent afterwards have the opportunity to enter into the covenant blessings with the consolation of recognising the worst thing they ever did as making a positive contribution to God's plan to spread His glory to the ends of the earth.

5   BEAUTY BEATIFIC!

St Anselm – good Christian Platonist that he was – held that paradigm value is one. My contention that aesthetic value is multiply integrated into the good of and for persons is but a fragment of that claim. I have commented on how formal aesthetic properties are partially constitutive of moral virtues and morally virtuous acts, how distributive and retributive justice are but species of aesthetic order.[17] Likewise, I have noted how aesthetic enjoyment of aesthetic goods is not only to be numbered among the intrinsic goods, but also is partially constitutive of sensory pleasures and the enjoyment of persons in intimate relationship. Finally, I have called attention to commonplaces about how the aesthetic properties of the cosmos as a whole and of an individual's life-history dramatically affect a person's survival and sanity, the goodness and meaning of his/her life. It follows that furnishing a person with satisfying relationships to aesthetic goods is one way to benefit a person. Likewise, the ability to contribute to the positive meaning of a person's life by overcoming evil with good, is in part a function of aesthetic imagination, of the capacity to weave evils into complex goods through subtle irony and reversal. All of these points are 'religion-neutral' in that they imply nothing about the existence of God, although they will not be acceptable to just any secular value-theory.

Yet, I agree with Penelhum that the logical problem of evil should be solved within the parameters of religious value-theory. To dramatise my contention that God's goodness to created persons involves showering them with aesthetic goods, I shall close by indicating how my theodicy, in effect, offers a select package of aesthetic goods as *sufficient* to guarantee God's goodness even to participants in horrendous evils. (i) First of all, I maintain, God Himself is the only good great enough to balance off horrendous evils, and yet as the incommensurate good not only 'balances off' but engulfs them. And what is so beatific about intimacy with God? One Biblical answer is 'the fair beauty of the Lord' (Ps. 27:6,11), 'the beauty of holiness' (Ps. 69:9), 'the glory of God' (Ps 24:7–10; 50:2; 63:2; 66:1; 76:4; 104:1; 113:4) – in philosophical language, a being a more beautiful than which cannot be conceived, even Beauty Itself! Analogous to 'sensuous' aesthetic values among physical things, God's beauty will be 'tasted' and 'seen' (Ps 34:8) and enjoyed.[18]

One might object that beauty is not the most frequently mentioned of Divine attributes in the Bible: more psalms celebrate the power and good will that stand behind the mighty acts which have instrumental value for individual and collective human ends, with His righteousness and covenant-faithfulness.[19] Yet, this observation does not undermine my point; for Divine beauty is featured in contexts which focus on the worshipful appreciation of God as He is in Himself, an activity which is our closest *ante-mortem* approximation to the beatific vision itself. Alternatively, one might protest that such aesthetic contemplation of God that values Him for His own sake is irrelevant to the traditional problem of evil which focuses on Divine *goodness to us*. Here my minimal aesthetic assumptions (iv)–(vi) (see 2.1 above) come to my rescue: aesthetic contemplation of God the incommensurate good, is itself an intrinsic good, one which is (as I claim) incommensurately good for the creature.

(ii) Second, I have insisted, as a matter of theodicy, that God will pay created personhood the respect of endowing each individual's life with positive meaning, which that individual himself can (at least from a *post-mortem* retrospective) appreciate (perhaps in addition to other meanings which are beyond the creature's power ever to grasp). Since God's beauty is – like His nature – omnipresent, His glory part of what we experience in our aesthetic contemplation of the beauty of nature and other persons here below (Ps. 19:1), our *ante-mortem* experiences of created beauty are given added meaning by such integration into our relationship with God.

(iii) Third, I have argued that the defeat of horrendous evils within the context of individual lives, requires aesthetic creativity as a dimension of Divine Wisdom and Power. (a) I have speculated that human pain and suffering is itself a vision into the inner life of God, perhaps even a mystic identification with Divine suffering. If so, Divine suffering must be integrated into God's Beauty, so that a creature might retrospectively recognise and prize his/her suffering as an excruciatingly intimate awareness of the Beauty that s/he now overwhelmingly enjoys. (b) Likewise, the soteriological plot line of the Synoptic Passion narratives serves as a model of how God can use the aesthetic techniques of tragi-comic irony and reversal to defeat our perpetration of horrendous evils within the context of our own individual lives.

In short, were we not so blinded by the lie of compartmentalised values, our hymns might sing how God, Himself Beauty unspeakable, the most relentless of its Lovers, the most artful of artists, freely expends unlimited aesthetic creativity to make all else in His image, to paint even our participation in horrendous evils into wonderful lives for beautiful children in a beautiful world![20]

Notes

1. I am grateful to Robert Merrihew Adams for helpful and extensive discussion and critique. My thanks go also to members of the Philosophy Department at Calvin College, where I presented an earlier version of this paper. I am otherwise indebted to the American Council of Learned Societies, the John Simon Guggenheim Foundation, and the University of California President's Humanities Council for grants that made this research possible.

2. Nelson Pike, 'Hume on Evil', *The Philosophical Review*, LXXII, no. 2 (1963), pp. 180–97.

3. Roderick M. Chisholm, 'The Defeat of Good and Evil', *Proceedings and Addresses of the American Philosophical Association*, XLII (1968–69), pp. 21–38.

4. Terence Penelhum, 'Divine Goodness and the Problem of Evil', *Religious Studies* 2, pp. 104–6.

5. Ibid., pp. 95–107; esp. pp. 98–100.

6. Ibid., p. 107.

7. Eleanore Stump, 'The Problem of Evil', *Faith and Philosophy*, Vol. 2, no. 4 (1985), pp. 392–423, 417.

8. Philip L. Quinn, 'God, Moral Perfection, and Possible Worlds', *God: The Contemporary Discussion*, edited by Frederick Sontag and M. Darrol Bryant (New York: The Rose of Sharon Press, 1982), pp. 197–215; esp. p. 203.

9. St Augustine, *On Free Choice of Will*, Book II, c.xi, secs 120–9; Book III, c.ix, secs 85–103.

10. St Augustine, *Confessions* X, 27: 'Late have I loved you, O Beauty, so ancient and so new . . . ' (in *Augustine of Hippo: Selected Writings*, translated by Mary T. Clark [New York: Paulist Press, 1984], p. 144); and 'Letter 147', c.22 (loc.cit., pp. 379–80).

11. Cf. Roland Andre Delattre, *Beauty and Sensibility in the Thought of Jonathan Edwards: An Essay in Aesthetics and Theological Ethics* (New Haven and London: Yale University Press, 1968).

12. Cf. John Hospers, 'Aesthetics, Problems of', *The Encyclopedia of Philosophy*, Vol. 1, pp. 35–56.

13. See 'Problems of Evil: More Advice to Christian Philosophers', in *Faith and Philosophy* (1988), pp. 121–43; 'Theodicy without Blame', *Philosophical Topics* XVI (1988), pp. 215–45; 'Horrendous Evils and the Good-

ness of God', *Proceedings of the Aristotelian Society*, Supplementary Volume LXIII (1989), pp. 299–310.

14. Dal Ratsch has observed that if God were conceived of as necessarily good to any created persons He makes, then, since it would be a necessary truth that any person God created would have a life that was a great good to him/her on the whole, no evils could constitute even *prima facie* reason to doubt this and so none could be horrendous. My replies are twofold: (i) I reject the notion that God is *necessarily* good to created persons. Just as I maintain that God has no obligations to created persons, so also I think His policy towards them is a matter of His free and contingent volition. (ii) In any event, it seems to me that there can be *prima facie* reasons for doubting even a necessary truth, and that these remain *prima facie* reasons, even when a person knows they will be defeated. Someone who believed (1) to be a necessary truth, could still hold that (2) constituted *prima facie* reason against its truth; and regard their *prima facie* incompossibility as creating – for anyone who believes them both – the problem of showing how the *prima facie* consideration against (1) raised by (2) can be defeated.

15. *Discourse on Method*, sections 5–6.

16. As I have said before, in 'Separation and Reversal in Luke–Acts', *Philosophy and the Christian Faith*, edited by Thomas Morris (Notre Dame, Indiana: Notre Dame University Press, 1988), pp. 92–117; esp. pp 93–4.

17. Cf. St Augustine, *On Free Choice of Will*, Book II, c.xi, secs 120–9; Book III, c.ix, secs 85–103.

18. Cf. Augustine, *Confessions* X, 27: 'Late have I loved you, O Beauty, so ancient and so new . . .' (in *Augustine of Hippo: Selected Writings*, translated by Mary T. Clark (Paulist Press, NY, 1984), p. 144); and 'Letter 147', c.22 (loc.cit., pp. 379–80), where Augustine insists that it is Divine Beauty that the mind's eye will see. In Western Christian theology, it is perhaps the Puritan divine Jonathan Edwards who took beauty the most seriously, making it not only chief among God's attributes, but also the replacement for goodness as the first principle of being. Cf. Roland Andre Delattre, *Beauty and Sensibility in the Thought of Jonathan Edwards: An Essay in Aesthetics and Theological Ethics* (New Haven and London: Yale University Press, 1968).

19. Karl Barth (in *Church Dogmatics* II.1 (Edinburgh: T. & T. Clark, 1957), pp. 651–7) displays considerable ambivalence about the notion of Divine beauty. On the one hand, he brings it up as an aspect of God's glory, which also involves reference to Divine power. On the other, he insists that God's beauty must consist in holiness, which one feels, is taken to have the flavour of righteousness.

20. There are a few hymns which do praise God for beauty: e.g., 'Fairest Lord Jesus' sings how Jesus is more beautiful than created beauties and Ps. 45:2 makes the same point when taken as referring to the Messiah; 'For the beauty of the earth' thanks God for created beauty.

6

Religion after Babel[1]
ROBERT MERRIHEW ADAMS

One of the many interesting and fruitful ideas in John Hick's *Interpretation of Religion* is that of a 'religious interpretation of religion'.[2] I wish in this chapter to apply that idea to some issues about the place of religious ethics in a pluralistic society, asking how one must understand the nature of religion if one is to understand oneself as fully and authentically religious in such a setting. My starting-point for the statement of the issues will be Jeffrey Stout's stimulating book, *Ethics after Babel: The Languages of Morals and Their Discontents*.[3]

1   THE 'MARGINALISATION' OF RELIGIOUS ETHICS

Stout speaks of 'the marginality of theology in North American society today'[4] – and it is theological *ethics* with which he is primarily concerned. It is by now a truism that contemporary American society is pluralistic and secularised and that religion is marginalised in it. There is certainly much truth in this, as there is in most truisms. It is obvious that religious institutions are less central to our society and culture than they traditionally have been in Western civilisation – perhaps largely because competing, secular centres of culture, service and social life are now so much stronger and more numerous. But we may be misled here also. Marginalisation is a spatial metaphor. What is marginalised is shoved or confined to the *edge* of something. Something else is in the *centre*. We must be clear about what is at the edge of what.

Our present concern is whether religious ethics is confined to the edge or periphery of public ethical discussion. What public ethical discussion? Stout seems at times to be thinking of ethical discussion that goes on in academia, and even specifically of what he calls 'secular philosophical thought'.[5] I can testify from experience that many philosophers are not easily interested in religious perspectives on ethics. This is a matter of professional and personal concern to me as a philosopher who is interested in religious ethics. But it would be parochial to identify professional moral philosophy, or even academic thought about ethics more generally, with the public ethical discourse of our society. Ethical discourse that is genuinely, fully public, in a democracy, would not be confined to the academy or to an intellectual elite, but would be generally accessible to citizens and would engage the interest of a large and diverse crosssection of them.

Is there in our society a fully public ethical discourse in this sense to whose margins religious ethics has been relegated? I doubt it. If religious ethical categories are relatively infrequent in our fully public political discourse, the most obvious reason, sadly, is that unambiguously ethical categories of any sort, religious or secular, are much less prominent in it than technological categories. And on those relatively infrequent occasions when a public issue is debated in clearly moral terms, identifiably religious voices virtually always take a leading part. As a white Protestant, perhaps I will not be suspected of bias in remarking that in the last few decades the American Catholic bishops and the African–American churches have provided some of the most effective leadership in focusing public attention on the moral dimension of public issues. And a President who is thinking of going to war is likelier to seek advice or support from a bishop or an evangelist than from a professor of philosophy. This undoubtedly reflects the fact that Americans are still in many ways a very religious people, and a large proportion of them do almost all their ethical thinking, whether about public or private issues, in an explicitly religious context. And we largely lack secular institutions that focus individuals' attention on distinctively ethical issues as persistently as many religious institutions do. In short, religious ethics is no more marginalised than secular ethics in relation to public debate in our society.

It is true, no doubt, that intellectually ambitious moral theology does not have the influence in American public life today that it enjoyed in the days of Reinhold Niebuhr and John Courtney Murray. But secular ethical theory probably does not enjoy *that* influence either. There are many possible reasons for moral theology's loss of influence. Increasing pluralism and secularisation of American culture is one. Perhaps the cultural impact of television is another.

There is yet another possibility, however, with which Stout's book confronts us. He argues that 'academic theologians have increasingly given the impression of saying nothing atheists don't already know'[6] – that is, that they have compromised the tenets of their traditions to such an extent that they have nothing left to say that is distinctive enough to command attention. Of course he knows that this is not true about all academic theologians, and he very briefly sketches six diverse ways in which he thinks some of them are trying to avoid such unorthodox conclusions.[7] But Stout is evidently not very optimistic about the success of these strategies. He doubts that they will persuade secular intellectuals that religious ethics is plausible enough to command attention. Either not distinctive enough or not plausible enough: that is the dilemma with which he believes theology is confronted. For many observers of the theological scene Stout's diagnosis will resonate with perceptions of a certain *malaise* afflicting academic theology in America, and not only in America.

In the face of such a *malaise* and such a diagnosis, what should be the aims and aspirations of religious ethics? The suggestion is strong in Stout's book that the ideal for religious moralists participating as such in public debate would be 'a common public theology'.[8] This idea seems to me both very questionable and deeply involved with basic issues about the nature of religion and the possibilities of religious pluralism.

2 A COMMON PUBLIC THEOLOGY?

Think of a free and open society, containing many religious and ethnic traditions and exposed to the great variety of cultural influences present, and increasingly communicated, in our world. It seems unlikely, on the face of it, that such a society would either reach or long maintain general agreement on an ethical theory of any comprehensiveness, much less on a theology. Even nineteenth-century America, Protestant-dominated as it was, can hardly be said to have had a common theology when its cultural leaders were as diverse religiously as, say, Ralph Waldo Emerson, Charles Grandison Finney, Mark Twain and William Jennings Bryan. To be sure, there were theological and Biblical concepts and images that would be generally understood and widely valued if employed in an ethical claim or argument; and such ideas are undoubtedly less widely appreciated today, due to increasing religious diversity, as well as to increasing religious illiteracy resulting from the educational failure of most American churches. But such shared ideas hardly constituted a theology. And if a thinker such as Reinhold Niebuhr had wide and public influence, as he did, it was certainly not by being uncontroversial, either in theology or in politics.

How then should we understand the grip that the ideal of a common public theology certainly has on the imagination of many theologians and students of religion? Some may simply be moved by the evangelistic desire that everyone should come to the knowledge of religious truth as they understand it themselves. But that is not the only motive at work here. There is also an interest in the relation of religion to society, state, and culture as such. This interest is articulated in some telling phrases of Stout's. He speaks of a change (which he does not expect) that 'might make some kind of theology central to the culture again', and of 'the inability of religious practices to serve as a unifying ideological center around which whole societies could order various goods, practices, and institutions'.[9]

These phrases resonate with important trends in the study of religion which focus on the role of religion as an organising aspect of society and culture. These trends affect theologians and biblical scholars as well as anthropologists. They draw inspiration from the study of societies in which religion seems to form a seamless whole with the rest of the culture. The embodiment of religion in a comprehensive 'form of life' in such contexts is understandably attractive to many religious minds, as well as fascinating to scholarly minds. And social and cultural studies are certainly enlarging our understanding of the history of religions.

But what are the implications for religion in a pluralistic society if we view the nature of religion primarily in terms of its social and cultural role? It seems clear that in a situation of religious pluralism, religion cannot serve the integration of society and culture as it typically does in religiously homogeneous societies. If we think that integrative role is of the essence of religion, we may be tempted to conclude that the religions apparently surviving in a pluralistic context can only be truncated, perhaps merely vestigial religions. This is a conclusion that religious persons who are committed to a pluralistic society will obviously want to resist.

Jeffrey Stout does not endorse such an extreme conclusion. He clearly recognises the reality of relatively private religious beliefs and practices in our pluralistic society, distinguishing 'the problem of public theology' from 'problems pertaining to the rationality of religious individuals'. It is the viability of *public* theology that he doubts. Nevertheless it is also 'the problem of public theology' that draws most of the attention that he devotes to theology in *Ethics after*

Babel.[10] And I think that religious moralists would be wise to be wary of Stout's efforts to assess their enterprise in relation to its social role. Religious moralists in a pluralistic society need to understand their role in way that does not require religion to be 'a unifying ideological center'[11] for the whole society. Otherwise they will be tempted, as Stout's argument suggests, to sacrifice the distinctness of their theological positions in a probably vain attempt to catch the attention of secular intellectuals.

Stout himself sings something of a siren's song at this point. He invites religious moralists to join in a 'movement toward historical specificity' in the study of religious ethics, and urges the need for 'a broadly humanistic account of those forces [that incline people for or against religious faith], an account capable of tracing their relation to changing historical circumstances and variations in moral language'.[12] The study Stout proposes is historical, descriptive and explanatory. Religious concepts will be mentioned rather than used in it. In John Hick's terms, I think we can fairly say that Stout's will be a *non-religious interpretation of religion.*

3 RELIGIOUS INTERPRETATIONS OF RELIGION AND ETHICS

Religious moralists and theologians are better advised to seek a *religious* interpretation of religion and ethics. In our context such a religious interpretation must surely seek to understand religion as something that can flourish in a full-blooded way in a pluralistic society. How can that be done?

One alternative is a retreat to a spiritual, if not a physical, ghetto. On this alternative, a richly-articulated religious tradition's role as unifying ideological centre for a whole society and culture is accepted as essential to a full religious life. Since pluralism prevents any one religious tradition from playing this role in the larger society, the religious community itself will take over as much as it can of the status of a whole society, creating strong, relatively impermeable boundaries between itself and the wider culture. Within these cultural boundaries, it may be hoped, as within the walls of a monastery, all of life may be permeated and organised by a single religious tradition.

Such a strategy of cultural encapsulation has been used with some success by minority religious communities in more than one historic context. It structured a considerable measure of religious pluralism in the Ottoman Empire, for example. And versions of it have been advocated by numerous religious thinkers in our society. But the isolation it involves of a community and its selves from alien influences seems to many of us likely to be unfruitful and lead to an unwholesome rigidity.

It may also be a particularly difficult strategy to implement in our situation. The traditional American form of religious pluralism, widely known as 'denominationalism', involves relatively permeable cultural boundaries between different religious groups. Some of our religious traditions, including mine, have never had strong cultural boundaries against outside influences; and it is probably too late to start building them.

What, then, are the possibilities of religious interpretation of religion and ethics for those of us who aspire to be authentically religious in a pluralistic society but without erecting impermeable cultural boundaries around our religious communities and traditions? This aspiration cannot be content with a view of religion as an aspect or dimension of a comprehensive social and cultural system. I grant that religious phenomena always have a social and cultural role, and there is usually something interesting to be said about them from a sociological point of view. But if religious thought, in a pluralistic society, sees its primary vocation in such a social and cultural role, it will be hard for it to find or retain its distinctive and authentic voice, for reasons that Stout makes clear enough.

Two points in John Hick's religious interpretation of religion may be helpful here. I refer, first, to what Hick calls 'the soteriological character of post-axial religion' and, second, to the importance of saintliness; and I should make clear that I am commenting at present only on these two points in Hick's complex and subtle theory. Hick describes the current major religions of the world as 'post-axial', meaning that they stem in one way or another from religious developments that took place in several parts of the world in what Karl Jaspers called 'the axial age', approximately 800–200 BCE. The older, 'pre-axial' religions, according to Hick, were 'centrally (but not solely) concerned with the preservation of cosmic and social order'; whereas 'post-axial religion [is] centrally (but not solely) concerned with the quest for salvation or liberation'.[13] On Hick's view, pre-axial religion is 'essentially conservative', post-axial religion is 'revolutionary',[14] '[C]entral to the post-axial movements [is the hope] for a radically new, different and better existence.'[15]

It would be too simple to identify the pre-axial outlook, as Hick understands it, with the conception of religion as a central, organising aspect of a total culture or social system. No pre-modern faith understood itself in sociological terms, and the post-axial religions certainly have provided organising principles to societies. But placing the essence of religion in its role as organiser of society and culture is certainly more congenial to pre-axial than to post-axial faith, as conceived by Hick.[16] A faith that actually does 'serve as a unifying ideological center'[17] for a whole society will not long remain revolutionary, if it ever was, as the sad experience of Marxism in this century suggests. 'The soteriological character of post-axial religion', I take it, is based on aspiration for a good that transcends any social and cultural system that has ever been realised in human history, or that we can expect to be realised by natural processes in the foreseeable future. Religious thought that is animated by such an aspiration can hardly suppose that religion is primarily an organising feature of such social and cultural systems. Seeing the nature, or the heart and soul, of religion in its transcendent aspiration may therefore free religious thinkers to pursue their distinctive religious themes without worrying too much about general cultural acceptance of their ideas, and also without feeling a need to retreat into a confined or narrowly sectarian cultural system that *can* be globally organised by their beliefs.

Hick regards post-axial religion as characterised by a certain individualism. It arose, he implies, in an 'emergence of individuality' in which 'religious value no longer resided in total identification with the group but began to take the form of a personal openness to transcendence'.[18] This personal openness to transcendence is for Hick the heart of a religious ethics. It connotes a transformation of human life that is primarily individual. Hick emphasises that religious ethics in a contemporary setting should be expected to have implications for political and economic liberation. However, he characterises this aspect of religious ethics primarily in terms of the social action of religiously-transformed individuals – indeed, the action of 'saints'.[19] Saintliness is clearly central to his view of religious ethics. Indeed, fruitfulness in 'the production of saints' is the main criterion he proposes 'by which to identify a religious tradition as a salvific human response to the Real'. The saints, for this criterion, may explicitly be 'both contemplative and practical, individualistic and political'.[20] But they are still individuals, and the criterion is concerned with the transformation of individuals in the first instance.

This focus on saintliness and the transformation of individuals has an important advantage for religious ethics in a modern pluralistic society. In such a situation, as I have argued, the distinctiveness of a religious tradition, or even of religious ethics more generally, can hardly be manifested in the organisation of the whole society. But it can be manifested in the organisation of an individual life. The lives in which it is most fully manifested are the lives of the saints. On this subject the religious moralist can certainly speak with a distinctive voice.

An oft-remarked feature of modern, 'secular' societies is a tendency for human lives to be lived in a plurality of institutions or spheres that are only loosely connected. Work, play, family, church, state – most of these come in many varieties, and each has its own style, its own priorities, its own meanings for various sorts of action. There is no integration of all this that each of us receives simply as a function of our ethnic identity. I think this does not make the integration of life and world impossible; but it does make it harder, and it makes it primarily a responsibility of the individual, rather than of the society. This individual responsibility for one's own integration goes hand in hand with individual freedom in a pluralistic setting. It does not follow from individual responsibility, however, that one must work *alone* at the task of integration. Religious traditions in a pluralistic society provide alternative social and symbolic frameworks for an individual's integration of life and world – frameworks rooted in long social histories. If the tradition does not retreat behind relatively impermeable cultural barriers, the pluralistic context may tend to destabilise integrations already achieved; but a perennial need for *re*integration need not be viewed, spiritually, as a disadvantage.

4 RELIGIOUS VISION AND PUBLIC ISSUES

My argument seems at this point to be assigning religious ethics an unfashionably individualistic role. And I am prepared to be somewhat unfashionable on this point. For it seems clear that if I am to see myself as both genuinely religious and culturally open in a pluralistic society, I must suppose that organising individual lives is essential to religion in a way that organising a whole society is not.

And yet religious moralists will rightly insist that they have something to say about the public realm. An ethics that has nothing to say about politics and economics and other issues of public morality cannot be complete even as an ethics of personal life. And religious views do have implications about public issues. Belief in transcendence, transformation, liberation, such as characterises post-axial religion according to Hick, gives rise both to critical judgements about present social arrangements and to visions of better alternatives. The 'radically new, different and better existence'[21] envisaged may well be social as well as individual. Post-axial religions are not defined by their social role, but they have ethical messages for society. Distinctively religious organisation of life, in a pluralistic society, will be private; but religion may address the public in distinctive voices.

The distinctiveness to be desired and expected in religion's public voices should not be exaggerated, however. To the extent that the aim of their prophecy is political repentance rather than religious conversion, they have only limited reason, in a pluralistic society, to emphasise religious distinctiveness, and much reason to seek common ground with people who do not share their religious faith. Perhaps the ideal for religious moralists, in addressing issues of public policy, is to say in a religiously distinctive way something that nonetheless has a more general appeal.

I will close with an example that may help to make clear what I have in mind. Theistic moralists find occasion from time to time to remind us that we are not God, and that comprehensive responsibility for the shape of human history belongs to God and not to us – not even to the United States Government. The somewhat euphoric reaction in this country at the end of the Persian Gulf war may be an important occasion for this sort of reminder, which may serve as a warning against the arrogance of power, as well as an argument against excessively utilitarian projects. The wisdom of this admonition will often be evident to people who do not believe in God. Everyone can see that, whether there is a God or not, we are not God. We are neither powerful enough nor good enough. Perhaps most important in the present context, we are not wise enough. We do not understand enough about the remote consequences of our actions, or even about their immediate impact on people quite different from ourselves. These evident truths sustain much of the theological reminder's import for political morality.

Yet I do not think the religious affirmation incorporated in the reminder is excess baggage or mere rhetoric for the purpose of social ethics. It matters here if there really is a God who can bear responsibility (so to speak) for the comprehensive shape of human history.

If we believe that there is, we may well bear with more equanimity, and even more hope, the recognition of our finitude, and may therefore be readier to deploy the thought that we ought not to play God. That thought, we may say, is 'at home' in certain religious views, though its wisdom will sometimes be apparent to most people.

Notes

1. An earlier version of this chapter was presented at a symposium of the Pacific Division of the American Philosophical Association, 30 March 1991, in San Francisco, at which John Langan and Philip L. Quinn were the other speakers. Quinn gave the lead paper, on 'Religious Ethics after *Ethics after Babel*: Tradition versus *Bricolage*'. Discussion with colleagues in the study of religion at UCLA, particularly Daniel Howe and Herbert Plutschow, provided inspiration for the writing of this chapter.
2. John Hick, *An Interpretation of Religion: Human Responses to the Transcendent* (London: Macmillan, 1989), p. 1.
3. Boston: Beacon Press, 1988.
4. Stout, *Ethics after Babel*, p. 187.
5. Ibid., p. 187. See also the references to 'secular intellectuals', 'the academy', 'an educated public', and especially 'the theologian's position at the margins of modern intellectual culture', ibid., pp. 164, 186f.
6. Ibid., p. 164.
7. Ibid., p. 185.
8. Ibid.: the phrase is quoted from p. 222; I will cite other pages that convey the suggestion.
9. Ibid., pp. 186, 289.
10. Ibid., pp. 187f.
11. Ibid., p. 289.
12. Ibid., pp. 122f.; cf. pp. 187f.
13. Hick, *An Interpretation of Religion*, p. 22.
14. Ibid., p. 27.
15. Ibid., p. 28.
16. Similarly, Mary Douglas sees the difference between 'primitive' and 'modern' religions precisely in the fact that the former do, and the latter do not, provide a unitary organisation for a whole society and its 'world'. See Mary Douglas, *Purity and Danger* (London: Routledge & Kegan Paul, 1966), p. 92; cf. p. 69.
17. Stout, *Ethics after Babel*, p. 289.
18. Hick, *An Interpretation of Religion*, pp. 29f.
19. Ibid., section 17.3.
20. Ibid., p. 307.
21. Ibid., p. 28.

7

Islam and the Hegemony of the West

MOHAMMED ARKOUN

Before discussing the possible evolution of the Arab world following the Gulf War, let us examine some of the important lessons of the war that will probably radically change the way in which the 'West' views Islam and the Arab world and that should free Muslims, and Arabs in particular, from the collective images that have dominated their behaviour, imagination, and demands since 1945–50.

The first lesson, it seems, is that an irremediable interdependence will continue to exist for years to come between the thinking behind 'Western' political domination and 'Western' philosophical and scientific reasoning, long billed as one of that culture's historical privileges. In order to delete the quotation marks that I have used for the term 'West', let us first define the temporal and spatial limits of the expression. The West, in the terms within which it has operated and asserted itself since the Yalta Accords, consists of secular and capitalist Europe, together with its two extensions: the socialist/communist USSR and liberal-bourgeois North America. Beginning in the 1950s, Japan has also joined in to strengthen, through its economic and monetary challenges, what has lately come to be known as the Group of Seven, 'the seven richest nations in the world'. Although they also are wealthy countries, Saudi Arabia and the Gulf Emirates do not form part of this group that manages the history of the contemporary world; the monetary wealth of these small, culturally conservative nations depends strictly on their investment in the banks and economic life of the West.

The West, as it is thus defined, has considerably reduced the presence of humanist Europe, forged since medieval times by Christianity and Greco-Latin culture: that is, by the inestimable contributions of the Mediterranean world. Islam and the Arab world are also linked to this Mediterranean heritage, which constituted, up to the nineteenth century at least, Humanist Europe. The historical rupture between Europe, which was subsequently transformed into the West, and the Mediterranean world has *a fortiori* given rise to the West's appropriation of trusteeship over Islam and the Arab world. The declaration of the 'death of God', followed by the 'death of man' and the discrediting of formal humanism, has reinforced the triumphant arrogance and cynicism of the economic and political reasoning of the West. International law, as defined in 1918 and again in 1945, is purely European and Western: the Mediterranean world, not to mention Asia and Africa, has never taken part in any aspect either of its development or its elaboration. Yet it has been in the name of law that colonial Europe in the nineteenth century and the West since 1945 have conducted all the 'legitimate' wars that we have known.

Today, we can no longer even speak of the unbearable contractions within the system of thought that continues to proclaim and impose the law, while at the same time exerting political hegemony over the world. The intellectuals, writers and artists who influenced opinion, in the sense of the ethics of the individual, until the 1950s, have completely ceded their critical function to the experts and media 'elite'. All this is occurring now in the most advanced democracies, which are in turn presented to the Third World as models of political freedom.

The *second lesson* has to do with the evolution of the Arab world since the 1950s: an evolution strictly controlled and orientated by Western domination. Dramatic events have punctuated the destiny of all the Arab countries and many of their Muslim neighbours: the creation of the state of Israel and the first Israeli–Arab war in 1948–49; the tripartite expedition to retake the Suez Canal in 1956; the elimination of Mossadegh in 1953; the Six-Day War in 1967; the fourth Israeli–Arab war in 1973; the Iran–Iraq War of 1982–88; and the rivalry between Khomeini's Iran and Saudi Arabia for control of Islamic fundamentalist movements in areas ranging from South Asia to the Muslim immigrant community in Europe. This rivalry is of incalculable importance, particularly in gauging the intolerable contradiction between the States of Law in the West and the attitude of these same states toward the satellite nations of the periphery. Saudi Arabia finances Islamic fundamentalist movements all over the world with the consent of the United States and Europe, yet a violent campaign against Islam is simultaneously being carried on everywhere in the West, portraying the faith as repressively ortho-dox, narrow-minded, xenophobic, and terroristic – even though

Islam itself is being inflamed and supported by the West's strategy of domination. Muslim immigration to Europe is the object of surveillance, distrust, rejection, even outright racism, while the Muslim states are riding tigers fed, protected, and emboldened by petrodollars. President Mitterrand has publicly admitted that France backed Saddam Hussein against Khomeini in order to contain the flood-tide of militant Shi'ism.

At the same time as these vast forces exercise their implacable control over history, political scientists, sociologists, and specialists in Islamic studies – the experts in all the relevant fields – are busy describing, classifying, and inventorying everything that is currently happening in Arab and Muslim societies as if these societies were freely creating their own history solely through the interplay of indigenous forces and struggles and other internally determined factors. Islam has thus become the absolute subject, the first and only source of all the evils and disorders that have afflicted these societies for the last thirty years.

In no way do I wish to imply the opposite of this vision, for there certainly are internal factors within Arab and Muslim societies that should be identified and measured by the proper analysts, but it is an irrefutable fact that certain elements – such as the coexistence of differing ethno-linguistic, cultural, and confessional groups never integrated into the nation; the state's fragility and lack of legitimacy; cultural, scientific and technical backwardness; runaway population growth; the complete absence or insufficient quantity of national resources; the colonial structure of economic exchanges, and so on – have all been aggravated and manipulated from the outside.

The *third lesson* of the Gulf War is that, over the past thirty years, contemporary Arab societies have been increasingly swept up first by the inflated imagery of nationalism and later by fundamentalist Islamic discourse, rather than by any realistic and clearly defined political will resolutely applied by the state. In fact, the state has been forced to adapt its discourse to the constraints and images that it itself has promoted and that were strengthened by independence. It has done so not only by including such imagery in official declarations, but even in educational programmes, legislation on the family, ideological functions assigned to the mosques, and the general manipulation of the past. Intellectuals who grow up in this context lose even their critical functions. We have just seen several of them, together with many political leaders, go along with the indignation, condemnation, and rage expressed by the majority of the population toward the West's 'aggression' against Iraq, thus postponing – 'till after liberation', as the saying went during the Algerian War – any critical analysis of the internal problems of Arab societies and governments.

This attitude was acceptable in the 1950s in the wake of more than a century of colonial domination, but now, after thirty to forty years of management of independent nations by national 'elites', it is no longer creditable. After the defeat of 1967, people began trying to pinpoint the causes and the consequences of the disaster in order to spare the Arab nation any such new catastrophes. Today, intellectuals who dare to speak out about the Iraqi leader's impulsive decisions, obstinacy, and military and ideological unpreparedness are censored before they can open their mouths; newspapers have even reported that 'the Arabs didn't lose the war'.

There has obviously been a change in the perception, attitude, and interpretation of the historical situation of 'Islam' and of the Arab world in relation to the West. The relevant issue here is not to find out whether some wonderful collective response is positive and productive or negative and self-destructive: it is to explain why Arab opinion, brushing aside its most vital problems, continues to give both Iraq and its leader the unqualified support that it denied Nasser in 1957. I cannot, however, answer this question here, because it would involve a lengthy and detailed enquiry into the Arab societies of the last twenty years. Let us simply emphasise that no alternative ideology seems able to impose itself in the 1990s, at least not in the way in which the orthodox Islamic solution replaced the 'Arab Socialist Revolution' after the death of Nasser. An immense ideological disillusion has succeeded the collapse of Marxism-Leninism, the setback of the mullah's Islamic Republic, and the sudden transformation of 'the Mother of all Battles' into 'the Mother of All Defeats'. The West has also gone through a crisis that has shaken it to its foundations and has left it in real disarray as it has tried to cope with the inanity of all the ethical and judicial declarations defending the legitimacy of the war, but the West will always be able to regain its arrogance and overpowering dynamism by returning to its institutional, secular heritage, to the conquests of the State of Law, to the efficiency of a well-rooted administration, and particularly to the privileges of a scientific, technological, and industrial advance unrivalled by the rest of the world. These are the factors upon which the domination of the 'model' of Western civilisation is based, even though the fresh philosophical, juridical, and ethical questions that have arisen out of the historical necessity of a new economic, monetary, legal, and cultural order on a planetary scale continue to be suppressed, evaded, put off, or simply transformed into themes for ideological polemics.

The *fourth lesson* ought to be expressed either as a question or as a conditional sentence. Can we conceive of the 'legitimate war', as Mitterrand called it, waged by the Allies against Iraq, receiving real legitimacy *a posteriori* thanks to a radically new policy of the G-7 (Group of Seven nations) toward the whole array of problems that have been building up in the Third World since 1945? It comes down to a question of asking ourselves whether or not the West's political thinking is capable of implementing the following changes:

(1) Does the duty of non-interference stop where the danger of non-assistance begins? This truly modern principle, adapted to the dangers that the majority of the peoples of the Third World have been living through ever since their so-called political liberation, was set forth by François Mitterrand during the late rebellion in China. Nevertheless, all Western diplomatic policies continue to proclaim absolute respect for national sovereignty and the 'right of peoples to self-determination'. Examples abound, we know, of direct or secret interference (I have pointed out above the support that the Saudis have given to fundamentalist Islamic movements all over the world with the assent of Western governments). A great deal of imagination and an active mental preparation are needed here to impose a new set of rules on international relations. What should be done in the face of all the regimes that oppress their people? How can we avert tragic scenes such as those of the boat-people being turned back from every country where they have sought assistance? Is it fair to say that the masses of immigrants from Eastern Europe, Vietnam, Cambodia, Albania, Africa, and the Arab world have moral rights to assert in the Western nations, when these same nations, for the last forty years, have imposed their dominion without ever agreeing to apply the very principle belatedly put forward by the French president? And can it be hoped, at least, that the United Nations will finally get busy finding ways and means of unwaveringly putting this principle into action?

(2) Communication between people has been largely supplanted by relationships between different nation-states, which function as private clubs. We know, however, that a great number of states have no claim to legitimacy from their people. We become indignant

after the fact, as we did with Ceaucescu, but we continue to make the mutual discovery of peoples dependent on the goodwill of their respective states. Once again, democracy abroad is held in check precisely by those societies in which it is the most solidly rooted, respected, and promoted: that which is beneficial and well-established among Western peoples remains ineffective and unrealisable for others still awaiting liberation. The mercantile success that has dynamised the Western economies has replaced understanding and peace among 'nations', and only nation-states are engaged in any real kind of exchange. France has been in close contact with Islam and Arabic culture ever since Napoleon's expedition to Egypt, yet present-day French ignorance of Arabs and Muslims and of Islamic history and culture is equal to that of the Germans and Scandinavians, who have only lately started accepting immigrants.

(3) Even more radically, can we hope that the critique of the bases of Western culture and knowledge will affect political reasoning to the point of saving the West from its own vision and hegemonic strategy? Can we conceive, in a West that holds all the instruments of power, that other cultures, religions, and paths of historical development will be more thoroughly analysed and better interpreted, and not kept at a distance, judged inferior, and neglected by hegemonic scientific culture? And when will the sciences of man and society finally accomplish this epistemological revolution? (I can already hear my 'Orientalist' colleagues protesting, telling me that what I am once again saying here has long been accepted, whereas the Arabs do not yet have their 'Occidentalists': a line of argument that is typical of hegemonic reasoning.) Can we imagine another revolution that would, this time, affect the way politics are practised, in which political elites and economic decision-makers would develop a new, integrated vision of cultures that had previously been ghettoised within traditions of archaism, religiosity, and outmoded notions of sacredness?

(4) Can we adjust the transfer of knowledge, of judicial and political models, of technologies, and of systems of production and exchange (I am not speaking here of arms) to the ability of people to accept, assimilate, and utilise them rather than to political voluntarism and state strategies for domination? We find that solidarity exists among nation-states trying to consolidate their position to the detriment of their own civil societies, which are neither consulted nor

respected in regard to their real needs, priorities, or deliberate refusal to accept certain policies. The Shah of Iran, with his brutal idea
of modernisation; Boumedienne, with his 'socialist' methods of tearing the peasantry away from the routine of their lives; Saudi Arabia,
which combines unbridled consumerism of material goods with a
radical refusal to accept intellectual and cultural modernity; Saddam
Hussein, with his strategy of regional power; all provide eloquent
testimony to whoever wants to pin down responsibility for the trag-
edies that have repeatedly occurred in so many societies.

What ethical principles, what types of knowledge, what political
culture can put an end to arbitrary reasons of state, to the voracity of
the merchant class, to pressures on economies obsessed with levels
of production, in order to instead respect the rhythm of the historical
evolution of peoples uprooted from their secular equilibrium a mere
fifty years ago?

Hegemonic reasoning wastes no time asking itself such questions,
and even less trying to answer them.

Let us turn now, though, to contemporary Arab societies and
see what, in spite of everything, they themselves must bear responsibility for.

THE ARABS IN HISTORY

In order to discuss the Arabs of today, it is necessary to adopt a long-
term perspective. In fact, I would like to emphasise the importance
of the following powerful paradox about them: the Arabs have isolated themselves over the middle term (1800–1990), and even over
the short term (1950–90), in order to nourish their revolt against
Western colonialism and imperialism, yet they are now turning to
their long-term history to search for ways and motives for their
present-day liberation within the early years of the Age of Islam
(610–32) and the Golden Age of their civilisation (632–1258). The two
periods work in a mythological mode that is only incidentally historical. The beginning of the Age of Islam provides the unsurpassed
and unsurpassable model for historical production in human
societies within the eschatological/messianic perspective of the Resurrection, the Last Judgement, and Eternal Life. The Golden Age
furnishes the Exemplary Figures of intellectuals, doctors of law,
saints, and heroes of civilisation, all selected, celebrated, and trans-
figured into Guides to Action in the present-day world.

This mythological relation with the past is only offset by a few rare historical studies, themselves imprisoned by outmoded methods, a corpus of apologetics, and a need to overstress 'values' and works in order to build them up to levels equal to or beyond those of the references claimed by the West. The ideology of anti-colonial struggle and, later, the nationalist discourse of the State, both favour this constant manipulation of the past by the present. The process ultimately leads to the restoration of the *Shari'a*, the religious law formulated by jurist–theologians between AD 661 and 900; to the generalisation, through sociological pressure, of individual and collective ritual conduct, even among immigrants to Western societies; and to the introduction, even into educational discourse and programmes, of a religiosity founded on a basically unrefined culture and then systematically disseminated via all the vectors used in the modern world for the transmission of information.

The concept of an *unrefined culture* is rarely taken into account by the sociologists and anthropologists of modernity. Yet it appears alongside modernity, even in societies stuffed with 'culture' and amply supplied with intellectual, artistic and scientific figures. Witness the functioning of the media, of political discourse, and even of certain aspects of scholarly commentary. Related factors in Arab societies exercise a multiplying effect: the omnipresent police-state, emanating from a single power; demography, combined with the uprooting of the peasants and nomads, which produces the powerful phenomenon of urban *populism*; continuing illiteracy; the absence of competent educational administrators; Western political manipulation; the destabilising effects of economic enclaves totally dominated by foreign industries; technocratic elites cut off from the immense populist social fabric; and the absence of social administrators receptive to a modernity that is critical of the human sciences and of society, while the vast populist sector vehemently and impatiently demands the material comforts provided by industrial production.

From the 1960s on, everything has swung toward the authoritarian state, one-party government, the division between the State and civil society, the expansion of populism and of unrefined culture, the apparent return of religion, the so-called 'revenge of God', and the discourse of dissatisfaction, of world-weariness, of frustration, resentment, demands – a discourse carefully channelled into denouncing foreigners, the enemies of Islam, and unrelenting imperialism. Here various elements are interwoven and foster a high level of confusion both in the social imagination and among certain observers who pretend to understand them. Let us once more specify what they are:

(1) The West's persistence in maintaining a strategy of exploitation, control, and domination is undeniable, and its effects are well-known.

(2) The states challenged by their social base have adapted to economic and monetary domination by the West because it has provided a certain well-being for their more modern sectors, which exist as enclaves in societies that are, in an overall sense, dedicated to populism. These states use nationalist discourse to cover up exchanges of advantages that they carry on with their homologues in the West: 'development aid', for instance, against bailing out the balance of trade.

(3) Civil societies are struggling to win fragmentary and precarious freedoms (the right to use parabolic antennae; the formation of solidarity groups parallel to bureaucratic mechanisms; business deals; glimpses of the West, that is forever being denounced in official nationalist discourse; the transformation of mosques into places of refuge, or, if need be, into springboards for discrediting the state, itself the immediate support of leaders shown to be capable of embodying resistance to internal and external forces of domination). In this way, contradictory modes of behaviour and portrayal multiply and spread to the point that 'intellectuals', completely renouncing any attempts at clarification, take the side of either the state or the populists (popular, or folk, culture is disappearing everywhere). This is done in order to give the appearance of 'scientific' validity to the ideological inconsistencies of a world-view that has been falsely constructed, though with full political awareness. As for contractors and other agents of economic activity, they are essentially mediators that assure the importation and distribution of goods; as representatives of large Western firms, they are incapable of strengthening investment networks in order to create, in their countries, an integrated economy offering a high degree of economic independence, as the capitalist bourgeoisie of Europe did from the eighteenth century on. Once again, the state has instead chosen to stop or discourage innovative initiatives, especially in areas which have been taken over by 'socialist' bureaucracy. It is interesting to compare, for example, the present-day economies of Algeria and Morocco.

(4) In all these modes of behaviour, these actions and reactions, Islam as a religion is neither cause, nor source, nor foundation: it is

a recourse, a refuge, an instrument, 'a bountiful fuel', according to the rich metaphor used by Hassan II when speaking of the 'fundamentalists'. In the discourse of its protagonists – the state and civil society – as it is reflected without critical analysis by journalists and political scientists, Islam is the Source-Foundation, the initiating Subject of history, the incorruptible substance, the transhistorical force of liberation and salvation in both this world and the next: it fulfils all grammatical, semiotic, historic, and eschatological functions that Allah has allocated Himself in Koranic discourse. The political and social discourse of all Muslim societies thus fulfils – especially since the triumph of the 'Islamic Revolution' of 1979 – the habitual function of *misrepresenting* the real stakes and determining factors of history: the profane becomes sacred; the contingent becomes transcendent; the human becomes divine; the ideology of combat becomes eternal and intangible religion; and, in the opposite way, spirituality is transformed into the ritual affirmation of group identity; the sacred is converted into a set of taboos or mandatory behavioural reflexes; and God becomes an ideological hypothesis invested with all the fantasies born out of a history divested from its people.

(5) The dispossession of the people's history, in all contemporary Arab societies, is an *historical* fact and not just a psychological one. Let us stress the geopolitical and historical status that is particular to these societies which were linked, beginning with the emergence of Islam, to the general destiny of the Mediterranean world, until that world was marginalised and secularised by the displacement of Western interests toward the lands bordering the Pacific and Atlantic Oceans. The competition between Byzantium and Islam, and between Islam and Christian Europe up to the eighteenth century, culminated in the age of European colonisation, in the carving-up of the Ottoman Empire, in the transformation of Arab societies into satellites of the Western powers that has continued until the present time. It would be impossible to say of these countries what Michelet wrote of his: 'France has created France, by a slow process, *of itself and upon itself*' (I have added the emphasis in order to differentiate a national history controlled by internal forces from one subject to the will of exterior forces, which, ever since the nineteenth century, have acted upon structural elements such as the tribal system in order to lay a better foundation for their own domination).

It is necessary, however, to take this analysis of dispossession one step further. How had Islam, which was the mainspring of the

'Arab' conquests and of the formation of an empire, become, by the thirteenth and fourteenth centuries, a mere shelter, and, secondarily, a lever for the resistance (*jihad*) to all the blows against the Muslim world (the Crusades, Spanish *Reconquista*, colonial invasions from the West, and Turkish and Mongol invasions from the East)? Islam *became orthodox* under the double demands of the struggle for self-protection and the narrow teachings of the brotherhood movements, which everywhere replaced declining central authority. It is this debilitated Islam, shrunken, ritualistic, dogmatic, and deculturated, which asserted itself during the nineteenth century and which later reemerged, in a more ideological form, after the 1930s (when Muslims began to compete with the *Salafi* reform movement).

What evolutionary perspectives remain open, considering all the situations, obstacles, and divergences that have just been described? Does the Gulf Crisis allow us to come to any new realisations or initiatives equal to the breakdowns and lessons cited above?

Let us first correct the too exclusively negative impression that might be conveyed by the description of the broad outlines of historical and political evolution that we have just portrayed. The facts and factors on which we have insisted could have their positive sides, or could abruptly change in significance in relation to Arab societies, whether or not the West modifies its policy, or the Arab states renounce their authoritarianism and agree to democratic collaboration with all their citizens. Demography is a heavy burden on a collapsing economy, but it is still a positive force if work is rehabilitated in all sectors. The provision of schools for the general population simply reinforces ideological designs and produces embittered graduates without jobs if Arabisation is understood to be a demagogic theme rather than a scientific and cultural undertaking on a national scale, and if teachers are poorly-trained, badly-paid, and lack basic freedoms. Let us keep in mind that in spite of all the structural upheavals that have taken place in Muslim societies, all the economic and political pressures, all the controls imposed on the citizenry, especially on women, the general tone of life among Arab peoples remains optimistic, the possibilities for progress and the mastering of history are considerable, and the gains of modernity are far from negligible.

It is these gains and the immense human wealth – the workforce, the enterprising spirit, the available resources, the sensitivity to utopias that can stir people to action, the national pride, and the ethical and religious ethos – that can change the course of history for the

better in the next twenty years. I do not believe that the fundamentalist fever will last unless it is aroused and nourished by a
powerful undercurrent, as it has been until now. Since nation-states
ultimately draw their legitimacy from universal suffrage and democratic institutions, they will no longer need to engage in ideological
excess among the populist masses in order to brandish the grandeur
of Islam. The immense task of effectively secularising society will at
last find adequate, direct, and critical expression in a discourse that
is both scientific and secular. Secularism will cease being a scarecrow
once citizens are freely able to choose their opinions, beliefs, and
ways of religious expression without social pressure. Religion will
then become, like Christianity in the West, a source of spiritual
enrichment for the self-sufficient, private individual, rather than a
civic duty that the citizen must comply with. Studies in the history of
religions and in religious sociology, philosophy, and anthropology
will multiply in the languages of the Islamic peoples, especially in
that of the Koran. This will be an essential step in the secularisation
of reflection and culture, and will thus focus on man, society, history
and the world.

Some will argue that this perspective leads to the same Western
solution that has so often been criticised and rejected. Is this to say
that the Western model is in fact universal and universally applicable? Why then have struggled so long merely to postpone an ines-
capable evolution?

This objection, so often raised in so many discussions, brings us
back to the fundamental polemical structure within which all examination of the links between religion, politics, society and culture
is always confined whenever Islam is in danger. We know how
Marxism has long reinforced this polemical structure in the West; a
secularising accentuation of secularisation in France, particularly,
has also contributed to a rigidification of positions. The road to a
new questioning that goes beyond the dualist thought which for
centuries has opposed the spiritual to the temporal, faith to reason,
the soul to matter, and good to evil, is being opened up in scientific
milieus that, even in the West, do not affect the public at large. This
is why the task of informing and of diffusing modern knowledge
must be intensified in all present-day societies in order to emerge
from polemics and simplistic oppositions between East and West,
spirituality and materialism, religion and secularism, and so on. The
mutually negative perception that has developed between 'Muslim'
and 'Western' societies is based on arbitrary images that have been

fostered on both sides by past and present confrontations which have often turned violent. Beginning in the sixteenth century, the longstanding rivalry between Islam and Christianity that sought to exploit the old symbolic common capital of monotheistic religions (revelation, the prophetic function, sacred scriptures) has given place to wars of domination. Moreover, the widening historical gap between Europe, which is forging its own modernity, and the Muslim world, which instead is retreating into mythological orthodoxies, has not until now, been the object of objective or detailed study, even among historians. Such study is, however, one of the necessary conditions for finally ending perceived mutual accusation.

These are the positive, clearly-defined tasks which the two worlds will have resolutely to attack in order at last to experience historical interdependence rather than confrontation, rivalry, and mutual exclusion based on false intellectual and cultural perceptions. The political task is to expand and spread the building of democracy in the world; the economic task is to institute and carry out changes based on fairness and openness; the cultural task is to encourage the free expression of all cultures and languages and to end the preeminence of Western reason and culture; the human task lies in working everywhere for increased flexibility in codes of nationality and in creating an international code of immigration.

If the international community commits itself to movement in this direction, if the Group of Seven countries redefine the notion of profit and their strategies for world investment, and if, for their part, the nation-states of the Third World finally feel sufficiently secure to renounce the policy of *nation-state-party-leader* in order to establish irreversibly, in all countries, states based on law, then history will judge that the stubbornness of Saddam Hussein and the heavy price paid by the Iraqi people will have made humanity take a decisive step forward in the endless struggle for liberation that is part of the human condition.

POSTSCRIPT (20 MAY 1991)

The text that you have just read was written in February 1991. At that time it was necessary to give the great decision-makers time to prove the sincerity of the commitments that they had solemnly undertaken under the eyes of world opinion. Dramatic in tone, the speeches of François Mitterrand were particularly promising, despite the touch of grandiloquence habitual to French society.

In another text, which I have decided not to publish, I defined hegemonic reasoning in the present-day world in the following way: a system of thought in which nothing can be said about anyone or anything in the world and in history, outside of the periodisation, time frame, conceptual structure, methodological norms, epistemological principles, and outlines of 'scientific' identification and positioning that were set by the West in the eighteenth century and were based on the West's own history. If any people dares to think, believe, perceive, and conceive in its own language or culture, and within its own ecological and historical experience, its creations will inevitably become the objects of ethnographic, or, at best, ethnological inquiry. If an Orientalist goes so far as to find some incipient movement among the Chinese, Indians, Iranians, or Arabs toward original forms or ways of political, cultural, or religious fulfilment, such a discovery will soon be reduced either to an exotic peculiarity with no potential for the future or to a phenomenon that has already been fully expressed and applied in the West. Thus, attributes of modernity such as humanism, practical law, the state of law, the rights of man, the human person, the separation of political and religious authority, the autonomy of legislative, executive and judicial powers, and philosophical attitudes separated from theological speculation, are all ultimately perceived as the discoveries and *original* creations of Western Europe, which has now become the West.

This incomparable epic of the human spirit does not keep the Western chancelleries from falling back on negotiations and compromises with states which support policies and principles completely opposed to everything that hegemonic reasoning so arrogantly demands; but that, of course, is part of the exercise of power.

World opinion accepts all that the Allies have done and *have not done* after the Gulf War without the slightest protest: suddenly Saddam Hussein has become necessary for regional stability, the Shi'ites have again recovered their status as dangerous fundamentalists, the Arab League has unanimously elected an Egyptian as Secretary-General, the Kurds have the right to humanitarian protection, the Palestinians continue to fall to the bullets of repression, the Prime Minister of Israel calmly declares that he will not give back a single inch of the occupied territories, and the French president quickly falls mute when faced with the New World Order.

We have to leave time for time, now and always. But during this painful waiting, people feel increasingly helpless, disillusionment paralyses them, and every opinion expressed by those once known as intellectuals or artists is met with derision.

Can we turn toward the men and women of religion, who regard all these events *sub specie aeternitatis*? I pose this question while thinking of the beautiful serenity of my friend John Hick, to whom I dedicate these pages. I know that we will find much more in them than my mere words and phrases have expressed. We have shared a common hope ever since we first met in Birmingham in 1977, and we have continued to develop the same critical criteria in regard to all religious traditions, for we are convinced that it is precisely these traditions that unscrupulous 'leaders' are going to draw on for the emblems, mottos, slogans, and symbols they will use to mobilise popular support and to make 'just' wars even more intolerable. It is my hope that works as modest as ours may have some impact precisely on this vast manipulation of the masses by their 'leaders'!

[*Translated by Hugh Hazelton*]

8

Christianity and Non-Christian Religions: A Neo-Darwinian Revolution?

JOHN BOWKER

Part of this chapter was originally included in a lecture for a symposium organised by John Hick in Birmingham. It is offered to him now with gratitude for his friendship, and for his courage in always facing the toughest and most demanding issues in the interface between theology and philosophy: *O si sic omnes.* . . .

When we think about Christianity in relation to other religions, the first thing we have to recognise is that Christianity began as another religion. It began as Judaism – or, to put it more accurately, it began as one among many attempts at that time to interpret how the revelation and action of God in the past among the Jews should be understood and expressed in the present. If there had been no sufficient reasons for the disentanglement of a different life-way (Christianity) from the existing, often very different, ways of being Jewish, then there would be no Christian problem of religions: there would only be the Jewish problem.

That is a more important point than probably it sounds, because the Judaisms from which Christianity departed were already competitive in relation to other religions in terms of truth, and some forms of Judaism at the time were strongly missionary. And it is important for a second reason as well: it has meant that Christianity from the start has incorporated the recognition that God does not deal exclusively with Christians. At the very least he has had dealings with his own chosen people; and much of the New Testament wrestles with the question of the status of the Jews in relation to God if Jesus is recognised as Christ.

What of the wider issue, the status of other claims, outside the boundary of Israel, to a knowledge of God? The engagement of Christians with that question in the early centuries was inevitably bound up with the answers already given to it in Israel. For at the very least, Christians had to recognise that if they understood their own relation to the Jews as being one of a new covenant in relation to the old, then however much the old might be regarded as superseded, it at least affirmed the continuity of God's action from the one to the other; so that, as Paul particularly emphasised, it could not be held that God's earlier action was a mistake. Thus the fact of God's redemptive initiative outside the boundary of Christianity was a matter of (Israel's) history; and since that history contained the unmistakable record of God at work outside the boundary of Israel (and recognised to be so), Christianity inherited an 'inclusive' voice in terms of the freedom of God's action in the world.

But another way of putting the same point was to recognise that God's initiative in repairing the broken relationships which the opening chapters of Genesis summarise led to a succession of covenants, beginning with Noah and ending (from the Christian point of view), not with Ezra, but with Christ. But that process (or at least the interpretation of it) carried with it the possibility of an 'exclusive' voice, for which the maintenance of the covenant community is seen to require a strong separation from whatever lies outside the boundary of the covenant process – including, eventually, in the rise of Christian anti-Semitism, the people of the older covenant.

Christianity thus inherited from Judaism a variety of different evaluations of other religions and philosophies, and of the possibility of a true knowledge of God within them, ranging from extreme exclusion to an acceptance that other religions and philosophies are different paths to the same ultimate goal, namely God. Thus Aristeas based his appeal to Ptolemy for the release of the Jewish captives on that ground (*Ep. Aristeas* 15):

> In the perfection and wealth of your clemency, release those who are held in such miserable bondage, since, as I have been at pains to discover, the God who gave them their law is the God who maintains your kingdom. They worship the same God – the Lord and Creator of the universe – as all other men, as we ourselves, O king, though we call him by different names, such as Zeus or Dis.

The logic of the argument is exactly the logic which was evoked over a great length of time in the biblical period, that if God *is* God, then he must be *God*: there can only be the one reality to which such language, prayer and sacrifice refer. If it is God who brought up the Israelites from Egypt, it is not other-than-God who brings up the Philistines from Caphtor and the Syrians from Kir (Amos 9:7), or 'that bitter and hasty nation' from Babylon (Hab. 1:6), or the Assyrians as a bee-keeper gathers his bees (Is. 8:18). Thus Aristeas was able to conclude:

> This name was very appropriately bestowed upon God by our first ancestors, in order to signify that he through whom all things are endowed with life and come into being, is necessarily the ruler and Lord of the Universe.

But that conclusion, which is by no means uncommon in Jewish writings of the period, did not lead into what would now be referred to as indifferentism – the view that if different religions have simply characterised the one reality in different ways, it is a matter of indifference which religion one chooses, since they are all pointing to the same goal. Indifferentist arguments certainly occurred in the Mediterranean world, but in general the Jews, even those who accepted the logical and biblical argument about God just summarised, remained equally clear that it is still possible to be *mistaken* about that one reality, in what one thinks or does in relation to it. Thus, as I have pointed out in *The Religious Imagination*,[1] when Josephus wrote *The Antiquities*, part of his purpose was to show that uncertainties and confusions among the Greeks about God can be resolved by attention to Judaism. His argument is not that the Jews worship another God, but that what God is, is more worthily and clearly established among the Jews:

> At the outset, then, I entreat those who will read these volumes to fix their thoughts on God, and to test whether our lawgiver has had a worthy conception of his nature (*phusis*) and had always assigned to him such actions as befit his power, keeping his words concerning him pure of that unseemly mythology current among others. (*Ant*.i.14)

So the Jews (or those among them who thought about such things) made exactly that combination of attitudes which (*mutatis mutandis*) has characterised the Christian understanding of religions ever since: that if God is God, then claims to a knowledge of God, if they are well-grounded, must be knowledge of *God*; but such claims are not necessarily well-grounded or unmistaken, simply by virtue of the fact that they are made: nor does a claimed knowledge or worship of God under different guises necessarily secure the individual or a community in a secure relationship with God.

It is in this way that Judaism was recognised by the Romans as being competitive and missionary – and indeed divisive – in the Empire. As the historian Tacitus put it:

> The Jews regard as profane all that we regard as sacred, and at the same time permit what we regard as abhorrent. . . . The lowest villains among other peoples abandon the religion of their ancestors and instead are continually sending tribute and donations to Jerusalem – thereby making the Jews even wealthier (*Hist*.v.4).

Seneca, who was a contemporary of Jesus and Paul, observed (according to Augustine, *de Civ.Dei* vi.11): 'The customs of that most despicable nation [the Jews] have prevailed to such an extent that they have been received throughout the world: the conquered have given their laws to the conquerors.'

Those are obviously the opinions of two men hostile to Judaism. But the attraction of Judaism to many non-Jews in the Mediterranean world was its clear and uncompromising allegiance to God – to the One who is *God*, behind and beyond the multiplicity of cults and philosophies. A Jewish philosopher like Philo could accept without hesitation that truth is achieved in Greek philosophy, but it is truth about God who has made his name and nature known among the Jews.

In exactly the same way, Christianity accepted that God can make himself known and can thus *be* known outside the boundary of the Jewish or Christian communities, but that such knowledge is often perverted and false, not yielding the individual into a saved relationship, the new covenant, with God. So the Apologists could both value the worth and beauty of much that had occurred in the classical world, not least in philosophy (so that Plato could be described as 'Moses speaking Greek'), and yet turn with passionate anger against the practices of pagan religion, in idolatry or in mysteries or in public shows. They could recognise *animam naturaliter Christianam*, and yet also insist, *spes mea Christus sola*.

The important point to grasp is that *both* attitudes are rooted in Scripture (in both Old and New Testaments), and that the history of the Christian encounter with other religions is *the history of the working out of emphasis*: should most emphasis be placed on the fact (or what was taken to be the fact) that this is God's creation in which he can be discerned, known, and worshipped, or on the fact (or what was taken to be the fact) that in Christ an atonement with God has been effected, as a result of which the confused and conflicting opinions of people about God have been replaced by the way that can lead them back to him?

Both emphases have drawn on texts for support. Thus in Acts 14:15ff., Barnabas and Paul refused to be acclaimed as gods by the people of Lystra, saying:

> Friends, what do you think you are doing? We are only human beings like you. We have come with good news to make you turn away from these empty idols to the living God, who made heaven and earth and the sea and all that these hold. In the past he allowed each nation to go its own way, but even then he did not leave you without evidence of himself in the good things he does for you: he sends you rain from heaven, he makes your crops grow when they should, he gives you food and makes you happy.

On a similar basis, Paul argued in Rom. 1:18ff. that the knowledge of God is perfectly possible, but that people have turned away from the one to whom reason once led them and have lapsed into irrationality: 'They knew God, and yet refused to honour him as God or to thank him; instead, they made nonsense out of logic and their empty minds were darkened.' (Rom.1:21). A very similar argument is developed in the speech before the Council of the Areopagus in Athens, in Acts 17:22–31: 'The God whom I proclaim is in fact the one whom you already worship without knowing it.'

On the other side of the emphasis are equally clear statements that the irrationality of which Paul wrote is not a trivial error of little consequence: '*All* have sinned and come short of the glory of God.' (Rom.3:23). It is to that situation that God addressed himself in Christ, 'reconciling the world to himself' (2 Cor. 5:19). Consequently, 'no man comes to the Father but by me'. (Jn 14:6).

We have now moved on to specifically Christian ground. Christianity, simply to exist, had to become separated from Judaism, since otherwise it would still be Judaism – or at most a sectarian relic of

Judaism like the Dead Sea sect. Why, then, did it eventually (and not without great struggle) become separate? And in so far as it did become separate in a world of sophisticated religious plurality, why did Christianity not exist more modestly as one possible way of salvation among many? Why, in other words, did the missionary urgency develop which carried Christianity across the Mediterranean world – and eventually far beyond – and which asked of people that they should transplant themselves, through baptism, into the new resourcefulness of Christ and the Spirit? It is precisely that urgency and demand which seem to carry with them the implication that other religions are inadequate or false. It is this which has seemed to create the problem of other religions in relation to Christianity.

When John Hick first addressed this issue, it seemed to him that the problem could be dissolved if it were to be realised that Christianity is not engaged (or should not be engaged) in enlisting allegiance to itself, but rather should be engaged in promoting an allegiance to God which can already be found in other religions. This is the famous 'Copernican revolution':

> The Copernican revolution in astronomy consisted in a transformation in the way in which men understood the universe and their own location within it. It involved a shift from the dogma that the earth is the centre of the revolving universe to the realisation that it is the sun that is at the centre, with all the planets, including our own earth, moving around it. And the needed Copernican revolution in theology involves an equally radical transformation in our conception of the universe of faiths and the place of our own religion within it. It involves a shift from the dogma that Christianity is at the centre to the realisation that it is *God* who is at the centre, and that all the religions of mankind, including our own, serve and revolve around him.[2]

But that is a very misleading way to state the requirement. We have already seen that Christianity is necessarily committed to the Copernican view, and has been from the very outset. The issue is not, and never has been one of theology: it has always been one of soteriology – how can men and women, and indeed the whole cosmos, be related to God in a condition which secures them for ever from destruction by sin, evil, death, the devil, or whatever? Of course

Professor Hick recognises this. His chapter on 'The Copernican Revolution in Theology' begins in exactly that way:

> Christianity has seen itself from the beginning as a way of life and salvation. Our next question is this: Do we regard the Christian way as the only way, so that salvation is not to be found outside it; or do we regard the other great religions of mankind as other ways of life and salvation?[3]

The question needs to be expanded a little, to express the point which Professor Hick is making, since otherwise it may seem to be implicit in the question that 'life' and 'salvation' are undifferentiated concepts in the great religions (and perhaps in the not-so-great also; see Hick, *An Interpretation of Religion*, p. 307). As matters stand, there is no logical reason why religious pluralism should not be 'writ large' into eternity (there might be *religious* reasons, but those in themselves could subvert Hick's argument). Thus, to put it crudely, where your treasure is, there will your heart be also; and if one person's heart is set on *nirvāna* and another's on the Muslim Garden, that is where, all being well, each will end up. On the other hand, one might have to ask the question in a much more sophisticated way: since other religions are unquestionably ways of what they describe in their own terms as life and salvation, are these ways efficacious in leading to the same condition that Christians, in their terms and tradition, have characterised as salvation? (Of course, someone asking the question from the standpoint of another religion would not put Christianity in the controlling position, but we are considering the issue of the salvation claims between Christianity and other religions.)

It is because John Hick answers that question so firmly and unequivocally in the affirmative that the issue of salvation, as a major part of the Christian tradition has seen it, disappears from sight and is transferred into an issue of theology – whether God is or is not at the Centre. If what counts as salvation can be isolated and its definition agreed, then methodologically it is straightforward to demonstrate the extent to which all religions exhibit it. This is the methodology of *An Interpretation of Religion*:

> The great post-axial traditions . . . exhibit in their different ways a soteriological structure which identifies the misery, unreality,

triviality and perversity of ordinary human life, affirms an ultimate unity of reality and value in which or in relation to which a
limitlessly better quality of existence is possible, and shows the
way to realise that radically better possibility. . . . Thus the generic
concept of salvation/liberation, which takes a different specific
form in each of the great traditions, is that of the transformation of
human existence from self-centredness to Reality-centredness.[4]

But is that list of impediments, for which salvation/enlighten-
ment is the remedy, descriptively realistic for the Christian tradition? Sin, still less aboriginal sin, is not an exact synonym for any of
them. And although John Hick may be deliberately avoiding reli-
giously-loaded terms, precisely in order to make the general and
universalising point, it will still remain the case that if the predicament is not described as the traditions (in this case Christianity) see
the matter, the remedy may not seem to be applicable either.

Thus it may well be true that 'for fifteen centuries at least the
Christian position was that all men . . . must become Christians if
they are to be saved';[5] and perhaps one might wish to call this the
Ptolemaic soteriology. But it is serious confusion to identify this
with Ptolemaic theology (see e.g. *An Interpretation*, p. 125). For it is
obvious that one could have a Copernican theology (that God is the
centre around which all people and all religions revolve, a position
which has always been implicit and usually explicit in Christianity),
and combine it with a Ptolemaic soteriology (which is also the majority voice in Christianity so far). The issue remains, therefore, not
whether God is at the centre, but how people are related to God in
terms of salvation.

But even on that issue it is important to note that John Hick makes
a highly selective use of history, despite his appeal to 'historical
relativity'.[6] He illustrates strikingly the ruthless vehemence of the
Ptolemaic soteriology, and there is no doubt that he could illustrate
it at even greater length, since it is unquestionably the majority
report in Christian history. He then argues that recently (which on
p. 123 means 'as long ago as 1854') modifying epicycles have been
added to the Ptolemaic theory – meaning by 'epicycles' attempts to
meet impossibilities in the original theory, not by abandoning the
theory, but by adding modifications to it.[7] The epicycles in the
soteriological case are such things as the theory of 'anonymous
Christians' or a theory of an atonement so objective that salvation is

already a fact, so that when, after death, all people are confronted by Christ they will recognise him for what he is.

But what complicates the issue as Professor Hick has presented it is that the 'epicycles', to continue to use his term, are not so recent as 1854. The possibility of people being saved who have lived outside the Christian boundary has been implicit and sometimes explicit in Christianity from the outset, precisely because Christianity attributed to Jesus – and no doubt learned from him, since it is explicit in Judaism – a Copernican theology. Even if God-relatedness (i.e. the covenant) was secured with one people (the Jews) proleptically (i.e. in advance of what will ultimately be the whole human case), Jesus came to realise that God-relatedness through faith is open as much to Gentiles as to Jews; and it is to *God*, now characterised as Abba, father, that they are related. That Christians subsequently emphasised what they believed to be the soteriological implications of Christology, thus creating strong boundary conditions of salvation in relation to Christ, is manifestly true. But what Professor Hick is really calling for is not a Copernican revolution in *theology*, but a questioning of whether the unalleviated Ptolemaic soteriology is correct, in view of the facts that (a) the Copernican theology to which Christianity is committed implied that people outside the Christian boundary can be God-related, and (b) the Ptolemaic soteriology is not, and never has been, the *only* account of salvation in the Christian tradition.

Thus to give only the most obvious example: both Aquinas and Calvin began their great summations of Christian theology (the *Summa Theologica* and the *Institutes*) with the same question and gave it the same answer: can there be a natural knowledge of God? Answer, Yes. But where they differ is in the status they give to such knowledge, especially in relation to salvation. Thus for Aquinas such knowledge may in some circumstances be efficacious (thus pointing already to anonymous Christians, long before 1854), whereas for Calvin the most it can do is to point up our culpability in doing nothing of worth on the basis of it. But this is a soteriological issue, not a theological one (except in the obvious sense that the former always raises issues for the latter). It is certainly not an issue about whether it is God who is at the centre of the universe of faiths. For the obvious point can be made, that many planets circulate around the sun, but only one of them is life-sustaining. To put (or keep) God at the centre of the universe of faiths does not of itself determine whether one, or more than one, is life-giving.

Thus the revolution that *may* be called for is a revolution, in the context of the neo-Darwinian fusion of genetics and selection, in the understanding of human nature and of what it would or could mean to be God-related. Sociobiology makes extremely strong claims for human universals (*not* for genetic determinism); and in its more sophisticated version (that of biogenetic structuralism) it makes the further claim that all human beings are prepared from genetic programmes for God-recognising behaviours – thus, to put it oversimply, the genes build the proteins that build the structure of our bodies, including those of the brain. We are thereby prepared for many fundamental behaviours, such as language competence; the genes do not determine which language we will speak, still less which particular words we will speak; but the gene-prepared competence is a human universal.

In the same way, it is clear that God-recognising and God-related behaviours are extremely fundamental in the brain (hence the strongly religious nature of young children), and that it makes obvious neurological sense to say, not 'Prepare to meet thy God', but 'Prepared to meet thy God'. Once again, the genes do not determine exactly what we will do with this competence, but the gene-prepared competence is a human universal.

But the Christian issue in relation to other religions will still remain whether the same genetic programmes create in us behaviours which can rightly be described under the category of 'sin', where the brain behaviours are operating us, instead of the operational centres of the brain operating them. The 'four Fs' of the limbic system would be an example. If the consequence of genetic programmes (which, after all, we did not choose but inherited) in the brain produce behaviours in us which can be described as wrong, then we are talking (in different language) about original sin – a concept which would then be much reinforced by post-Durkheimian sociology. For in these instances the issue of soteriology is being returned to the centre. What *does* need to be done if the universal human condition is to be brought to the transcendence of its unchosen but profoundly wounding inheritance? The neo-Darwinian revolution in anthropology does not dictate the answer to that: it is encouraging to John Hick's programme on the one side, because it makes unsurprising the natural human capacity for God: it is discouraging on the other, because it reinforces the realisation of the earliest forms of Christianity that the composition of many of our abject or sinful behaviours (and thus of a character which is imbued with them) precedes our choice or learning. If this latter is taken as seriously as Paul, for example, took it, then the neo-Darwinian revolution in soteriology may have the effect, not of tending toward indifferentism, but rather of emphasising that the distinctions in religious anthropologies are irreconcilable. For while it will translate into perceptions of aboriginal sin, it will not translate into conceptions of karma. Even then, of course, it will still be a matter of argument how the consequence of Christ in relation to the transcendence of gene-constrained possibility is extended to others. And here again, the consequence of the neo-Darwinian revolution needs to be taken very seriously indeed; for the more that is known and understood of the ways in which gene programmes set limits to the possibilities of individual and group behaviours, the more this revolution demonstrates that the cultural relativity, which has been so dominant for at least a century, is false; and in that case, the programme which is so important to John Hick, in relating the values of different cultures and religions to each other, becomes a serious possibility for the first time.

Notes

1. John Bowker, *The Religious Imagination* (Oxford: Oxford University Press, 1978), pp. 113f.
2. 'The Copernican Revolution in Theology' in John Hick, *God and The Universe of Faiths* (London: Macmillan, 1973), pp. 130f.
3. Ibid., p. 120.
4. John Hick, *An Interpretation of Religion* (London: Macmillan, 1989), p. 36.
5. Ibid., p. 120.
6. Ibid., p. 132.
7. Ibid., pp. 124f.

9

John Hick on Life after Death

JOHN B. COBB, JR

I

No concern has played a greater role in the history of religions generally than that of death and what, if anything, lies beyond. Some have theorised that awareness of mortality is at once the clearest distinction between human beings and other species and the heart of religion. Today also the question of life after death fascinates masses of people.

Much has happened in the modern West to undercut belief that physical death is not the end. The sense of reality emerging in the post-Enlightenment period has rendered such ideas problematic if not absurd. Intellectually dominant views of the human soul tie it so tightly to the body that its survival of bodily death is precluded. The universe itself is seen as having no 'place' for the continued existence of the dead.

Meanwhile psychological and sociological analysis cut against acceptance of the reasons for belief, emphasising their negative aspects. The unwillingness to accept one's own mortality is seen as ego-inflation, a form of immaturity. The positing of a future life that rectifies the injustices of this one is criticised as justifying present injustices rather than energising us to overcome them.

The force of the combined arguments for incredibility and undesirability has caused the theological community to lapse into silence on this important question. The rhetoric of resurrection has continued to play a major role, and in some theologians, such as Wolfhart Pannenberg, a decisive one. But even when eschatology has been reinstated as central, as in Juergen Moltmann, it is difficult to find answers to the ordinary believer's question as to what can be expected after death.

In the context of this silence John Hick had the courage to publish quite detailed speculations on this question. It would be too much to say that he thereby restored it to a central place in professional theology, but at least he helped to give explicit discussion of the topic a certain respectability. This was no mean accomplishment. As one who had tried to keep the topic open, but only at the periphery of theological thought, I want to express my gratitude and admiration. The proper way to do so, I judge, is to take seriously Hick's work on this topic and to engage it appreciatively and critically. To simplify my task I am limiting my critique to one book: *Death and Eternal Life*.

The question about what happens after death could, in principle, be one of mere idle curiosity, but in fact it is rarely that, and it is certainly not treated in that spirit by Hick. Although he judges ideas dispassionately according to their supporting evidence and intrinsic credibility, he also judges them in another way which he sometimes calls religious. He believes that there are legitimate human concerns by which theories can also be evaluated.

Although there is no systematic treatment of these considerations, they appear with special clarity in his critiques of other positions and especially in a section entitled 'The basic religious argument for immortality'. This argument consists primarily in showing that the humanists' complacency about life as intrinsically rewarding is possible only for an elite few, that for the vast majority of people throughout history the human potential is fundamentally unfulfilled. The religious spirit refuses to accept this evil as the final reality.

Hick tends to present his own vision as alone satisfying the demands of this religious spirit. As a basis for evaluating his claim I propose to discriminate some of the concerns of religious people that go beyond what humanism (in Hick's sense) allows.

First, most people are not content to cease existing or for others whom they love to do so. If this life is all there is, many feel, evil has, irredeemably, the last word. Only continued personal existence opens the door to the justification of reality.

Second, there is a deep dissatisfaction with a world in which the righteous suffer and sinners flourish. Even among persons not otherwise very religious – or particularly vindictive – one finds the conviction that Hitler *should* suffer for his crimes far more than he can be imagined to have suffered before his death. More generally, as people face the high correlation between ruthlessness and worldly success – the fact that the morally scrupulous and personally sensitive so often finish last – they crave the assurance that the radical maldistributions of rewards in this life be compensated in another one.

Third, the concern about justice takes another form as well. It sometimes focuses not so much on the lack of correlation between virtue and success as on the drastic inequity among starting-points. Some are born with good health, good physique, intelligence, and cheerful disposition into loving families of culture and wealth. Others are born sickly, malformed, dull-witted, and melancholic to unwed mothers who do not want them and can offer them few opportunities. What could be more unjust than that? Some feel that there *must* be a reason and that this reason must be what one has come to deserve through a previous life.

Fourth, for many people the deepest question is not justice but meaning. The meaningfulness of life is bound up with making a difference, and this relates to the future. But most of what happens seems to make very little difference in the ongoing course of affairs and is soon forgotten. Time assigns it all to oblivion, both suffering and joy. Why work for goals transcending one's own immediate enjoyment if all alike is swept away? Does 'eat, drink, and be merry' after all embody the highest wisdom? Against this dissolution of all importance, many protest that what is lost in the world is not finally lost, that indeed the temporal endures in the eternal or everlasting.

Fifth, the whole course of events, with all its injustice and suffering, seems to make no sense unless it is moving toward an end that is truly worthy of attainment. Only by affirming such a consummation can the world as we know it make sense. This may be conceived historically as the classless society, apocalyptically, as the coming Kingdom of God, or even cosmically.

With so many motifs involved in concerns for life transcending this one, it is inevitable that religious visions satisfying some concerns do not satisfy others. It is also inevitable that those who feel particular concerns intensely are deeply dissatisfied with visions that neglect or minimise them. Sometimes they dismiss these visions contemptuously.

It can also happen that religious people join with those Hick calls humanists in believing that reality is such that some religious concerns simply *are not* satisfied. In Hick's case, for example, although there is no disposition to belittle the religious concern that there be some reason for our unequal starting-points in life, he finds it unfulfilled. When he explores what we know about the explanation for this inequality, he sees that the space for reasons based on a previous life is vanishingly small. In any case, explanation in terms of a previous life simply postpones the issue. Arbitrariness must simply be accepted with regard to the initial starting-point of the soul's career. It is on this rational–empirical ground that he sets the otherwise valid religious concern aside.

For Hick the first and last of the five concerns are overwhelmingly important. Only a final consummation can make sense of the world and justify its creator. And only the participation of all persons in this End can render it a true consummation. Hick has worked this out by viewing the purpose of all things as the perfecting of souls or persons, so that the End of the process will be the fulfilment of all.

The concern for justice as the suffering of sinners and the reward of the righteous is drastically subordinated in Hick's theory to the dominant theme. Hick strongly opposes the tendency of those preoccupied with rewards and punishments to posit that decisions in this life are eternally determinative of one's fate. He sees rewards and punishments much more as the working-out of the inherent consequences of moral and spiritual attainments and flaws rather than as externally imposed. Nevertheless, he does not deny that there can be a great deal of suffering after death as a result of viciousness in this life and that true virtue greatly speeds the course toward fulfilment. Hence, it can be argued and I personally would argue, his vision satisfies the legitimate concern for justice without falling into the distortions of which most Christian eschatological thinking through the centuries has been guilty.

The concern about how temporal passage undercuts meaning plays an even smaller role in Hick's religious sensibility. This may be because his own vision does give meaning and importance to all that happens as part of the long journey to fulfilment. It is probably true that the modern preoccupation with meaninglessness arose as confidence about life beyond death receded. For those such as Hick who are secure in this belief, the ways in which recent philosophers and theologians respond to the threat of nihilism has little resonance. Instead, their efforts are quickly dismissed as failing to provide for the fulfilment of those who, in this life, are drastically unfulfilled.

In many ways I find Hick's formulation remarkably successful in meeting the religious needs of humankind. As I have sorted them out, not all are equally well-treated, but none are simply neglected, and several are met very well indeed. Hence the theory deserves close examination to determine whether it can withstand more thoroughgoing analysis and criticism.

Obviously, one line of criticism would be as to whether the evidence warrants the speculation. Hick's general method in this book is to determine whether a theory *could* be true. If it could be true, satisfies deep-seated religious needs, and accords with such evidence as there is, Hick believes the speculation is warranted. The reader suspects, in light of his other writings, that the degree of confidence he has in his own basic conclusions is connected with his conviction that there is a supremely powerful and benevolent God and that the course of events must finally be understood in light of this reality. Hick believes, quite plausibly, that only some such view as the one presented in his book is compatible with this deep-seated Christian tradition.

II

As I turn now to critique, two options lie before me. I can engage in internal criticism, that is, pointing out difficulties within Hick's formulation and vision as judged by criteria he accepts. Alternately, I can engage in external criticism, challenging some of Hick's assumptions from my somewhat different philosophical and theological stance.

My choice is for the former approach. I shall analyse the inner coherence of Hick's vision and the extent to which it meets criteria that are important to him. Nevertheless, I know that my critique is affected by the angle of vision with which I approach his work. This leads me to notice and highlight certain problems in his position and not others. Hence it seems a matter of honesty to note certain key differences between my general conceptuality and his.

First, our views of the relation of divine power and human agency differ somewhat. Hick believes that God's control of environmental agencies combined with the way God has created us can assure us that all will eventually be redeemed. I see a larger role for change and for the perverse exercise of freedom even in an infinity of time.

Second, Hick thinks in terms of a beginning and final End of creation. I believe the interaction of Creator and creatures is everlasting.

Third, Hick thinks of persons, selves, or souls as the objects of redemption, whereas I think of individual occasions of experience. This means that I pay particular attention to Hick's treatment of personal identity, and it is indeed with this topic that I begin. But because I have chosen the path of internal criticism, I am approaching the topic in terms of Hick's own formulations.

'Personal identity' is a term used in a number of contexts to refer to quite diverse things. Sometimes it refers to the question of how one is and is not identical with oneself. Sometimes it names a stage of maturation in which a certain integration is attained. Sometimes it points to the question of how and to what extent one is the *same* person in successive moments or time periods. It is the last of these issues that is important in this discussion.

In ordinary usage and reflection at least part of what is meant by saying an old woman is the same person as the little girl of seventy years ago is that her body has developed and changed continuously. Assuming that the death of the body ends this type of continuity, any claim that the same person continues to live after bodily death highlights the question as to what other continuity or identity there may be that allows this idea to be meaningful at all. Hick understands the problem well and gives considerable attention to it. His conclusions are subtle and nuanced. My judgement, nevertheless, is that his basic claims require a doctrine of personal identity stronger than the one he can reasonably assert and that what he can reasonably assert leaves unsatisfied some of the concern for meaning in and of this life that he has dismissed.

The deep underlying intuition of Hick's vision, I think, is that all the injustices and suffering of this life can be accepted as part of a larger good if we can expect that all the mistreated sufferers will eventually fulfil their human potentiality. All manner of evil, including inequity and injustice, can be understood as occasions for growth as long as that growth can be seen as continuing beyond physical death. Hence, we can all participate meaningfully in a meaningful process. The problem with which he wrestles, and which I am highlighting, is whether those who will eventually fulfil human potentialities are *the same* as those who now live and suffer.

This could be affirmed quite unequivocally if we held that the true self or *I* is a transcendent or transcendental reality or a metaphysical substance only secondarily identifiable in its phenomenal, empirical, and experiential manifestations. But this type of doctrine has problems of which Hick is fully aware. At a minimum he does not want so to relate his vision to a doctrine of this kind that only those who accept the metaphysics in question could follow his reasoning. As one who does not accept that kind of metaphysics, I appreciate his move.

But if identity through time is not metaphysical in this sense, then how do we understand it? So far as I can tell from Hick's account, our answers to this question are largely in agreement. Identity depends partly on conscious memory and anticipation and perhaps even more on continuity of experience from moment to moment.

Hick understands that conscious memory and anticipation cannot carry far toward full identity even over the space of one life, much less over many lives in highly diverse forms. Memory and anticipation can realise and appreciate the continuity of self over a considerable period, and they can clarify what is involved in continuity. But they cannot successfully identify the person now with a successor a thousand years hence.

This means that, from the point of view of the person *now*, fulfilment in a distant future personal experience, however connected with one's present self, does not go far toward reconciling one with present injustice and misery. It is already difficult to persuade an adolescent boy to forgo gratification because an old man – his future self – will pay a high price. To speak of fulfilment thousands of years in the future will seem irrelevant. Even though an adult may see the point of delaying gratification better than a youth, the advantages to a truly remote figure hardly play much role.

It is the more detached observer, perhaps the philosopher, for whom the remote advantages give meaning to the present struggle. This is not unimportant. We are all observers and philosophers as well as participants, and our participation is affected by our observation. But we must be clear that it is not our natural egoism that is satisfied with the promise of fulfilment thousands of years hence. It is instead our need to believe that the whole course of events makes sense. Hick himself makes this very clear. He is writing as a highly-advantaged person for other highly-advantaged persons. Among these persons, he grants, it is possible to declare life worthwhile whether or not it continues beyond the grave. But he calls on this elite to recognise that what is satisfactory for them is profoundly unsatisfactory when we think globally. It is for the sake of a satisfactory vision of the whole that we need to accept his theories.

Hick softens the point that those who are fulfilled are the same persons who now are unfulfilled in a second way as well. He emphasises the relational character of human existence, how we genuinely participate one in another. And his ultimate vision accentuates the unity of all constituted through this rich interconnectedness. Just how the members of this final unified humanity are individually related to present-day individuals is left open. The point of these comments is to say that perhaps this is not as important as Hick's formulations in general imply. Perhaps the perfecting of persons leads them to transcend the need for personal existence. Perhaps contribution to the perfection of the whole finally suffices. Hick himself seems almost to come to this conclusion, but not quite.

His resistance arises, of course, from a deep concern for justice. We feel that the final fulfilment should be for the one who now suffers. That someone or something else in the remote future benefits does not seem fair. However, I have tried to show that the limited continuity asserted by Hick helps very little with respect to this concern. The view of life after death that does respond to it is one of rewards and punishments following shortly after death where memory of this life is still vivid. The anticipation of such an afterlife *can* have existential meaning here and now in the midst of injustice and suffering.

I have noted above that Hick's proposal does not ignore this concern. In his view the experiences of the soul at death are largely a function of what the soul has become in this life. Hence in so far as the individual's usual cry for justice is concerned, the period soon after death, which can readily be anticipated in this life, is decisive – not the remote future perfection of an individual soul.

Although I have argued this point in a way that is internal to Hick's position, I have acknowledged that my emphasis is influenced by my somewhat different ontology and anthropology. Hick's agreement gives the impression that for him the person is the ontological unit and therefore the moral and religious one. For him, even though the connection between the person at an early epoch of development and the person in final fulfilment is vague and tenuous, nevertheless, it is decisive for the adequacy of the eschatological doctrine. My view is that the ontological unit is the momentary experience. In the human case this momentary experience is tightly connected with past and future momentary experiences through memory, anticipation, and unconscious continuity, just as Hick affirms. These connections give rise to persons and to personal identity through time. As long as memory, anticipation, and unconscious continuity are strong, personal identity is indubitable, but as they fade, so does personal identity. It is not an absolute, an either/or. It is instead a matter of degree. Hick's own account shows that this identity fades off into triviality over extended periods of time and through the drastic changes he describes.

From my point of view this weakness of his position does not obliterate the value of an eschatological vision of the sort he offers. The sense that our present struggles can contribute to an ultimate fulfilment of creation is an invigorating and empowering one, allowing us to believe in the meaning of life and history. But this is independent of a sense that we will personally participate in that fulfilment. My judgement is that Hick almost acknowledges this point.

Hick continues to see the eschatological issue as that of the final redemption of each person. There is no concern about the redemption of the events or experiences that constitute the person's long journey to that end. These are justified as means to the end of final redemption and only in that way. The present suffering does not *seem* justified to the sufferer by its contribution to the redemption of the person at a remote time and in a very different form because existentially personal identity cannot be felt over such distances of time and changes of character. But the philosopher, concerned to justify God, is satisfied.

III

Because Hick is satisfied with this, he dismisses rather contemptuously a variety of eschatological views characteristic especially of twentieth-century Protestants and important to me personally. Pannenberg, Tillich, Barth, and Hartshorne all fail his criteria for the same reason. They fail to provide for the changed conditions and new opportunities after death that alone could justify the misery of the masses in this life. Instead they preserve in some transformed way the life that has actually occurred. It is hardly too much to say that Hick sees no value whatsoever in these eschatologies. But all of these thinkers are concerned to affirm that what *has* happened is redeemed rather than to treat it as a step in a long process toward a remote end. In their varied formulations what has occurred is resurrected at the end of history, at the end of bodily life, or moment by moment. The resurrection has in it the element of judgement, but it is also a fulfilment or perfection of precisely those events or experiences that constitute that personal life. Nothing is lost.

Hick's polemic against this eschatology is based on his judgement that for most human beings their lives are too miserable to be worthy of preservation. In his view only the unusually fortunate, the elite, can take any satisfaction in the resurrection of what has been.

One certainly cannot dismiss Hick's objection out of hand. The eternalisation of misery hardly seems an adequate response! But we have seen the limitations of Hick's response as well. The fact that some being in the distant future whose supposed identity with the present sufferer is realised by neither, will enjoy blessedness hardly seems a satisfactory affirmation.

Much of the issue here is factual in a broad sense of that term. First, has most of human experience over the millennia been so miserable that it is best forgotten and lost? Hick apparently believes that this is so. But is it really true that hunters and gatherers, for example, were for the most part miserable? It is probably true that if Hick or I were now forced to try to eke out an existence as hunters and gatherers we would be miserable for a short time and then die, but the evidence from contemporary hunters and gatherers suggests that although their lives are probably more difficult than those of their ancestors before the appearance of civilisations, they still enjoy life at least as much as university professors. Indeed, studies of happiness show that although relative standing in a society does affect happiness, absolute living standards do not. It is not at all certain that feudal serfs were less happy than contemporary waiters and taxi-drivers, or that the latter are so miserable that their lives are of no positive value to them.

The problem remains that history is full of horrors: famines, slaughter and slavery are all too prevalent. There are lives so wracked with pain that death is truly a blessing. What can the resurrection of such lives be?

But before judging that all this evil and misery is best lost and forgotten forever, consider the outstanding example from our own century, one that surely ranks with the worst horrors of any age – the Holocaust. Let me say that I for one can take some satisfaction from Hick's view that each of its victims lives on, benefiting from any moral and spiritual growth that occurred. Nevertheless, I cannot say that this alone suffices. In all probability not all grew morally and spiritually through the agony. Presumably some were morally and spiritually degraded. The consequences of such imposed degradation are just as negative, in Hick's scheme, as degradation that occurs quite responsibly and wilfully. That eventually in some future life this handicap will be overcome does not seem an adequate way to deal with the Holocaust. For many Jews, it is important that they – and the world – remember.

One might suppose that the reason for remembrance is pragmatic – to alert us all to danger that may recur, to evoke action before it is too late. Certainly that. But there is also a deeper sense that the final betrayal will be to forget the agony in general and in its details. The fury engendered by the attempts to rewrite history so as to deny that the Holocaust occurred points to the sense that the deepest evil is obliteration.

The point of this in the present context is to protest Hick's quick dismissal of concern for the resurrection of the past. Of course, if such resurrection meant that the agony simply continued forever, we would find little consolation in that! But none of the proponents of resurrection mean that. They are struggling to affirm in their varied ways that God transforms as well as preserves, that the event or personal life in God, while retaining its concrete particularity, is also both judged and redeemed.

Hick acknowledges that his own eschatological vision is hard to conceive. The same is true for this one. At present this is not the issue. The issue is whether the concern for the preservation of what has been is an authentic and legitimate one. I believe it is. I believe that recognising this does not invalidate Hick's concern for growth beyond death, but I also believe that Hick's concern does not displace this one.

IV

Thus far I have focused on the five ways for going beyond humanism. I have supported Hick's affirmations of the first and the fifth – personal life after death and the hope for an inclusive fulfilment. I have suggested that personal and cosmic destiny should be more fully distinguished than he allows. I have affirmed his way of dealing with rewards and punishments as well as the inequities of birth. But I have stressed the positive importance of undergirding the meaning of life with a doctrine of the resurrection of events in God.

The emphasis on this distinct idea may be heightened by the lack of certainty about any final consummation of the whole, an uncertainty entailed in a different doctrine of God.

Perhaps the lack of assurance of a permanent, ideal conclusion to the whole process also accents my concern to distinguish personal destiny from cosmic destiny. But I propose to conclude this essay by discussing personal destiny not from that perspective but rather from a perspective that is more nearly internal to Hick's own vision. What does the importance of loving God say about personal destiny?

Hick speaks movingly about closely-related matters. He sees the progress of the person as toward egolessness. In the egoless state there are no boundaries separating us one from another. We become one in a quite radical sense. It is this eschatological vision that, even in Hick's mind, most strongly qualifies the full personal identity between ourselves and these remote egoless beings.

I would accent that these egoless beings, if not embodied, would ultimately cease to exist as members of a personal sequence. From moment to moment they would draw upon the community and anticipate the further enrichment of the community. They would not juxtapose a personal past or a personal future to the communal past and communal future.

In the Buddhist vision on which Hick draws for part of his theory something like this seems to be the final word. After death we are given the choice of egoless existence or of persisting as egos. Hick and the Buddhists assume that most of us will persist in clinging to personal existence; so the journey goes on. I share with Hick and the Buddhists the speculation that as long as we *want* to continue to be persons, this will continue, even though I do not see that it provides much identity over long periods of time.

The theistic vision can add an element rejected in the Buddhist one. Buddhism points to detachment from ego as the way of becoming free from suffering. Christianity calls for moving away from ego through an equal love of others and loving God with all our hearts. These two methods are, or can be, complementary: the weakening of ego can open us to others; the love of others and of God can weaken the ego.

Here I am emphasising human love for God. I do not believe that God can be served except in and through the creatures. But the collective love of all creatures and, in and through them, of the Love that animates them all is something beyond the love of each severally. To love God with all our hearts would be so to love God that the importance of our fate as separate persons fades. Our joy would come from contributing to God's life.

It is Charles Hartshorne who most powerfully expresses this vision. For him the meaning of life is not the preservation of what has been or the growth into something better for our personal benefit. It is the joy of giving to God, the one wholly worthy recipient of all that we can be or give.

Hartshorne is sometimes dismissed with the jibe that this is great for God but worthless for us. There is some point to this. As long as we love ourselves a great deal and God very little, it is an almost inevitable reaction. But it is disappointing that Hick is also so unsympathetic. Surely in the long run he wants us to become lovers of God who go beyond the ego that now blocks that love!

The difference is perhaps that Hick rightly observes how rare is any real approximation to such egolessness in our world. Hartshorne speaks the last word but neglects the need for a long process before most of us will be ready to hear that word. Until we are ready to hear it, the accompanying cessation of personal existence may appear as bad news rather than good. But in the long run, everlasting personal existence is not true blessedness. In the end – God.

10

The Pluralism of Religions
LANGDON B. GILKEY

This chapter in honour of John Hick represents a meditation on pluralism, the pluralism of religions – the burning issue which Professor Hick has done so much to raise for all of us. This is, I will suggest, a much wider, and for our wider culture, more existential issue than plurality in religion may first appear to be. But for a number of reasons it has, as a foundational issue, arisen there, among the religions – and like most new and significant appearances in history, it is unavoidable, awesome, fascinating, terrifying and potentially most creative. Plurality is not new; there have always been other religions. What is new is the dawning recognition of what I have come to call 'rough parity' between them, and so a new relation of *dialogue*, of mutual respect, of the recognition of truth, of some sort of truth, in the Other, and thus a stance of listening as well as of proclaiming and instructing. This sort of relation has been very real and fruitful between Jews and Christians for some decades; it is gradually appearing also, for example, between Christians and Buddhists and Christians and Confucianists.

All this is not just an intellectual flurry among professors. Concurrent with these new discussions, other religions have appeared in our day in *power* among us and even on our turf; the mission flow now moves in an opposite direction. This, then, is not just a matter of religions recognising each other as in some sense of parity; in the real world they have been revealed to *be* at parity, and each knows this in a new way. Each senses this new day among religions with excitement and expectancy – but also with more than a dash of dread; for the angel of fellowship brings with her, as a lurking companion, the spectre of relativity – and there our puzzlement begins to be a troubled puzzlement.

Now to many in the wider secular culture, especially the universities, this sudden realisation that religions are 'at parity' and so in some sense 'relative' appears to be normal enough, only perhaps a bit tardy: it seems high time indeed that the religions recognise this

111

and stop pretending one of them was superior! Thus the new plurality, or recognition of it, is taken as one more result of the gradual
spread of secularity – of the loss in a secular world of the possibility
of an absolute and dogmatic faith and the evident relativisation of all
standpoints. To me, however, this view represents for the academic
a comforting but a false interpretation. That various other standpoints are relative to one another *within* an assumed universal horizon is no real pluralism: then our *own* hold on reality is neither
shaken nor challenged. Thus it is with the University: its empirical,
historical consciousness, setting everything in its context, relativises
all that it studies – except itself as a mode of human consciousness.
And its implicit naturalistic metaphysics – namely, that the only
relevant factors that are at work are those available to empirical
and historical inquiry – can relativise all modes of religion. But the
modern naturalistic horizon implicit here *itself* remains as yet un-
challenged and unshaken; it remains for its holders – a *universal*
horizon, the horizon of the one universal rational culture available to
humans, if not yet, then surely in principle. With regard to *real*
plurality, plurality as parity of all fundamental viewpoints, this
secular understanding of religious relativity is not even close.

The attitude of the modern secular consciousness, the attitude of
much of the academy, to other cultures and other religions in fact
resembles what is called the *inclusivism* of liberal religion: of Buddhism, Hinduism, Sikhism, liberal Christianity and Judaism. This
has been an extremely impressive attitude in which all other religions are accepted, tolerated and even admired – but still interpreted
as to their worth and validity according to the criteria, the consequently absolute criteria, of the interpreting faith. The relativity of
a *fundamental* viewpoint: of one's own interpretation of reality and
value, and of one's own cognitive hold on that reality and value, that
relativity is far different – and that is what the new pluralism in
religions represents for those who seek to live within and so to think
from one of these religious standpoints now recognised as at parity.

Is an ultimate relativity possible, can a truth be held to be true if
we see it as relative to other perspectives? Can a method and the
form of consciousness it represents – for example, the modern empirical consciousness on which the University lives – be held to be
valid, even useful, if other modes of consciousness, other ways of
dealing cognitively with reality, are given parity with it? As is evident, the issue of truth, while by no means all there is in a given
religion, is vital to it. Religion is for the participant a mode of inter-

action, of encounter, with the real – whatever shape the latter may take; the symbols and rites of a religion – its doctrines or teaching, its modes of worship, its sacraments – disclose or manifest or communicate what are taken to be realities or powers on which we depend. To most of us, for example, the Buddhas at the Art Institute are magnificent aesthetic objects; to some of us they are pointers to our own psychological quest; to the authentic Buddhist, however, they are symbols of *śūnyatā*, the nothingness that pervades all that we take to be reality. Again, religiously the *rationality* of the concept of God, is not of supreme importance; what *is* important is the power of that symbol to communicate to us the reality of the divine ground, and the power of the divine call to each of us, what is therefore *true* about things and about ourselves. In that sense the component of truth is vital to religion as it is to any fundamental mode of consciousness, including the modern naturalistic consciousness. Correspondingly, if we suddenly recognise, in a way that we cannot   escape, that our own symbols, the system of symbols in which and through which we seek to live, the 'reality principle' for ourselves, are *relative*: if it appears that God is only one way of speaking of ultimate reality, that God's command for justice is relative, possibly to the indifference of all things, and that the forgiveness of God – what is that but a relative truth and a relative hope among a lot of contrasting truths? If, I say, we suddenly recognise *this*, we are shaken, as well as puzzled, fascinated and lured. A fundamental viewpoint – and a living religion represents precisely that – has grave and intelligible difficulty with the recognition of its own relativity – which is why we speak in that case of disillusionment and despair on the one hand and of conversion on the other. Since, therefore, it is impossible to live without some fundamental viewpoint on the reality and value of world, community and self, it seems *ab initio* impossible to live within such a total relativity.

The impossibility of a total relativity becomes perhaps more apparent when we speak of action in the world – and none of us can escape this. History is full of the Intolerable: Nazi brutality, the Holocaust, racism and segregation, imperial and economic oppression, widespread poverty and discrimination, rampant sexism: these are intolerable, and a vocal *no* of protest and political acts of negation are both called for. If at this point we embody in our life a relativity, a wavering or an evasion, we barely exist, we are a shadow or worse – and even we, especially we, can hardly bear to live with ourselves. But this 'no' in protest and in rebellious action, this taking a stand,

implies and necessarily implies, standing *somewhere*: that is, somewhere in a 'world'. It posits an objective world, an interpretation or
seeing of reality that is affirmed, and affirmed in the action. We
cannot act in the world – and act we must – without affirming along
with that action a view of human nature, an understanding of
human authenticity, a vision of society, or history and hence of
cosmos. No protest but asserts truth as well as a complaint; no
revolution but affirms a new world and with it an entire vision of
history; no action for liberation but announces an entire theology.
We cannot avoid an affirmation of a truth, even of *the truth*, unless
we go permanently to sleep – and even that dreaming inaction
dreams out an implicit aesthetic metaphysics! The existence, and
with that every action of humans, especially political actions, even
more liberationist actions, embody an understanding of reality, of
themselves in reality, and so a view of truth and of good. Though
many in the academy prefer to think of metaphysical visions and
ontological affirmations as representing only the claims of *others*,
there is no academic method of analysis or of cognition, nor any
form of private or public action that does not presuppose, entail and
embody an understanding of what is real and therefore a claim of
what is true about what is real. An unanchored relativism is impossible, and so the descent into total relativism represents a threat to
our existence as well as a puzzle to our minds.

Religion, therefore, is not alone in inescapably affirming an understanding of truth, of the way to the truth and hence of what is
authentic – what is, in fact, an 'ought' – about human life, society and
the universe. The University, although everything within the scope
of its inquiries becomes *ipso facto* relative, is not *itself* relative to itself;
nor are its methods of inquiry, the ontology they imply, and the
values on which all this rests held to be relative. The problem of
parity, therefore, is a real problem, a stubborn Zeno-like paradox,
faced in our present mainly by the religions which now view one
another in a new light. On the one hand they must recognise the
Other as also having truth, a truth commensurate in some way with
one's own; and on the other their participants are under the necessity, the unavoidability, nevertheless of standing somewhere, if they
are genuinely to participate in the religion as an ultimate standpoint
and especially if as participants they are to be and to be at work
creatively for liberation in the world. The drive for liberation and the
parity of pluralism sit down very uneasily together. Let us, therefore, explore a way, if perchance there be one, out of this dilemma.

We will begin by seeing what we might mean by 'parity'. Certainly this is neither an empirical nor a theoretical judgement of equality, the equality of all religions or standpoints. Such a judgement would require a criterion of religions that itself transcends all of them. Many claimants to this role of criterion are available, especially, probably, modern liberal humanism – but then in this role it discloses *itself* as non-relative, as one fundamental view assessing all the others, and we are back in inclusivism. No, by parity we suggest not an assessment of all relevant religions but what is called an 'heuristic principle': a method of *approach* to the other religions, a way of meeting them and relating to them. It abjures and denies the claim – which, though diplomatically repressed, is frequently present – of superiority, the quiet confidence of the hidden possessor of an absolute standpoint, and with it a tolerant but secure certainty that one really understands the other on one's own terms better than they understand themselves on their terms. So Christians have dealt with Jews from the beginning; so liberal Christian missionaries regarded other religions, perhaps especially American Indian religions; so Hindus and Buddhists have historically viewed others – and so the academy, viewing each of them from a 'scientific' perspective, regards them all. No, this new attitude denies such a superior vantage point; it recognises, however painfully, its own perspective as relative and not universal – and thus it can listen to the other in order to learn and not just in order to take notes on them or to gain time to argue. It recognises the Other as Other, as *really* different, as presenting a really different world, a world that cannot be reshaped into our world, a world that cannot – and should not – become merely a colony in our religious or cultural empire.

These last remarks, with their evocation of the now-vanished colonial imperial world, suggest what is perhaps the main *cause* of this new attitude among the religions. To be sure, important theological changes, and changes in ethics – in how Christians believed in what they believed and what they thought they ought to do in the world – had in the nineteenth and twentieth centuries prepared the way. But to me the major cause of 'parity' lies in the social and historical spheres, namely in the sudden yet effective disappearance of the domination by the so-called Western nations – politically, militarily and even economically – over the entire globe, a disappearance that, ironically enough, took place precisely with their victory in the Second World War. Those nations had enjoyed an astounding dominance for four centuries; one or another of them

ruled every corner of the earth to which the others allowed them to
go – and between them they almost owned it all. With that power
came a sense – now seen by us as an illusory sense – of their own
superiority and the superiority of their culture (recall *A Passage to
India*); and with that superiority came a certainty, a faith in the
permanence and the universality of their culture, a confidence in its
identity with fundamental purposes of history itself. Western self-
consciousness, and Christianity with it, saw itself as the culmination
of history's developments, in science, medicine, technology, education, political and social institutions, morals and finally in religion.
At last history had achieved a universal consciousness, the authentic
way of knowing, and with that the authentic way of being human.
Accordingly Christianity – 'Protestant, free-church' Christianity, as
President Burton of the University of Chicago said in 1922 – represented the future and thus the universal form of religion, the
culmination of the world's other forms of religion. This consciousness, political, cultural, moral and religious, has now almost van-
ished along with its political, social and military base – though not
without a trace. It lingers in the conservative and certainly the fundamentalist churches, in most of official Washington, and perhaps
most evidently in our universities – but its undergirding support in
the realities of the world's political, social and cultural institutions
has begun to dissolve. The Western nations now perforce *share* power
among other nations and cultures, who are in no way their colonies,
others who will develop modern technical and industrial civilisation
in their own ways. And all this new pluralism will be increasingly so
in the future. The first cultural and spiritual institutions to come to
awareness of this new historical moment have been the religions;
each in principle is beginning to recognise and acknowledge its
relativity among the others and so its rough parity with the others.

   Now that we have understood some of the causes of this new
situation, let us return to our thoughts about how to begin to deal
with it. We must, we said, recognise at the outset the finitude, the
partiality of our own religious standpoint – that it represents one
perspective on the mystery of existence and not the final, absolute
truth, the standard and criterion for all other perspectives. Thus we
listen to them, knowing now that we do not understand them better
than they understand themselves.

   Why, we may next ask, should we listen to these Others, these
very different and to us strange, bizarre ways of looking at the world
and of being human? What do we have to learn from them? Again,

events have made us aware, not only of our relativity, but also of serious *faults* in our most fundamental attitudes, both secular and religious – or to put it more precisely, faults in the Enlightenment consciousness, and in the Christian and Jewish traditions that have together formed us, that have been the creative ground of what we are.

First, our relation to nature, and so our most fundamental attitudes, secular and religious, towards nature, have in recent decades been revealed as a disaster. These attitudes, and the technical and industrial power to enact them, have deep roots in our Western religious and humanistic as well as in our scientific and technological traditions. All are at fault in the present assumption that nature represents only an objective and material resource for our use during the week and, on weekends, a place for relaxation and escape from reality elsewhere. With this consciousness we have been set free to exploit nature at will, limited only by the vacationing needs of the exploiters. Since our collective greed is almost infinite, this domination over nature by our technical skills can lead paradoxically to our own self-destruction. Other religious traditions, African, Native American, Indian, Chinese and Japanese have much of great value to teach us of our human relation to nature.

Secondly, it has long been recognised that the West – in both its Greek and its biblical roots – uncovered and developed into its most clear and powerful form the sense of the inwardness, reality and value of the human person – that is, the depth, creativity, integrity and value of human being, even in the least of its representatives. Now, although this treasured base of our humanism as of our best politics is authentically Western, nevertheless this too has become precarious. Such has been our fascination with what we can know about reality outside of us, and with our concurrent power over the external world – in scientific inquiry, in technological power, in industrial production – that we have progressively forgotten, ignored, or even denied the inward. And now the inward appears in much of our common life as merely subjective, infinitely varied, almost unreal – a firm base neither for a sense of private integrity and reality nor for public policy and action. Ironically, therefore, many have with good reason turned away from our own Western religious communities, filled as they are with public activities but often empty of creative possibilities for inward renewal. And they have entered religious communities from Asia in order, as many have said to me, to find again through ordered spiritual techniques

the reality of the me that is me, the inside of this active organism –
the integrity and value that my existence and my being incarnate. If
Western religious communities are poverty-stricken, it is in techniques for spiritual renewal, for disclosing to awareness and for
inward appropriation the reality of our inward being and its
relatedness to its divine ground. They can well replenish these
shrunken resources with help from the Zen, the Vedanta and the
Sikh communities. Strangely enough, it is these Others that can give
back to us the forgotten treasures of our own spiritual traditions.

Finally, modern history has disclosed to us the demonic possibilities of religious absolutes at every level. Many of the churches learned
part of this lesson in the seventeenth century. When each confessional community, each church, claimed absolute truth for itself,
only evil ensued: religious intolerance, religious persecution, religious wars. That each denomination holds only part of the truth has
been a lesson well-learned by most, though not all, churches within
Christianity. However, it was not, I believe, until our own century
that this lesson began to be made plain at the level of religious
traditions as a whole. It is in this century that different cultures and,
so, different religions have begun to encounter one another on a
somewhat equal basis and to look in new ways at their own history.
With this new encounter and this new look, the demonic historical
effects of our religious absolutism on other groups outside our own
religious tradition have become plain to all of us, on Native Americans, in South America, on the African and the Indian continents
and on the cultures of East Asia. In each locale, the very surrender of
the self to its God has, as Nishitani Keiji remarks, resulted in the
divine call to that self to subdue others outside its tradition. The
same absoluteness which grounds the self's surrender to God *also*
can impel the self's imperial domination over those outside. There
appears here a tragic paradox in absolute religious commitment: the
committed self gives itself to its God, its ideals, its ideology – and
becomes thereby precisely a terror to all outside the orbit of its faith.
We know this now (but not before!) concerning the Crusades; we
know this in our own history with the Native Americans; we are
coming to recognise it in the intertwining economic and missionary
interests in the building of our empires – and we see it clearly now
in all virulent political ideologies: in orthodox communism ('hardline',
as we call it), in right-wing Americanism, in fundamentalist Islam.
It means that no religion can regard itself as absolute and still be
loyal without contradiction to its own commitment to love and

respect the neighbour. And the same paradoxical dilemma confronts liberal democracy when it in turn comes into conflict with another political, economic, or social perspective. Thus we must listen to the Other; and we must recognise our own relativity at the deepest level, even the relativity of our own ultimate framework, our own deepest ultimate concerns. Although we cannot live without a standpoint, we must relativise our own standpoints, our own absolutes – if we would live creatively and fruitfully in history.

How is this to be done? We return to our puzzle: how do we articulate and live from a viewpoint, an understanding of things that nonetheless we recognise to be *a* perspective, relative, one bounded, so to speak, by Others? How can a fundamental viewpoint be affirmed, elaborated *and* acted upon, and yet be seen to be relative? It has long been plain in logic, in philosophy and in theology that fundamental presuppositions or axioms cannot be proved; we now face the added difficulty that they must also be qualified, understood as transcended, limited and complemented. Is this not a contradiction, an impossibility?

One answer in religion – and the same will be proposed in culture – is to seek an 'essence' that transcends all particular religions; to divest our own religions, say Christianity, or Judaism, of what seems to be unique and, so to speak, gritty and unyielding about them – in Christianity its emphasis on Christ and in Judaism on chosenness and Torah – and to concentrate alone on what seems universal. In these two cases this universal essence is perhaps theism, their belief in a divine reality that is benevolent, or perhaps their ethical and political emphasis on human liberation. But this way out is no way out. Each of these: a generalised theism or a political liberationism, valid and good as they are, are still particular, implications of and so, in fact, dependent aspects of these two particular religious traditions. General essence of religion turns out to be not general at all but itself particular, a particular view of cosmos, history, society and human being. Thus neither one of these fits other religious traditions, for example, non-theistic Buddhism, any better than do orthodox Christianity or normative Judaism. And hence, again, if we seek to unite via an 'essence', either each particular religion is not so much accepted in its Otherness as it is reshaped into something it is not, into something much closer to what we, the proposers of the Essence, regard as 'true religion'. It is not possible for finite temporal beings, be they scientists, philosophers, or theologians, directly to conceive and so helpfully to propose the universal. We can only approach the universal indirectly, dialectically, through negation as well as affirmation – this much we have learned.

The alternative is therefore a paradoxical alternative, affirming and articulating one's own position in the light of its relation to other positions, developing its own uniqueness in dialectical relation to the Others. This means, first of all, interpreting, for example Christianity, primarily in the light of its own sources in scripture and tradition, in using its own historic symbols: God, Christ, creation, fall, incarnation, and the call to liberation, and beginning with its own historic media of grace – community, Word, Sacrament, and saintly life. It is through these media that whatever truth Christianity represents about reality, about human being and about nature in history has been known. All that is there said about God, about God's requirement for justice and liberation, about God's love, and about the promise – yes, the universal promise – of redemption through that love, is inextricably linked to these particular and special points of disclosure. That 'essence of Christianity', which we had sought to abstract and replant elsewhere, turns out to be unknown and so uncertain without what is unique and particular about Christianity: scripture, covenant, Christ and community. And the same holds for each religious tradition; for example, the universal elements of Buddhism are quite dependent on the higher consciousness achieved in Buddhist meditation, and thus it is quite a particular mode of consciousness. It is like seeking to establish the University's consciousness while eliminating its scientific method and spirit. To relinquish the particularities of divinity is, therefore, not to retain that call to liberation, that love for the neighbour or that universal promise of salvation; rather it is to lose the ground for affirming each of these – or at least to be sent to find something like them secured in some other way, for example in Buddhism or in humanism. But that way, that new foundation, is in the end itself a particular way – and so there we are, back again in finitude and in particularity. Thus an ecumenical theology begins with the effort to establish its own integrity on its own sources and in its own terms – in, as we have said, the light of the Other, in relation to that new presence which now we cannot escape.

What does that mean: 'in the light of the Others'? First, it means listening to the Others as the Others present their particularity as a complement, even as a dissimilar alternative to our own, not as a derivative from our own. The lacks and faults of our own tradition: in our case the relation to nature, the cultivation of inwardness through meditation, the intolerance of other views – can then be healed; a reshaping process, in the light now of one's own authentic character, can take place. Dialogue can here help us to rethink in our *own* terms what we have learned from the greater creativity of the Other, from its revelation of the mystery of being and of non-being within which we all live and on which we all depend. Theology begins with its own sources, but now it also rethinks or revises them, not only in the terms of our contemporary experience, but *also* in the light of our creative dialogue with our neighbour, with the Other who stands over there and thus sees things we do not see and cannot see from here.

Secondly, and most difficult, it means holding our faith: our understanding of reality, of ourselves, of others and of our obligations and destiny, in such a way that we can live from its nurture, see with its wisdom, act by its requirements and hope from its promises – hold it with absolute passion; *and yet* that we know it to be relative, one perspective on the mystery of being and non-being. Thus Christians know that in and through Christ we experience the truth, and yet there are other truths; that the revelation we live from is a true revelation, and yet there are others. We have, as Reinhold Niebuhr once said, the truth, and yet we know also that in a sense we do not yet have it. Is there, can there be, a truth, an ultimate or foundational truth, that is yet relative? Can the radical relativity experienced in modern physics but buttressed there by the universal constant and the universality of mathematics, be borne in the realm of existence, of religion – of politics and of ethics?

I believe it can. The articulation of this puzzle is to me the present's most fascinating, if not its most immediately pressing, requirement in theology. It represents a deeper penetration into the mystery of our finite contingency and temporality, our boundedness in time but also our limitation by others different from ourselves. Others are also related, as we are, to what is real, what is true and what is good. Our century has been exposed at ever-deeper levels to the terror of the relative, of the groundlessness and foundationlessness of contingent life: we are neither self-sufficient nor universal but mere *parts* – and all we are: our thoughts and our faiths, even the sacred media of both, themselves subsist within the finite and the temporal that engulf us. We have available to us no universal foundation, nor can we directly articulate what one might be. Yet, as we have seen, to be it all we must become related, in our particularity, to what transcends us, to what is not relative, and to affirm and live from that point. The ultimate structure of things, the ground, the order, and the unifying end – this mystery is *there*; our relativity depends on it and cannot remove it lest we cannot be or act at all. Our relative affirmations point to it; they affirm it and negate it at once. We must live from this mystery as it has disclosed itself to us: in science, in values, in history and in our religious tradition – we have no other place either to start or to live. But now we know that whatever the truth and value of what we say and affirm, there are other ways of saying and affirming – and to these also we must listen if we are to hear the divine word and know the divine mystery.

One final word. The relativity of pluralism has begun to engulf the religions, and it is felt with mingled excitement, relief and terror throughout the contemporary religious world. The shadow and the promise of this relativity has not yet reached the edges of the academy – though they are felt in anthropology as in religious studies; nor is it yet articulate in the wider secular culture. The form of consciousness that forms the University: empirical, analytical, historical; intensely rational, individualistic, liberal, this-worldly and yet fundamentally progressivist – and, with all this, inescapably reductionist – this forms of consciousness has been immensely creative for all aspects of our common modern history. And yet it is not at all either as universal nor as everlasting a mode of human consciousness as we have held it to be. It now appears First World, Western, Northern hemisphere – if not otherwise ethnic- or even gender-specific. In fact it may well be much more temporally, spatially and culturally particular and limited than are either Christianity or Buddhism, and it has as many severe lacunae as they do. Like them it has penetrated with great success into other cultures and effected many conversions there – though most of the latter have moved here. And like them it has done a very great deal of good as well as much that is ambiguous. This expansion will increasingly help to effect a process of the modernisation of the rest of the world: in technology, in science, in industry – and to some extent in social institutions, politics and so on. However, these other cultures, having absorbed these influences, will reshape all of this in their own terms, as they have done many times before. And, what is even more important, they will create other forms of 'modern' consciousness than our own, as different as Japan, China, India, Islam and Africa are at present from us. At that point, *plurality* will appear within contemporary culture and even at the edge of the University. How then will we recognise these Others, these other modes of fundamental consciousness: Islamic, Buddhist, Hindu, Sikh, Confucian – Indian, Japanese, Chinese, African? Are they to be at parity with us or still regarded as 'backward', 'undeveloped' in relation to us – to be understood on our terms and in our categories? And if they are recognised as genuinely different, as *also* valid in their own way, how *then* do we articulate, revise and reaffirm our own treasured standpoint, our methods of enquiry and of understanding, and our own traditional ideals and values? When this day comes there will be as much excitement and hustle, accompanied by *angst*(!), on this issue among philosophers and philosophers of science, in area studies and in the social sciences, as there is beginning to be now in our seminaries and divinity schools.

11

John Hick and the Question of Truth in Religion
BRIAN HEBBLETHWAITE

John Hick's writings on the philosophy of religion reveal an increasing tension between his commitment to critical realism regarding the cognitive fact-asserting nature of religious language, on the one hand, and the key devices which he employs in order to work out and defend a philosophy of religious pluralism, on the other. In this essay I shall argue that it is the Kantian element in Hick's epistemology that both enables him to hold these two basic positions together at one and the same time, notwithstanding the tension, and also accounts for the threat which Hick's religious pluralism now poses to his critical realism.

Hick's commitment to critical realism is evident from his inaugural lecture at Birmingham in 1967[1] to his contribution to the Realism/Anti-Realism conference in Claremont in 1988.[2] These two pieces reflect decades of polemic against the so-called 'Wittgensteinian fideism' of D. Z. Phillips, as well as against earlier 'non-cognitivists', such as A. J. Ayer, R. B. Braithwaite, and J. H. Randall. Hick has, of course, been more concerned with religiously sympathetic figures such as Braithwaite, Randall and Phillips (and, latterly, Don Cupitt) than with the anti-religious logical positivists such as Ayer. And indeed it is the former who represent the greater threat to Christian self-understanding: for they challenge a cognitive or realist conception of the faith not from outside but from within. This issue – whether or not Christian God-talk is referential, conveying truth about transcendent matters of ultimate concern – was spoken of by Hick in 1967 as 'theology's central problem',[3] and it has continued to preoccupy him to the present day. Hick still holds that religion, whatever else it is, is 'fact-asserting', including, that is, truth-claims in the sense of putative articulations of how things really or ultimately are. Thus, in the Claremont paper, he argues that the cosmic optimism of the great world faiths depends upon a realist interpre-

124

tation of their language. Only if it is *true* that the world has a transcendent meaning and a future goal that will indeed be realised in the end, have they genuine hope to extend to suffering humanity.

That this commitment to critical realism remains, despite Hick's more recent espousal and defence of a philosophy of religious pluralism is clear from the way in which this pluralism is expressed. Each major 'post-axial'[4] world faith constitutes a possible salvific path from self-centredness to Reality-centredness.[5] The vehicle of each such path is religious experience; but it is the testimony of (nearly) all forms of religious experience that they are experience *of* transcendent, ultimate Reality – albeit under various guises. Salvific experience, therefore, in its many forms, points to a transcendent Real as its source and goal.[6] There are thus implicit truth-claims about the transcendent embedded in (nearly) all the practical life-transforming and life-reorientating religious traditions in the post-axial history of humankind.

But if an underlying cognitive realism is retained throughout the corpus of his writings, Hick's understanding of the truth-content of such implicit claims has undergone a sea-change. Whereas in early books the cognitive aspect of religious experience was articulated in the language of biblical faith in a personal God revealed in Christ,[7] in later writings Hick speaks of an Ultimate, or a Real, manifested now in the personal representations of the theistic faiths, now in the impersonal representations of Theravāda Buddhism or monistic Vedantic Hinduism.[8] What enables continuity, in Hick's overall view, despite this pretty drastic change, is a basically Kantian epistemology concerning both the nature of truth and human access to truth.

As is well known, for Hick, religious truth is grasped, in faith, through a particular way of interpreting experience.[9] Faith is defined as the interpretative element within religious experience. This involves the application to the religious case of a more general epistemology of interpretation. All experience is experiencing-as. Raw experience is indefinite or ambiguous until interpreted as significant in some specific way. This occurs at every level of our experience – natural, moral and religious. Even at the level of our experience of the natural world, the mind is active in applying a range of concepts to what is given, so that we construe ourselves as living in a material world of interacting objects. The ambiguity, at this level, is minimal. Ordinary everyday experience presupposes a basic realist interpretation, even though our everyday world-view involves a selection of practically-relevant features of the given. Moral experience is less immediate. It involves seeing the sphere of interpersonal life as imposing certain demands and obligations upon us. It is quite possible to miss or turn a blind eye to such significance. Religious experience, in its Christian mode, involves experiencing the whole world as God's creation and the sphere of God's providence. Our whole lives become a response to the immanent presence of this transcendent Spirit, and we look, in faith, for an eschatological consummation, beyond death, when all ambiguity will be resolved. For ambiguity is at its greatest in the case of religious experience. Our whole world and our own lives *can* be experienced naturalistically. On Hick's view, this would be a systematic error, but it is quite rational. Equally rational is the decision of faith, whereby the religious interpretation is allowed to structure our whole life-world. Such a faith perspective, Hick believes, is true and will be confirmed as true in the end.

The Kantian element in all this is the stress on the contribution of the knowing mind to the interpretation of experience as naturally, morally, or religiously significant. This contribution is not arbitrary. There are less and more appropriate ways of so structuring our experience as to gain access to reality; but since at each level reality is apprehended through our own interpretative concepts, we only know it as it appears to creatures endowed with sensible, moral, and spiritual faculties such as ours. Kant is not in fact mentioned in Hick's earlier writings on 'experiencing-as', except in respect of our experience of a categorical moral demand; but that Hick's whole epistemology is fundamentally Kantian is confirmed by the Gifford Lectures, where Kant's seminal distinction between noumenon and phenomenon, between the thing in itself and how it appears to beings such as ourselves, is explicitly transferred from the basic case of our knowledge of our perceived environment to the more controversial case of the epistemology of religion.[10]

By this time, of course, the religious interpretation is not restricted to its Christian mode. There is an intriguing parallel with the story of post-Kantian general epistemology here. For Kant the world appears to beings endowed with faculties of sense and understanding such as ours in only one, shared, way. Even though we do not have access to the world as it is in itself, the world as it appears, the phenomenal world, is a uniform, public world that we all experience similarly and that Newtonian science explores and describes systematically. Post-Kantian philosophy has lost this confidence. The possibility of many different, perhaps systematically incommensurable, ways of interpreting the data of experience has been explored by writers such as Quine.[11] Hick now sees a comparable plurality in ways of interpreting the world religiously. Whereas in the early writings, religious faith was spoken of solely in Christian terms – as experience of a personal God of creation, providence, and eventual redemption – now, in the more recent writings, this is seen as only one of a range of phenomenal representations of the ultimate noumenal reality that are not only possible but actual in the history of religions. Hick's so-called 'Copernican revolution', like Kant's, transfers much of what used, pre-critically (or even critically, in Hick's case) to be ascribed to the object of religious experience to one way in which that unknown noumenal object appears to those of us nurtured in a particular religious tradition. Hick now employs a neutral term, 'the Real', for the ultimate transcendent, noumenal, religious object, and re-locates the God of Judaeo-Christian theism among the various 'personae' of the Real, that is, the set of ways in which, for certain traditions, notably those of Semitic origin – but also for devotional Hinduism and other Eastern and African faiths – the Real is represented as a divine Thou, evocative of worship, and sustaining human beings in a variety of life-transforming ways. In these personal modes, the spiritual resources of the transcendent are experienced as grace and love. But there are other traditions – equally resourceful in spiritual, life-transforming, power – which represent the Real, phenomenally, through various 'impersonae' – that is, interpretations of the Real as a non-personal Absolute, as Brahman, in Vedantic Hinduism, for example, or Nirvāṇa or Śūnyatā in the various Buddhist schools.[12] In these traditions of interpretation, union with the absolute yields peace, bliss, and unlimited compassion. The ethical and salvific effectiveness of all these ways of religiously 'experiencing-as' forbids our attempting to 'grade' them from some allegedly neutral standpoint.[13]

Let us now ask how the question of truth in religion fares in this newer pluralistic context. Previously, as we have seen, it was the concepts supplied by the Christian tradition that enabled Hick to interpret his religious experience, cognitively, as experience of an ultimate, personal, source of grace and love, to be encountered unambiguously, though still mediated through the (now-risen) Christ, in the eschaton. These were basic religious truths, both disclosed in and evocative of Christian salvific experience. Despite the interpretative processing involved, Christian faith gave cognitive access to the noumenally real as actually being personal and gracious. But now, in the pluralist context, nearly all these alleged truths are transferred to the phenomenal level. They cease to be true of ultimate reality as it is in itself. One might still say that they remain true of that reality *as it appears* in one of its personalist manifestations. But Hick himself is more inclined to speak of them now as *myths*, expressive of religiously appropriate attitudes, namely attitudes conducive to ethical and spiritual transformation – from self-centredness to Reality-centredness.

We encounter this shift regarding the truth-content of religious beliefs at what might be termed its half-way stage in the book *Truth and Dialogue*,[14] which came out of a 1970 conference in Birmingham on the apparently conflicting truth-claims of the world religions. The conference was dominated by the contribution of Wilfred Cantwell Smith and reactions to it. For Cantwell Smith, religious truth is not propositional, cognitive, or fact-asserting, but rather personal – a life-transforming quality of sincerity and commitment – as persons inwardly appropriate their faith's spiritual power and vision. In his own essay in that book, Hick endorses the practical orientation of Cantwell Smith's view, but points out that a religion can only become true in the latter's existential, personalistic sense if it is already true in a more universal and objective sense. Neither Christianity nor Islam could become true if there were no God. Hick, therefore, retains his critical realistic account, even when endorsing the practical, personalist approach. (It is clear that the same must in fact be said of Cantwell Smith himself, as later work has shown.[15] The problem of conflicting truth-claims therefore remains. Hick goes on to consider the hypothesis that all the great religions are in contact with the same ultimate divine reality, but that their differing experiences of that reality, shaped over centuries in different historical and cultural contexts, have received different conceptualisations in their respective theologies. It is this basically Kantian distinction between experience and interpretation that enables Hick to graft his emerging pluralism on to his longstanding critical realism. At this stage the suggestion is of complementary rather than of rival truths.[16] Hick is optimistic here about the possibility of convergence and the discovery of common ground, even between the personal and non-personal experience of what he still calls the divine. At the doctrinal level, however, he is already resorting to the language of myth, as one way of dealing with a disputed doctrine such as that of reincarnation.

'Myth' becomes an increasingly important category in Hick's writings during the 1970s and 1980s, most notably and notoriously in connection with *The Myth of God Incarnate*.[17] There 'myth' is defined as 'a story which is told but which is not literally true, or an idea or image which is applied to someone or something but which does not literally apply, but which invites a particular attitude in its hearers',[18] and it is used particularly of the Incarnation which must, indeed, be 'demythologised', if the pluralistic hypothesis is to be sustained. This definition of myth, not surprisingly, has been attacked as being purely subjectivist and expressivist; but, of course, that does not do justice to Hick's intention. The 'myth' of God incarnate may express an attitude to Jesus, but the attitude in question is still one of reverence for and commitment to one who has enabled and whose memory still sustains the Christian form of salvific encounter with God. So there are still underlying truth-claims about God involved in mythical talk about Jesus. The situation is very similar to that of Hick's own reply to Cantwell Smith.

In subsequent writings, this notion of the mythological is greatly extended. Indeed, in the Gifford Lectures, it is suggested that talk of God (as of Nirvāṇa) functions mythologically *vis-à-vis* the transcendent Real.[19] Hick is clearer now about the implicit reference to the Real – we might call this the residual truth-claim in the pluralist hypothesis – that underlies the attitudinal definition of myth. Myths express appropriate attitudes and responses that enable salvific realignments with the Real. I notice, however, a certain residual tension between what Hick says at this point about the mythological function of religious language and what he says at the end of the book when explicitly addressing the problem of conflicting truth-claims. In the penultimate chapter it seems that all the doctrines of all the religions refer at the phenomenal level only to personae or impersonae of the Real. In so far as they refer beyond the phenomenal to the noumenal Real, they function mythologically. But in the final chapter, the category of myth appears to be restricted to specific narratives like those of creation, incarnation, or eternal life, while the primary underlying affirmations may yet be discovered to be complementary.[20] It must be said that the bulk of the Gifford Lectures favours the former rather than the latter view. The final chapter seems to revert to what I called the half-way stage where complementarity still remains a possibility. The main thrust of the Gifford Lectures lies in the direction of extending the category of myth to cover all aspects of phenomenal manifestations of the Real. Personae and impersonae alike are phenomenal, and everything we say about them is therefore mythological *vis-à-vis* the Real. In other words, Hick has become less optimistic about cognitive complementarity, and tends to fall back on comparable salvific efficacy.

This means that the ultimate referent of religious language – the noumenal Real, lying behind all phenomenal representations – becomes more and more vague and unknown as Hick's Copernican revolution gets further developed. As with Kant's noumenon, virtually nothing can be said about it. We have no cognitive access to it. Only a practical faith – the aforementioned salvific transformation from self-centredness – bears witness to the unknown Real responsible for such effects in all the different (indeed incommensurable) forms of spiritual life.

But it may well be asked whether it is necessary to retain such a vague transcendent reference point. Just as post-Kantian phenomenalists and constructivists accept Kant's analysis of the contribution of the knowing mind to what it knows but drop all reference to an inaccessible noumenon lying behind the phenomena, so Don Cupitt now suggests[21] that Hick's religious 'personae' and 'impersonae' can be appropriated as human social constructs without the postulation of a transcendent Real behind them. They may still be spiritually effective in the lives of different communities of faith even if there is no ultimate object of faith at all. On Cupitt's view, Hick's ever-receding noumenal object has become so vague as to be entirely redundant. It is in this sense that the Kantian element in Hick's epistemology, developed and deployed in defence of religious pluralism, has become a threat to his critical realism. And, of course, if the single noumenal Real is dropped, the variety of salvific life-ways becomes unproblematic.

It is worth pondering the reasons why Hick wishes, against Cupitt and all non-cognitivists, to retain a transcendent noumenal Real, even though we have no access to it as it is in itself. There is no doubt that Hick believes that religious myths do express experiences and attitudes that are not self-supporting. In the context of both personalist and impersonalist faiths they are responses to, evoked by, and sustained in relation to, something from beyond both the natural and the human worlds. Intriguingly, Hick's well-known notion of eschatological verification still provides the litmus test of the fact-asserting nature of religious language. For it is an implication of all the great faiths that human beings are not snuffed-out at death but caught up into a further purifying process which will demonstrate, less and less ambiguously, that their beliefs about an ultimate resource of spiritual transformation were true. Once again there has been a pretty drastic change in Hick's assessment of the details of this eschatological hope. No single heavenly scenario will now perform this role. The ultimate will continue to be manifested, albeit less ambiguously, in a variety of phenomenal forms – but the fact that this process continues beyond death will verify the critically realistic claim that the personae and impersonae of the Real are indeed of the Real and not purely human constructions. For purely human constructions are bound to end for all of us at death.

A footnote in the Gifford Lectures bears this out.[22] In his book, *Theology and Religious Pluralism*,[23] Gavin D'Costa had argued that eschatological verification would require the prediction of a single ultimate future state, which would thus refute the pluralistic hypothesis. Hick replies that 'the cosmic optimism of post-axial religion expects a limitlessly good fulfilment of the project of human existence. But this fulfilment could take many forms'. So even in respect of eschatological verification our predictions, and perhaps our post-mortem experiences themselves, retain the character of mythical representations. The only residual truth-claim in the cognitively realist sense is that there will be some such limitless good fulfilment beyond death.

It is worth attempting to list the residual, underlying, noumenal truth-claims to which Hick remains committed, despite the increasing weight he places on different phenomenal manifestations in the religions of the world. They are:

1. There is an ultimate transcendent Reality, to which all human religions, in their very different modes, are historically and culturally shaped responses.
2. Salvific religious experience, leading to transformation from self-centredness to Reality-centredness, is not a purely human possibility. Religion, in all its different forms, involves spiritual resources from beyond.
3. Human life will be extended, beyond death, towards some form of perfected consummation in the end.

It is difficult to see that there are any further assertions of transcendent fact which Hick could now endorse in the light of his pluralistic hypothesis. All other religious assertions function

mythologically, expressing attitudes evoked either by historical figures or merely phenomenal representations.

Two questions may be posed regarding Hick's now minimal critical realism. In the first place, can these three residual truth-claims
resist the threat of collapse into redundancy in the light of purely
expressivistic, constructivist, alternatives? And, secondly, can
religious believers be expected to accept that these three residual
truth-claims represent the cognitive heart of their traditions' central
doctrines? The first question is a question for philosophers of
religion, the second for the respective members of each community
of faith.

Both questions seem to call for answers in the negative. It is highly
dubious that religious experience alone can be thought to carry the
weight of sustaining such minimal and vague claims concerning the
transcendent. Even if it is conceded that all the world faiths may be
construed in this way, that they *must* be so construed seems very
implausible in the light of the alternative accounts (by no means all
hostile or reductive in any pejorative sense) that are now available.
The second question can only be answered from within a particular
faith community; but it seems that Buddhists as well as Christians,
Hindus as well as Muslims, will resist the relegation of their most
characteristic doctrines to the level of appearance, functioning only
mythologically *vis-à-vis* the Real.

Any challenge to Hick from the realist side of this debate must go
right back to the Kantian epistemology which has allowed this gradual
process of erosion towards the affirmation of an increasingly minimal set of truth-claims about the transcendent, in the interests of the
pluralistic hypothesis. Kant greatly overestimated the contribution
of the knowing mind to how what is known appears. This is most
obviously true of space and time, which must surely be admitted to
be relational dimensions of the world as it is discovered to be in itself
– and to have been long before human minds evolved. But it is also
true of the categories and concepts in terms of which we process the
data of sense and understand ourselves and our world. Our basic
categories are required by and evoked by the very nature of what we
encounter all the time, and our concepts, though partial and selective, are likewise determined by the given nature of things as we
discover them to be. Similarly our moral experience is of objective
demands and claims that impose themselves upon us in the dictates
of conscience, irrespective of and sometimes despite social condi-
tioning. And if we admit the force of reason and revelation as well as

that of experience in the sphere of religion, we will, at least in the context of the religions of Semitic origin, find ourselves constrained to affirm that ultimate reality is personal and not impersonal, graciously active and not inert, and to hope realistically for a consummation beyond death that will take the form of a perfected communion of love and not absorption into a featureless Absolute. Christians will go further than this in claiming that God's personality and love have been definitively revealed in the Incarnation, whose truth they therefore maintain.

The upshot of this discussion is that, when we have firmly rejected, as we must, Kantian epistemology in all its forms, we will find ourselves able to make many more discriminating truth-claims in religion than Hick's pluralistic hypothesis can allow. Among them will be a different hypothesis concerning the relation between the truths contained in the Christian tradition and the truths contained in other religions.[24]

Notes

1 John Hick, *God and the Universe of Faiths* (London: Macmillan, 1973), Chapter 1.
2. To be published in D. Breitkreutz (ed.), *Is God Real?* (London: Macmillan, forthcoming).
3. *God and the Universe of Faiths*, loc. cit.
4. This phrase goes back to Karl Jaspers. See John Hick, *An Interpretation of Religion* (London: Macmillan, 1989), pp. 29ff.
5. John Hick, *Problems of Religious Pluralism* (London: Macmillan, 1985), p. 44.
6. *An Interpretation of Religion*, Chapter 11.
7. *God and the Universe of Faiths*, Chapter 3.
8. *An Interpretation of Religion*, Chapters 15 and 16.
9. John Hick, *Faith and Knowledge*, 2nd edn (Ithaca, NY: Cornell University Press, 1966), Chapter 5.
10. *An Interpretation of Religion*, pp. 240ff.
11. W. V. Quine, *Ontological Relativity and Other Essays* (New York: Columbia University Press, 1969).
12. *An Interpretation of Religion*, Chapter 16.
13. *Problems of Religious Pluralism*, Chapter 5.
14. John Hick (ed.), *Truth and Dialogue* (London: Sheldon Press, 1974).
15. W. Cantwell Smith, *Toward a World Theology* (London: Macmillan, 1981).
16. *Truth and Dialogue*, p. 152.
17. John Hick (ed.), *The Myth of God Incarnate* (London: SCM Press, 1977).

18. Ibid., p. 178.
19. *An Interpretation of Religion*, p. 351.
20. Ibid., p. 374.
21. In seminar discussion.
22. *An Interpretation of Religion*, p. 361.
23. Oxford: Basil Blackwell, 1986.
24. See now G. D'Costa (ed.), *Christian Uniqueness Reconsidered* (Maryknoll, New York: Orbis Books, 1990).

12

The Difficult Limits of Logic

ANDERS JEFFNER

Anyone who has dealt for any length of time with John Hick's works seems to arrive at an absolutely unavoidable conclusion: philosophy is of enormous importance in theology. Most readers of the volume at hand would likely regard that statement as being a truism. But it may be worthwhile to keep in mind that many eminent theologians have furiously denied its validity. I intend to take up one such theologian from my own religious tradition and elaborate on one of the aspects distancing him and John Hick; we will find that this distance seems considerably shorter when the discussion is complete. The theologian I have chosen is Martin Luther.

Luther's extremely negative statements about philosophy and the use of reason are widely known.[1] But when these passages from his works are analysed by Lutherian scholars, a somewhat modified and more intriguing picture emerges. A balanced and well-grounded account in the English language of the main lines of Luther's criticism of philosophers is found in Chapter 2 of B. A. Gerrish's study, *Grace and Reason, A Study in the Theology of Luther* (Oxford, 1962).[2]

It is not my intent here to enter the general debate on Luther's view of philosophy and reason as expressed in the different stages of his enormous production. I shall delimit my analysis to his later important disputations where he is explicit and gives examples to prove the impossibility of using philosophy in theology. Two disputations are of particular interest: *Verbum caro factum est*, 1539 (John 1:14), and *De divinitate et humanitate Christi*, 1540.

'*Idem non est verum in theologia et philosophia*' (The same is not true in theology and philosophy) says Luther in the first of the above-mentioned disputations.[3] When he argues against Schwenkfeldt in the second disputation, he initially admits, '*Haec est philosophica solutio*' (This is a philosophical solution), but immediately adds, '*sed nos*

135

dicimus theologice' (but we speak theologically).[4] What is his intended meaning? Does he reject all philosophical tools in his theological work? It can be tempting to ascribe such views to Luther. But when he gives examples of a wrong use of philosophy in theology, it is clear that he does not mean philosophy in general; rather he refers to a special use of philosophy in theology, i.e. the application of rules of logic to theological propositions. Luther opposes this use in his disputations. When he makes the claim that 'the same is not true in philosophy and theology' he means that the same conclusions do not follow from identical premises in philosophical argumentation and theological argumentation.[5]

The disputations contain many examples which, according to Luther, show that an argument can be logically conclusive and have true premises without resulting in a true conclusion. Here are two of his examples:

Omnis essentia divina est pater	The whole divine essence is the Father
Filius est essentia divina	The Son is divine essence
Ergo filius est pater	Consequently the Son is the Father
Omnis caro est creatura	All flesh is a creation
Verbum est caro	The Word is flesh
Ergo verbum est creatura	Consequently the Word is a creation

Luther says that these premises are true and the logical structure is correct. In philosophy the conclusion therefore follows, but here reasoning concerns theology and the conclusion is false. There are three interpretations of Luther's words which lie close at hand, all of which are wrong as far as I can see.

The first interpretation is that Luther adheres to a theory of double truth. However, what he says is not that we are expected to accept the proposition in the conclusion as being true. Rather it is simply false that the Son is the Father or that the World is a creation. He means that these false propositions are a result of using a good logical tool outside its range of application. *Nos negamus principia dialectica esse vera in hac materia.* (We deny that the dialectical principles are true in this matter.)[6]

But if ordinary logic (which according to Luther is good in philosophy) cannot be used in theology, does there exist a special logic for theological propositions? It is a second possible interpretation to ascribe to Luther theories of a logic of faith. Such ideas were objects of discussion in Luther's day. The nominalist philosopher Robert Holkot, for example, tried to develop a *logica fidei*, but Luther rejected such ideas early, and kept to his position in his later disputations.[7]

There is also a third interpretation, tempting for modern readers, i.e. Luther is on his way to a Wittgensteinian theory of religious language. He means, perhaps, that Christian theology constitutes a language with a peculiar grammar which cannot be corrected in accordance with the grammar of some other language. Luther expresses himself in the disputation *De divinitate et humanitate Christi* in a way that seems to support this interpretation: *'Spiritus sanctus habet suam grammaticam* (The Holy Spirit has His Own grammar.) Gerrish has touched upon this possible interpretation in his very informative article on Luther published in Edward's *Encyclopedia of Philosophy*. However, such an interpretation makes too much of what Luther actually said. He refers to one special theological principle concerning the application of terms to God and Christ, i.e. the *communicatio idiomatum* (exchange of predicates), and moreover does not claim anything other than that certain theological terms have a meaning which is impossible to apply logical rules to, or which can be confused with a non-theological meaning and thus lead to logical mistakes.

The correct interpretation of Luther's theses concerning arguments such as the syllogisms quoted above seems to be that the syllogisms are wrong not because of their logical form but because of their *materia*, i.e. the meaning of the words constituting the premises. Ordinary logic, which is good, is misused in the example because of the special theological meaning of the terms.[8]

Does this mean, then, that Luther rejects all use of ordinary logic in theology? It is quite possible to imagine such a radical position. Some mystics come close to it and it holds true for a modern noncognitive interpretation of religion. But in actual fact this position has nothing to do with Luther. A substantial part of his theological work consists of arguments that follow the ordinary rules of logic, and he does not express doubt when arguing with help of Godsentences. To take just one example at random, he says in his Small

Catechism that God promises to do good to those who keep His commandments. *Therefore*, Luther says, we shall gladly live according to the commandments. Luther can also accuse his adversaries of not following the rules of logic.[9]

Now it is clear that Luther, far from rejecting philosophy in a sweeping and casual way, is touching upon a classical and complicated problem still alive among philosophical theologians. A modern philosophical theologian must admit that logic cannot automatically be applied to theological sentences. The abundant literature on symbols and metaphors demonstrates this fact. On the other hand, few are willing to set logic aside in their theology. If this were the case, such a book as John Hick's *Evil and the God of Love* (1966), would be of little importance. But most Christian readers of that book, philosophers or not, feel that it deals with a very fundamental problem in their faith, a problem created by the use of logic on the most central theological propositions. An important question now emerges: How shall we draw the demarcation line between those theological propositions which fall outside logic and those which can serve as premises in a logical reasoning?

Our analysis of Luther's position up to this point has led us not away from philosophical theology, but to one of its main problems. I do not intend here to discuss the problem in general as I have dealt with it in other writings.[10] However, I will attempt to ascertain whether Luther can help us single out one set of important theological sentences that fall outside logic, and will discuss some consequences of Luther's position.

Luther never formulates any principles for the restriction of logic in theology. Bernhard Lohse says that the only principle one can find in Luther's work is that a clear truth known by revelation invalidates logical laws.[11] This seems to be a sheer *ad hoc* principle, but if we look at Luther's example, I think we can discern an interesting pattern. All examples in the disputations of theological reasoning falling outside the sphere of logic concern the same theological theme. I think this can be concentrated in the following wording which can be called 'the Nicene principle of incarnation': God as Father has given birth to a Son and this Son has been incarnated in Jesus. Now we can reconstruct Luther's position thus: Sentences which build up or develop the Nicene principle of incarnation fall outside the range of logic. These sentences have a special mystical meaning in theology.

A position such as Luther's is easy to understand from a modern point of view. The Nicene principle of incarnation is the key sentence in a religious narrative, whether we call it a story, a model or a myth. The sentences building up this religious narrative cannot be handled as straightforward scientific propositions or, couched in the terminology of Luther's day, the rules which hold in philosophy cannot be applied in this instance. Doing so would lead to theological absurdities of the kind of demonstrated by Luther's syllogisms. I think that most theologians will agree up to this point. Frances Young is in line with Luther when, in John Hick's *The Myth of God Incarnate*, she writes that the simple equation Jesus = God 'turns "myths" into "science"'.[12] This, however, is only the beginning of a long series of well-known problems. Many theologians have asked themselves if the sentences which in their direct meaning constitute a narrative might, taken together, have an indirect cognitive meaning.[13] Here the theological roads part. We shall look at some of the main alternatives.

One possibility is to deny that there is an understandable cognitive meaning expressed by this Christological story. Luther, of course, would not have dreamt of taking such a position. The reactions to *The Myth of God Incarnate* show that a majority of theologians still see this alternative as a threat to the very core of Christianity, and as far as I can see, many of the contributors to this much-debated book agree with their opponents in admitting an important indirect meaning to the story of incarnation.[14] But if we accept the idea of an indirect cognitive meaning, which I do myself, we encounter a new fork in the path. This holds true even if we refrain from discussing the modern problem of the historical Jesus, a problem which has no connection to Luther's day.

The indirect meaning expressed by the Nicene principle of incarnation can be seen as cognitive but absolutely impossible to formulate in direct propositions. Luther's sentences about the mystery can be interpreted along these lines. The Christian believer can grasp the meaning, but cannot express it other than by telling the story. In this case, the Nicene principle of incarnation falls completely outside the limits of ordinary logic. The idea of an ineffable cognitive meaning seems to me possible to defend, and perhaps there are good reasons to ascribe such a meaning to the incarnation story, but it is very difficult to argue that such a story is completely untranslatable into a direct language. Those religious persons who earnestly relate the narrative, generally believe it to contradict such a statement as, 'There is nothing remarkable in the relation between Jesus and God'. They consequently take it for granted that we can derive some direct propositions from the Nicene principle of incarnation, propositions that follow the accepted laws of logic. I think that this much must be accepted if we are to remain within the borders of Christian theology. But at this point the next need for a choice asserts itself.

Can we formulate the indirect meaning of the Nicene principle of incarnation in any positive propositions about God, in propositions that directly state something about the nature of God? There are metaphysical traditions, both Platonic and Aristotelian, in the Christian doctrinal world which have permitted to a certain limited extent such positive propositions and they can, of course, be handled according to the rules of logic. This holds true even if the propositions about God contain analogical predicates. However, I know of no philosopher today who can consistently defend a metaphysical theory which permits a translation of the Nicene principle of incarnation into analogical propositions about the nature of God. This does not, of course, exclude the possibility of being able to say something about God in an analogical way, for instance, 'God loves mankind'.[15]

Let us, however, immediately look at the other alternative for those who adhere to the idea of some understandable cognitive meaning behind our principle. According to a long theological tradition, it is possible to derive negative direct God-sentences from the Nicene principle of incarnation. Although we cannot translate the Nicene principle of incarnation into direct propositions about God's nature, nor even into analogical sentences, we can understand so much that we can exclude a set of statements about God and Jesus as false and thereby encompass something of the divine mystery. Such a tendency can be clearly seen in the writings of the Eastern fathers of the church. Also according to this alternative, we can apply logical principles to the incarnation narrative. If it can be translated into negative statements about God and Jesus, then it of course contradicts a set of sentences, for example, 'Jesus was an ordinary sinner', or 'The relation between God and Jesus was the same as between God and St Peter'. Such an apophatic or negative theology seems to me to be an unavoidable part of a Christian doctrine and a reasonable way of handling the Nicene principle of incarnation.[16]

But then the most difficult problem remains. Which sentences will be negated if we spell out the indirect meaning? This question can only be answered on the basis of religious experiences by a comparison between the narrative of the incarnation with other Christian narratives, with direct analogical God-sentences, and with our scientific and moral convictions. To balance these parts against one another is not easy. It belongs to the theological art of the religious man; it is not a scientific task.

Let us carry out a test. Does the Nicene principle of incarnation and its narrative expounding contradict the sentence 'The biological father of Jesus was a Roman soldier'? Luther would of course have answered with a resounding 'Yes'. For my part, I must admit that I am not a good Lutheran in this matter.

It is a difficult project to point out the limits of the use of logic in theology even if we take a small area and a reasonable starting-point such as Luther's view of the Nicene principle of incarnation. Philosophers and anti-philosophers in theology have here a common field to cultivate.

Notes

1   One of the most influential books in modern Swedish cultural life is a very critical investigation of Christian doctrine and modern theology, *Tro och Vetande* by Ingemar Hedenius, (Stockholm, 1949). Serving as its motto is Luther's comment on reason being 'the Devil's Whore'.

2.   In writing this essay, I have found the following three Luther studies to be particularly helpful: Bengt Hägglund, *Theologie und Philosophie bei Luther und in der occamistischen Tradition* (Lund, 1955); Bernhard Lohse, *Ratio und Fides, Eine Untersuchung über die ratio in der Theologie Luther* (Göttingen, 1958); Reijo Työrinoja, 'Proprietas Verbi, Luther's Conception of Philosophical and Theological Language in the Disputation Verbum caro factum est, 1539' in Heiki Kirjavainen, Risto Saarinen, Reijo Työrinoja, *Faith, Will and Grammar* (Helsinki, 1986).

3.   WA, 39, II, 1.

4.   WA, 39, II, 100.

5.   This has been clearly demonstrated by Työrinoja. See op. cit., p. 153.

6.   WA, 39, II, 12. Cf. Työrinoja, op. cit., p. 157.

7.   See Hägglund, op. cit., p. 43.

8.   See Työrinoja, op. cit., p. 156f. Cf. *'Certum est tamen, omnia vocabula in Christo novam significationem accipere in eadem re significata.'* WA, 39, II, 94.

9.   See Lohse, op. cit., p. 117.

10.   See my *Kriterien christlicher Glaubenslehre* (Uppsala: Uppsala Univ. Acta Univ. Uppsliensis, 1976), Chapter 6, and *Theology and Integration* (Uppsala: Uppsala Univ. Acta Univ. Uppsliensis), Chapter II.

11. Lohse, op. cit. p. 117.
12. Frances Young, 'A Cloud of Witnesses' in John Hick (ed.), *The Myth of God Incarnate* (London: SCM Press, 1977), p. 35.
13. For a discussion of indirect meaning and a definition of 'indirect statement', see my *The Study of Religious Language*, (London, 1972), p. 15.
14. See Maurice Wiles' two articles, 'Christianity without incarnation?' and 'Myth in theology', for example, pp. 9 and 159, in John Hick (ed.), *The Myth of God Incarnate*. If one compares Wiles' ideas with those of John Macquarrie in his contribution to A. E. Harvey (ed.), *God Incarnate: Story and Belief*, the differences in their basic positions seem to be very small.
15. For an interesting attempt in modern times to formulate a theory of analogy, see the appendix in Joseph Bochenski, *The Logic of Religion*, 1965.
16. Perhaps St Cyril of Alexandria holds this opinion when he writes in his commentary to John 10:15, 'For the Father alone knows His own offspring, and is known by His own offspring alone. For that the Father is God, and the Son as well, we both know and believe, but Their ineffable nature is in its essence utterly incomprehensible to us and to all other rational creatures.'

13

Religious Diversity and Religious Truth
GORDON D. KAUFMAN

> It never occurs to most of us . . . that the question 'what is *the*
> truth?' is no real question (being irrelative to all conditions) and
> that the whole notion of *the* truth is an abstraction from the fact of
> truths in the plural, a mere useful summarizing phrase like *the*
> Latin Language or *the* Law. . . . Truth grafts itself on previous
> truth, modifying it in the process, just as idiom grafts itself on
> previous idiom, and law on previous law. . . . Far from being
> antecedent principles that animate the process, law, language,
> truth are but abstract names for its results.
>
> William James[1]

Anyone who works as a Christian theologian today increasingly
comes up against the problem of the enormous diversity in religious
claims about truth, as one moves from one religious tradition to
another. John Hick has done more than any other individual, perhaps, to push theologians to acknowledge the significance of this
fact for their work. As will become clear in this chapter, I am not in
agreement with Professor Hick's way of addressing the problems
raised by religious diversity, but I do want to express my deep
appreciation for all that he has done to lead many of us to see its
importance for theology today.

Unlike historical or scientific truth-claims – which can be exam-
ined and assessed in the light of public criteria that are widely
accepted even in what are otherwise very different political, social
and cultural situations – there is little agreement on questions of
religious truth, or on how disagreements in this field should be
adjudicated among Buddhists and Moslems, Hindus and Christians.
Each tradition seems to have worked out what it will regard as
'true', and what criteria establish this to be true; and if other tradi-

tions disagree with these judgements, so much the worse for them. Most religious thinkers seem satisfied to live out of, and hold themselves responsible to, only the resources of their own tradition, paying little attention to the fact that other equally thoughtful and sincere folk hold quite different views. If dialogue is pursued, it is largely more for purposes of gaining information about another way of life, or perhaps with the intention of converting those who differ from one's own way of thinking, rather than addressing the broader question of what this enormous diversity and disagreement means for our understanding of religious truth itself. What does it really mean to speak of religious *truth* (or truths)?

In this chapter, although I write as a Christian theologian, I am not interested in attempting to set out an argument for specifically *Christian* truth: rather, I want to examine some aspects of the broader and more general question of the peculiar character and status of religious truth and religious truth-claims. This is a question which needs to be more directly faced, in my opinion, by those aware of the religious diversity of humankind. Should – or can – we regard the various claims to truth made in the different religious traditions as somehow all true? Or are they all false – religious claims about truth being in fact a sham? Or is each such claim a partial and inadequate version of some ultimate truth toward which it reaches but which no religious tradition has succeeded in articulating adequately? Or should we each say (as most often happens in our actual practice, I suspect) that it is really only in my own tradition that the ultimate truth which brings salvation and fulfilment to human beings is to be found? – where others agree with the way my group thinks, they are basically on the right track; where they disagree decisively, they must be in the wrong. I do not think any of these – all too common – answers to our questions about religious truth are very satisfactory; and what I would like to do in this chapter is propose a somewhat different way of thinking about this whole nest of problems.

I recognise, of course, that the question of religious truth(s) can be approached from many different angles – from the point of view of the needs of religious proclamation or catechetical instruction, or the necessity for prophetic criticism of political oppression or social injustices, or the conditions that facilitate quiet meditation to nourish the soul, or the tendencies of religious piety too easily to deceive itself. All of these perspectives – and more – on the nature and problems of religious truth are valid and important, and would need to be considered in any full treatment of this subject. I cannot, of course, even begin to undertake that here. The most that I can do in this paper is to take up some of the special problems which the fact of religious diversity poses for our attempts to conceptualise religious truth today, and then propose a model which can, I think, help (those of us interested in these issues) address them more fruitfully. The important questions about how this model bears on the other concerns about religious truth just mentioned – and how they must be made to bear on it – will have to be left for other occasions.

I

What we are faced with here today is not, of course, a completely novel set of issues. Wherever dissimilar communities and traditions have confronted each other with different religious claims, men and women have been aware of the possibility and the reality of strong disagreements on religious issues, disagreements with the potential of exploding into bitter wars and leading to brutal oppression. Consciousness of what we today would call religious differences (and of the importance of these) has been widespread among human beings for thousands of years; and in some civilisations, for example in India, religious diversity has been recognised as a problem that itself called for religious interpretation and understanding. The approach that was developed in India – that there are many roads leading to the top of the mountain, and different individuals and communities should follow the road which they find most accessible and helpful – seems attractive to many religious thinkers around the globe. This position appears to take for granted that all (or nearly all) religions are concerned with essentially the same basic human questions, and they each offer answers that, in one way or another, meet the deepest religious needs of humans. Despite all appearances of diversity, then, humankind is actually one at its core; and the various religions are all concerned with addressing these needs of women and men to break through the illusions and partialities and evils of life, thus coming into touch with Reality. On this view it is a mistake to suppose that there is real disagreement among the religions on questions of truth: though they frame their interpretations of religious need and religious meaning in quite different ways, they all are concerned with the one ultimate Truth and ultimate Reality which answers to our deepest human problems.[2]

This is a very ancient, and at the same time quite modern, answer to the question we are exploring here: essentially it denies that religious diversity cuts as deeply as I claim in this paper, and asserts instead that at bottom all religions are one. Clearly, this is one way to handle the problem; but I do not think it is satisfactory. It requires us – in the name of a deeper and more profound knowledge, available only, perhaps, to a few philosophers – to turn away from and largely ignore what seems on the face of it so obviously true: that the various religions really do make different sorts of claims: that they understand what human life is all about in quite dissimilar ways; and that in the different parts of the world where they have been able to shape human living and acting, they have each brought into being (over many generations) significantly different forms of human existence. As nearly as we can see today, there are many quite distinct ways of being religious and of being human – human existence is pluralistic through and through – and although it is, of course, possible to deny this obvious fact in the name of some allegedly special insight or knowledge, there is no more reason to accept *that* particular religious claim as true than there is to accept any of the many other particular religious claims with which the world today confronts us. What is needed instead, in my opinion, is an approach to human religiousness that begins in and with this enormous diversity and difference itself, and – instead of playing down its significance – seeks to show its import for our understanding of human existence and religious truth.

What does this mean, to begin 'in and with this . . . diversity . . . itself'? How can we do this? Let us call to mind how and why we moderns have become so conscious of this question. Two points should be noted in this connection. (1) The immense increase in contacts between persons and communities with very different cultural and religious backgrounds and forms of life – made possible by modern methods of communication and transportation – has impressed upon many today the fact that human beings are capable of living and thinking, feeling and acting, in enormously dissimilar ways: and there appear to be, thus, many ways of being human. (2) In connection with these increasing cross-cultural contacts in the modern world, there has emerged the attempt to understand these matters *historically*, i.e. in terms of the processes – the successions of historical events – through which these diverse patterns have developed, to understand them in terms of the historical experience and the historical activity and the historical creativity of human beings in their quite diverse historical settings around the globe; this mode of understanding and interpretation, moreover, has proved to be both convincing and illuminating to many. With the emergence of modern 'historical consciousness' (as it is often called) – both partially created by, and itself further contributing to, the development of modern methods of historical study – a profoundly deepened sense of human diversity and pluralism has appeared. Modern history and cultural anthropology have supplied what Clifford Geertz has called 'thick descriptions' of the variant forms of human life that have developed in different times and places;[3] and we have begun, in consequence, to appreciate the richness of meaning and value which these variant forms of life have opened up for human experience. Historical consciousness, together with historical and anthropological studies, have helped to create our modern awareness of the significance of religious and cultural pluralism; and it is through our historical consciousness and reflection on its meaning (I want to argue), that we can uncover the wider import of this pluralism.

Wilfred Cantwell Smith has pointed out that our growing awareness of the history of human religiousness – made available by modern studies in the history of religions – can provide us with an overall framework within which each of the known religious traditions can be given a significant place and be meaningfully interpreted, without in any way compromising its integrity. Every religious community and tradition grew up within a historical context provided by other communities and traditions. From this context it acquired many of its beliefs and practices and in relationship to this context it defined and understood itself, developed its own distinctive institutions and ways of living, worked out its particular conception of the world and the place of human beings within that world. It is now possible to see, Smith contends, that the wide religious history of humankind is actually a single interconnected whole, and only this whole can today rightly be regarded as the proper context for understanding and interpreting the myriad particular expressions of human religiousness.

The new emergence is the recognition of the unitary religious history of humankind. . . . [The] static notion of an 'Islamic religion' [for example] gives way, once one looks more closely, to a dynamic notion of Islamic religious history . . . [and] the notion

. . . of Islamic religious history gives way to the truer concept of an
Islamic strand in the religious history of the world. The same is even
more obviously true for the Buddhist case, and is becoming increasingly visible for the Hindu, the Jewish, the Christian. . . .
What is beginning to happen around the earth today is the incred-
ibly exciting development that will eventually mean that each
person, certainly each group, participates in the religious history
of humankind – as self-consciously the context for faith. . . .
Christians will [not] cease to be Christian, or Muslims Muslim.
. . . Christians will participate, as Christians, in the religious
history of humankind; Muslims will participate in it as Muslims,
Jews as Jews, Hindus as Hindus, Buddhists as Buddhists. . . . For,
ultimately, the only community there is . . . is the community,
world-wide and history-long, of humankind.[4]

Our modern world no longer consists of nations or civilisations or
peoples which can regard themselves as existing more or less au-
tonomously, in independence of each other. We have become interconnected with each other in countless ways: what happens in one
part of the world economically or politically has its effects on us all;
we breathe a common atmosphere, and we all suffer from its growing pollution; we live together under the threats of ecological and
nuclear disaster. Although culturally we are increasingly aware both
of our diversity and of our interdependence, the meaning of this for
our religious institutions and traditions, and for our religious self-
understandings, has barely begun to dawn upon us. It is important,
however, that we find a new and more adequate way to think both
the diversity and the interconnectedness of our human religiousness, if our various religious heritages are to contribute positively to
the building of a world in which we, in all our differences, can live
together productively and in peace. Fundamentalistic reifications of
religious positions still frequently appear around the globe, offering
legitimation for dangerously parochial religious and social movements and practices which, in their divisiveness and destructive-
ness, are a threat to all humanity. We need a way to understand our
religiousness which can honour the integrity and meaning of each of
the great religious traditions and yet open them to appreciation of
and reconciliation with each other. Historical understanding and
interpretation of human religiousness can help to make that possible. I want to suggest in the remainder of this chapter that such

historical understanding can lead to a new approach to the problem of the diversity of religious truth-claims.

II

Human beings have been confronted, in their varying circumstances of time and place, with quite different contingencies and problems. In their attempts to address these they have drawn, of course, upon the resources of knowledge and wisdom and skill made available to them through traditions and practices passed on by earlier generations; but they have also used their own inventiveness and ingenuity, as they sought to deal with new and unexpected issues and difficulties. Each new generation added to the traditions it had inherited, deepening and enriching and refining them in response to the new circumstances which it confronted. What ultimately became regarded in a tradition as valuable and important – indeed, as true – emerged in connection with the attempts of women and men to address the concrete problems with which life confronted them. Over the course of time, in each developing tradition, certain modes of thinking and acting, of meditation and practice, proved increasingly helpful in defining and diagnosing some of the more difficult problems and ills faced by the society, thus making available treatments and remedies that were healing and in other ways effective. These modes of understanding and practice became honoured and respected and preferred to others – regarded as good and right and true, to be followed if humans were to find some way to survive the terrors and evils of life in a threatening world. In the various religious and cultural traditions developing around the globe there emerged quite naturally, thus, diverse ways of picturing and understanding human life and the world – that is, significantly different conceptions of what is *true* about human existence and the context within which it falls.

It is important that we do not confuse the conception of truth which developed in these (pre-modern and even pre-philosophical) religious traditions with our modern, highly reflective notions. Religious truth in these early stages was not essentially a piece of information about what is the case, a statement of 'fact' in our modern sense (heavily influenced, as it is, by scientific ideas); nor was it a highly reflective, carefully-argued metaphysical claim about 'ultimate reality'. Truth was, rather, a symbolisation or articulation of that which was 'useful', as the Buddha put it, to bring fullness of life to human beings, 'salvation' or 'enlightenment' or 'liberation' from the various sorts of bondage to which humankind is heir. 'I have taught a doctrine similar to a raft', the Buddha said; 'it is for crossing over' to the other side, not something to be grasped or clung to.[5] For Jesus, also (at least as represented in the Fourth Gospel), religious truth was an eminently practical matter: 'If you continue in my word, . . . you will know the truth, and the truth will make you free' (John 8:31f). Here truth is understood as that which makes possible 'abundant life' (10:10); indeed, Jesus declares himself to be 'the truth' (14:6). For these great religious teachers truth appears to have been essentially the practical insight or wisdom – the vehicle – indispensable for proper human living and dying, not a collection of metaphysical dogmas or other speculative beliefs. In time, of course, this practical wisdom often became formulated in terms of quite specific truths and practices to be passed on from generation to generation. And in some cases these truths became formally fixed as bodies of belief (creeds or confessions) to which all members of the group were expected to subscribe, while in others the tradition remained more informal, though it nonetheless came to have great authority in ordering the lives of women and men who took religious matters seriously. But in all these cases 'truth' and 'truths' were largely matters of practical commitment and belief.[6]

Since religious truth came into being this way in connection with the very practical problems and difficulties and even emergencies in human living, it should not surprise us to discover profound disagreements regarding this liberating or saving truth among the religious traditions of humankind. In each case the understanding of truth(s) and practice(s) was defined and shaped largely by the particular problems being addressed as well as by the previous experience of the society. Meditation and reflection on the problems of life was largely limited to the specific issues discussed, and to the ways of framing those issues, which had already emerged in the previous history of the particular culture involved. What came to be regarded as true in the different religious traditions was a function of the way in which each had come to picture or conceive human-life-in-its-environment; and this symbolic conception or picture was itself defined and shaped in many respects by the metaphors and images, and even the grammar and syntax, of the language in and through which it was articulated. Religious traditions structured by significantly different symbolical patterns came to have profoundly different understandings of reality and truth.

For example, consider the basic symbolic patterns that came to structure Buddhist life and reflection on the one hand, and Christian on the other. Buddhist patterns of religious symbolism appear to be essentially 'holistic' in character; Christian patterns, in contrast, are dominantly 'foundationalist'. The differences between these two patterns of experiencing and thinking, I want to suggest, explain a great deal about the differences between these two religious orientations.

Consider first the Christian case: why characterise Christian symbolism as essentially 'foundationalist'? This is not difficult to understand. Christian faith is a form of *monotheism*, the idea that there is a single reality – God – which underlies and gives rise to all other realities without exception. God is 'the creator of all things visible and invisible', as the creeds put it; and that means that everything that exists depends for its being on God, but God's reality, in contrast, depends on nothing other than Godself. God alone has *aseity*, is self-existent; God is the ultimate ground or foundation on which all else rests. Thus, at its deepest level Christian faith and understanding begin with grasping a *distinction*, the distinction between creator and creation. Until and unless we understand that there is a single *ultimate* reality with which we humans have to do, and that we ourselves – as well as all the other realities to which we are related – are derivative, transitory and contingent, are finite beings and thus not ultimately reliable, we will not be able to grasp what Christian faith is all about. For at its very heart Christian faith is a claim about our alienation from this God on which we depend in all respects, and about the healing of this alienation through God's own reconciling work – a healing which also restores our proper relations to the rest of the created order. I call this underlying creator/creation pattern – with its radical asymmetrical dualism – 'foundationalist': the central structural features of this symbolism are nicely caught up in the metaphor of foundation-and-superstructure (for without the foundation the superstructure could not be at all). For those who see all human problems through 'foundationalist' eyes, the really important religious questions are about the ultimate ground or foundation on which all human life rests, and about our relationship to that ultimate ground.

The foundational metaphor, however, is not the only one which can provide a way to grasp the human situation in life, though it has been a prominent and fruitful one. Another metaphor with quite different implications is drawn from the idea of an organic whole. Our experience of our own bodies – made up, as they are, of hands and feet, stomach and brain, skin and bones, each distinguishable from the others and yet all interconnected and interdependent in such a way as to be parts of a unified living organism – may well be the originary source of this second metaphor. In any case, *holistic* symbolic patterns are those based on metaphors that emphasise the mutual *inter*connectedness and *inter*dependence of all things, rather than the 'absolute dependence' (Schleiermacher) of all finite beings on some ultimate self-subsistent *foundation*. I am certainly no authority on these matters, but as nearly as I can see, the basic Buddhist symbolic pattern is essentially holistic in character. On the one hand, Buddhists resist the reification of anything and everything which women and men can directly identify and name – anything of which they can speak and know – in their insistence that all things are 'empty' (*śūnya*). The frequent use of the symbol of 'emptiness' (at least in Mahāyāna Buddhism) tends to weaken foundationalist tendencies in this tradition, since it undermines every symbolic claim about some 'absolute' or 'utterly independent' reality; even emptiness, we are told, must be understood to be empty.[7] On the other hand, the idea of 'dependent co-origination' (*pratītya-samutpāda*) emphasises the mutual interdependence and interconnectedness of all things with each other, as in an organic whole, an organism. In this vision of the world, then, human lives are seen as essentially integral moments or passing phases of this interdependent network of transient realities always coming into being and passing away; and it is the realisation of this that both makes possible and constitutes human release from the evils of life. This is a very different picture of the human, and of human problems and prospects in the world, than that conveyed by Christianity's foundationalist pattern.

Each of these metaphors ('holism' and 'foundationalism'), through providing an illuminating way to grasp the ultimate structure of things, has its own distinctive plausibility; and there appear to be no independent criteria on the basis of which a rational choice between them might be made. Moreover, each can be developed into a powerful framework within which human beings gain significant understanding of important features of their situation, and of major problems with which life confronts them; and they each suggest ways to address these problems. However, as we can readily see, these metaphors and their implications – when worked out, as in

Buddhism and Christianity, into detailed symbolic pictures or conceptions of human-existence-in-the-world – will necessarily contradict each other in important ways. It is not germane to our purposes here to examine these contradictions; but we do need to take note of certain implications of this profound difference between the symbolic patterns of Buddhism and Christianity for our understanding of the problem of religious truth. How should we interpret the fact that these two religious traditions understand the deepest truth about reality, and about human life in the world, in such diverse, even contradictory, ways? Should we take it for granted that only one of these positions (at most) can be right and true, the other thus being false? Or is there some other way to interpret differences as fundamental as this?

The existence of such striking differences in the fundamental 'symbolic patterns' that give world religions like Christianity and Buddhism their underlying structure and meaning suggests that it is a mistake to regard religious conceptions of human-life-in-the-world – and thus religious truth-claims – as straightforward expressions of direct insight into or knowledge of the nature of the world and the human place within it. Rather, these conceptions appear to be built up in the course of long histories through refining and developing the potential of certain 'root metaphors' (Stephen Pepper)[8] to provide illuminating ways of grasping and holding together wide reaches of human experience and knowledge. It takes many generations (as we have noted) for overall pictures of the world and the human to be constructed; and it is only from within well-articulated symbolic frameworks of this sort that the kind of (religious) experiencing and reflecting, meditating and knowing, which is capable of uncovering and addressing the deepest problems and evils in life, can occur. Hence, the appearance of new insights and understandings – one thinks, for instance, of the deepening conceptions of 'sin' and 'salvation' in Christianity, and of *duḥkha* (suffering) in Buddhism – is in fact essentially a nuancing and deepening (and perhaps further unifying) of the available symbolic resources. All such developments, of course, amplify and extend the tradition in significant ways. Thus, the momentums of the profoundest metaphors and symbols of each tradition become reinforced and deepened as history rolls on, and a symbolic pattern of increasing refinement emerges, enabling humans to come to terms with their problems more effectively. In this way the great religious traditions have grown and developed into vehicles of enormous insight, meaning, and truth for human life. But in each case what they have to recommend as 'true' is grounded, ultimately, on the metaphorical and symbolical resources which they have acquired through their history.

This analysis suggests that it is no longer feasible to think of religious truth in more or less simplistic monolithic terms, as if there were some single unified pattern of truth to which all religious truth-claims approximate and in terms of which all should be assessed. Rather, as modern historical understanding enables us to see, there are a number of (quite dissimilar) patterns of religious understanding and religious truth, each of them intelligible and persuasive in its own terms but standing in some tension – or even contradiction – with the others on certain fundamental issues. Through most of human history, however, religious reflection and thought has – in parochial fashion – taken for granted the absolute finality and normativity of the truth(s) and practice(s) made available in its own local tradition(s), judging all else by these standards. It should be apparent that such parochial religiousness does not – and cannot in principle – address the issues which religious pluralism poses for us today.

What moves, then, are open to us? It no longer seems reasonable to continue to follow the essentially provincial approach characteristic of most religious (and philosophical) traditions in the past – attempting to evaluate the significance and validity of these various overall symbolic patterns simply and directly in terms prescribed by our own (rival) pattern of meanings and criteria – since the symbolic and linguistic patterns underlying our criteria of judgement may well be as parochial as those others which we are seeking to assess. Does this drive us, then, into a complete scepticism about all religious truth, or into a relativism which prevents our making any judgements at all? I do not think so. What it does demand is that we reconsider our conception of religious truth itself in light of (a) the way it develops historically, and (b) the large disagreements with respect to it which we find in history. A pluralistic conception of truth, I want to suggest now, or a conception of pluralistic truth, can provide us with a way to address the issues we face here.

III

In recent years there has been increasing emphasis on the importance of religious dialogue, that is, wide-ranging conversation among representatives of various religious traditions about matters of belief and practice, about values and meanings, institutional arrangements and patterns of symbolism, question of morality and justice and human well-being, about religious truth-claims. Often in such dialogues the conversation is confined to imparting and acquiring information and knowledge about the several religious traditions represented, with special care being taken not to call into question important religious beliefs of any of the participants; were this to occur, it is feared, the spirit of open interchange might be undermined. The presence of such protective constraints means that although various truth-claims of the different religious traditions may be presented, serious examination of issues of religious *truth* – that is, of what is to be taken with religious seriousness across the lines that distinguish the traditions – seldom occurs. Our parochial, somewhat monolithic, ways of thinking about what religious truth is and how it is to be understood divide us against each other in ways which make such discussion quite difficult.

In place of the absolutistic conceptions of truth which we have inherited from our several religious traditions, I suggest that we attempt to think in terms of a dialogical and thus pluralistic conception. Experiences from everyday conversation, particularly the free and spontaneous conversation that can occur among equals such as friends, can provide us with a model for developing such a notion.[9] Traditional conceptions of religious truth and its dissemination appear to be connected with fundamentally *authoritarian* models, such as teacher/student or guru/disciple, in which truth is something *known* to one of the parties – i.e. is essentially a *possession* of one of the parties – and is then communicated to, passed over to, the other party who receives and accepts it. A unidirectional relationship or movement of this sort characterises much traditional religious thinking and practice with respect to truth – consider the special authority given to sacred texts by readers and interpreters, and especially by religious communities; the religious importance of prophets to whom God is believed to have revealed divine truth, or otherwise 'enlightened' persons whose insight into the truth is thought to go far beyond that of ordinary folk; the authority of most religious teachers in relation to their disciples; the importance in many religions of the activity of preaching to audiences (large or small) who remain basically hearers, recipients of the word; the authority given to traditional doctrine or teaching by most religious groups. In all these instances truth appears to be understood on the model of *property*, something that is owned by one party, and thus is not directly available to others, but which can be passed on or given over to others if the owner so chooses. If we move away from this property-model of truth, however, to a model based on the experience of free and open conversation, a quite different conception comes into view.

In sharp contrast to many formal religious 'dialogues', in which all of the participants have specific agendas in mind which they wish to pursue in representing properly their respective communities and traditions, a typical conversation among friends often proceeds quite spontaneously. Though in each remark the speaker is attempting to 'say something' that is fitting at that moment – and in that respect has something 'true' in mind – the 'truth' which may emerge in the course of the conversation cannot be understood simply by taking up these individual speeches one by one, as though each stood on its own feet. For the interchange may have developed 'a life of its own' (as we say), and it may have moved in directions no one anticipated and lead to new insights and ideas which none of the participants had previously considered. (Here the difference between our conversation-model and most interreligious dialogues – where formal papers are prepared ahead of time and then published afterwards, often without significant alteration of the text – is obviously quite marked.) Thus conversation is itself sometimes the matrix of significant creativity in human life. Let us see if we can unpack a bit the way in which this creativity-in-conversation occurs; and then I want to point out the significance of this model for our understanding of religious truth.

Some light can be thrown on this creativity if we take note of the mixture of determinateness and indeterminacy which is characteristic of every word used and every speech made in a conversation.[10] Each word in a language has, of course, certain fairly definite meanings and uses; but these actually fade off into each other, and into a rather indefinite penumbra of meaning that surrounds the word. The various participants in a conversation understand each other because of the relative determinacy of meaning of each word spoken – a meaning made even more definite by the particular context (in the sentence, in the ongoing conversation, in the private and the common experience of the participants) in which the word is used at this particular moment. But the penumbra of connotations and indeterminacy surrounding each word's relative determinateness of meaning, taken together with the diverse kinds of experience and history undergone by each participant in the conversation, make it inevitable that each hearer will grasp and attend to something slightly different from the others and from the speaker. Thus different responses are called forth from the different hearers, and the conversation proceeds down pathways not expected by the original speaker or by any of the others. (This may be an exciting and happy development on some occasions; on others it may be tragic, ending in the bitter enmity of hitherto friends.) An intervention by speaker B moves the conversation in a way that A had not intended; and a succeeding intervention by C moves it on a slightly different tack, not anticipated by either A or B, so that when A responds again, it will be with a comment not directly continuous with his or her earlier remark, but one which takes into account what B and C have unexpectedly said. And thus the path of the conversation as a whole, though definitely continuous, is not a direct working-out of the original intention which A (or anyone else) was attempting to express.

If this pattern of conversation is allowed to proceed for a while, it may depart radically from the apparent subject-matter of A's original remark, going down quite unexpected pathways that none of the participants have followed before. Sometimes, in an exciting conversation of this sort, where new ideas seem continuously to be bursting forth, the participants are 'carried away' by the flow of the conversation itself, which has come to have a seeming intention of its own. These can be moments of high 'spirit' for human beings, even of 'ecstasy'; they are moments in which the creativity of the social process is being directly experienced. This social experience, in which a spirit of the group comes alive and takes over, does not mean that the individuals cease to act as free agents in their own right: they each contribute to the conversation out of their own freedom, not under some external compulsion. And yet that freedom is led beyond anything any of them could have deliberately 'decided' to think or to say; it is a moment of creativity which only the group process makes possible. In the course of this sort of conversation, new insights or meanings appear which, though not directly intended by any of the speakers, are of great interest to them; indeed, these may become of greater interest to the speakers than what they themselves had originally intended in their own contributions. The freedom and creativity of the participants, far from being in any way diminished by their participation in the social process, has actually been expanded and extended by it; and the conversation proves to be the matrix in which *new truth* emerges for them, truth that goes beyond anything they had known before. It is truth grounded in what each had to contribute to that conversation, but truth which could not have been either discerned or formulated from the standpoint of any one of the participants.

This model, by leading us to focus on the way truth *comes into being* rather than on its existence as a possession that belongs to someone, can assist us in our reflection on religious truth. Here it does not seem particularly illuminating to regard truth as a possession at all, even a possession belonging in common to a community (e.g. the group of friends who are conversing together). Rather, truth is perceived as a process of becoming, a reality which *emerges* (quite unexpectedly) in the course of conversation – a reality which, if the conversation continues, may continue to break in upon the participants. It is a reality which will harden and die away, however, if the participants in the conversation attempt to reify it into legalistic definitions and formulas which thereafter are regarded as authoritative bits of knowledge, to be respected and revered and learned but not to be criticised and creatively transformed in further conversation. I call this a 'pluralistic' or 'dialogical' conception of truth, because here – instead of taking truth to be a property of particular words or propositions or texts which can be learned and passed on (more or less unchanged) to others – it is identified as a living reality which emerges within and is a function of ongoing, living conversation among a number of different voices.

We can see better what is involved here by contrasting a conversation with a lecture. In its very form a lecture expresses an essentially monolithic and finitistic conception of truth: it suggests that truth is the sort of thing which can be presented quite adequately by a single voice in continuous ongoing monologue, and which can be brought to a satisfactory conclusion at a particular point in time. The model of conversation suggests, in rather sharp contrast, that many voices, representing quite different sorts of experience and points of view, are required even to begin to articulate truth; and, indeed, that truth demands a kind of open-endedness into an indefinite future (conversations are often simply broken-off for extraneous reasons without being brought to any 'conclusion'), and therefore even a plurality of voices is not fully adequate to truth. In conversation every voice knows that it is not complete in itself, that its contribution is in response to, and therefore depends upon, the voice(s) that came before, and that other voices coming after will develop further, modify, criticise, qualify what has just been said. Free-flowing conversation presupposes a consciousness of being but one participant in a larger developing yet open-ended pattern of a number of voices, each having its own integrity, none being reducible to any of the others; and it presupposes a willingness to be but one voice in this developing flow of words and ideas, with no desire to control the entire movement (as in a lecture or other monologue). When truth is conceived in these pluralistic and dialogical terms, no single voice can lay claim to it, for each understands that it is only in the ongoing conversation as a whole that it is brought into being. In this model, truth is never final or complete or unchanging: it develops and is transformed in unpredictable ways as the conversation proceeds.[11]

It would be foolish to argue that this notion of dialogical truth can answer all questions or should displace all other conceptions. Truth manifests itself in many different forms – scientific and historical knowledge, mathematical formulae and logical proofs, religious teaching and poetic insight, the surprising intuitions of persons of unusual sensibility, ordinary common sense, and many more – and these will continue to play important roles in ongoing human life and to require diverse modes of conception. I do want to suggest, however, that a pluralistic understanding of truth, based on the model of what can occur in serious conversation, is much better fitted to the needs of contemporary interreligious dialogue than the ordinary monolithic conceptions taken for granted by most participants; and it may, perhaps, come to be seen as fitting for religious life generally, as we find ourselves increasingly forced to grow into a single interdependent humanity. For this is a model which demands that all participants in the dialogue – that is, each of the different religious traditions represented – enters into conversation with the others on equal terms: all are there to participate with the others in the search for truth; none is there claiming alone to possess final religious insight or understanding; each wishes to contribute whatever it can from the riches of its own tradition to the ongoing conversation, and will be listened to respectfully and attentively; all expect to learn from the others, through appropriating with appreciation what they have to offer, and through opening themselves willingly to probing questions and sharp criticism. Each participant in the conversation posits the others as substantive contributors in this collective pursuit of (religious) truth, and thus is open *in principle* to contributions from those others – instead of these several voices each presuming it is fully capable of expressing (by itself) what needs to be said. Through such a process of free and open conversation on the most profound religious issues – a conversation that will have to continue for years, even generations – it may be hoped that deeper religious truth than that presently known to any of our traditions will in due course emerge.

Historically, all too often, religious knowledge has taken authoritarian forms, with truth believed to be accessible only to special elite groups who could interpret sacred texts and explain obscure ideas. Under these circumstances, the path to knowledge and truth was a more or less direct movement toward those (texts and personages) regarded as ultimate *authorities* in these matters, with little open discussion and criticism along the way. All of this fostered hierarchical social patterns easily subject to abuse: religious knowledge and power were in the hands of the few, and the masses of ordinary people were expected simply to believe what they were told and to obey. The conversational model of truth which I am proposing here, in contrast, is not hierarchical and linear but is instead essentially dialectical. It is democratic, open and public – a model which encourages criticism from new voices and insights from points of view previously not taken seriously. This conception of religious truth avoids the nihilistic tendencies of an unqualified relativism, for it is *truth* – with its unique and undeniable claims upon each voice in the conversation – that we are concerned with here; but simultaneously, in its acknowledgement that this truth is *pluralistic* – that no one voice or formulation can possess or adequately express it – this conception undercuts the tendencies, so prominent in traditional views, to become absolutistic, dogmatic, imperialistic.[12]

Modern historical studies have shown that it was often through internal dialogue and external exchange that religious truth in fact grew and developed in each of the great traditions (although this has not been well-understood and was often resisted). Religious truth has always been, thus, pluralistic in character, emergent from conversations among many different voices over many generations; and the efforts made, from time to time, to freeze it into authoritative monolithic forms have always failed. If the great religious traditions could come to understand their deepest insights and truth in the historical and pluralistic way that I am proposing in this chapter – that is, as contributions to the ongoing larger conversation of humankind on the deepest issues with which life confronts us all – we would move a step further toward finding a way to live together on our small planet as a single, though pluriform, humanity.

IV

Earlier in this chapter I suggested that if we understand religious symbols, practices and claims in historical terms, we will be able to appreciate and honour all aspects of their meaning. It is important to admit now that the pluralistic conception of truth which I am proposing here does not quite fulfil that promise. For the *authoritarian* and *absolutistic* characteristics of traditional religious truth-claims are not, in fact, given full respect in this more democratic, open, dialogical understanding. What I am suggesting here is that in the modern world, at least those parts of the modern world which emphasise democratic values and the necessarily public character of knowledge and truth, hierarchical patterns of the traditional sort no longer are appropriate or justifiable. On this point modernity and most traditional religions strongly clash; and we are forced to choose between the older religious models and this newer one which is consonant with our historical knowledge about the development of human religiousness and is demanded by our modern democratic values. If we make the move to a conception of religious truth as essentially pluralistic in character, we will, thus, be significantly modifying more traditional understandings of religious insight and knowledge; and this must be forthrightly acknowledged.

This openness toward some of the values of modernity does not mean, however, that our pluralistic conception of religious truth is simply *secular*, one which is not based on important traditional moral and religious insights. In fact this conception expresses well – better than any monolithic notion can – religious understandings of human finitude, and it incorporates moral insights appropriate to those understandings. Our pluralistic/dialogical conception is based on the recognition that truth-claims are always made by *particular finite human beings*, with their own particular limitations of vision, insight and understanding, and their own propensities to prejudice and self-interested falsification; precisely for these (religio-moral) reasons, no human claims to incorrigibility or absoluteness are justifiable. In entering into conversation with others on religious questions, therefore, a proper humility about one's own position and a respect for the other is always called for; and this requires willingness to listen to the other who sees things differently, allowing oneself to be criticised and corrected by the other when appropriate. Moreover, it demands that we open ourselves to conversation with any and all who care to participate with us on free and equal terms.

Through most of human history our epistemic traditions – religious, philosophical, scientific – have been elitist and thus esoteric. In contrast, a pluralistic/dialogical conception of truth can help to break down all forms of exclusion and domination – whether based on authoritarianism, elitism, or any other form of unfair discrimination – while encouraging in their stead the practice of a truly democratic interaction in the consideration of matters of ultimate import and concern.

Notes

1. *Pragmatism* (New York: Longmans, Green and Co., 1910), pp. 240–2.
2. John Hick in particular (in recent years) has been developing a full philosophical articulation of this approach. An early statement of his developing views is to be found in *God and the Universe of Faiths* (London: Macmillan, 1973); his most recent – and most thoroughly worked-out – statement is in his Gifford Lectures, *An Interpretation of Religion: Human Responses to the Transcendent* (London: Macmillan, 1989). Here he concludes that the variety of doctrinal and other claims made in various religious traditions actually reflect 'experiences that . . . constitute different ways in which the same ultimate Reality has impinged upon human life.' He argues that the 'important ideas within different traditions which on the surface present incompatible alternatives . . . can be seen on deeper analysis to be different expressions of the same more fundamental idea'; for instance, where there are 'rival conceptions of the Real as personal and as non-personal . . . the Real in itself is the noumenal ground of both of these ranges of phenomena'; and the various 'mythic pictures [in the different traditions] are true in so far as the responses which they tend to elicit are in soteriological alignment with the Real . . . [They] may each mediate the Real to different groups of human beings; and . . . in fact do so, as far as we are able to judge, to about the same extent' (pp. 373–5). Hick regards the position he has worked out as 'pluralistic'; in my opinion, however, it is utterly monolithic, for according to him there is a single universal philosophical framework – one known to John Hick and articulated by him quite straightforwardly – that takes up into itself *all* religious conceptions, however diverse, and explains that, as far as truth is concerned, they all come down to *essentially the same thing*. (The quotations just given make precisely this point.) Although this position resolves the problems of diversity by moving to a very abstract ultimate unity, there is much to be said for it; but I cannot go into that here. It obviously differs sharply from the 'pluralistic' conception that I seek to articulate in this chapter – a conception which goes so far as to attempt to conceive even what we call 'truth' in thoroughly pluralistic terms.

3. See 'Thick Description: Toward an Interpretive Theory of Culture', in *The Interpretation of Cultures* (New York: Basic Books, 1973).

4. *Towards a World Theology* (Philadelphia: Westminster Press, 1981), p. 44.

5. See Walpola Rahula, *What the Buddha Taught* (London: Gordon Fraser, 1967), pp. 12–14.

6. See W. C. Smith, *Belief and History* (Charlottesville: University Press of Virginia, 1977), and *Faith and Belief* (Princeton: Princeton University Press, 1979).

7. For a full discussion of the notion of emptiness, see Frederick J. Streng, *Emptiness: A Study in Religious Meaning* (Nashville: Abingdon Press, 1967).

8. Stephen Pepper, *World Hypotheses* (Berkeley: University of California Press, 1961).

9. In human life there are, of course, many different sorts of situations within which conversations occur, most of them shaped in important ways by differences in status, roles, class, gender, levels of education, and other factors which generate domination/submission power differentials of many sorts. These all affect the flow, content, freedom and spontaneity of conversations in many different (often hidden) ways. I bring up this truism to make clear that the model of conversation which I will be discussing in the next pages – the 'free and spontaneous conversation that can occur among equals such as friends' – is very specific and perhaps somewhat idealised, and my observations with respect to it (about 'creativity', for example) obviously may not be applicable to other quite different conversational situations. I want to emphasise that in this brief examination of certain features of some conversations, I am not claiming that conversation generally is a satisfactory model of what human interaction overall should be: that would be a gross oversimplification. (For some discussion of the problematic character of conversation as a model of ideal human interaction, see Sharon D. Welch, *A Feminist Ethic of Risk* [Minneapolis: Fortress Press, 1990], esp. Chapter 7.)

10. Cf. Wolfhart Pannenberg, *Anthropology in Theological Perspective* (Philadelphia: Westminster Press, 1985), pp. 370–6.

11. In recent years there has been increasing interest among philosophers and theologians in conversation or dialogue, as a proper goal for intellectual activity, instead of the more traditional pursuit of truth (cf., for example, R. Rorty, *Philosophy and the Mirror of Nature* [Princeton: Princeton University Press, 1979] and *Consequences of Pragmatism* [Minneapolis: University of Minnesota Press, 1982]; J. Habermas, *Theory of Communicative Action*, 2 vols. [Boston: Beacon Press, 1984, 1987]; R. S. Bernstein, *Beyond Objectivism and Relativism* [Philadelphia: University of Pennsylvania Press, 1985]; H. Peukert, *Science, Action and Fundamental Theology: Toward a Theology of Communicative Action* [Cambridge: M.I.T. Press, 1984]; F. Fiorenza, *Foundational Theology* [New York: Crossroad, 1984]; D. Tracy, *Plurality and Ambiguity* [San Francisco: Harper and Row, 1987]; P. Hodgson, *God in History: Shapes of Freedom* [Nashville: Abingdon, 1989]). My suggestion that (religious)

truth should be understood to be specifically pluralistic and dialogical in character is in harmony with this growing interest in conversation and 'communicative action'.

12. It will be obvious to the readers of this chapter, I am sure, that many of the most difficult questions about (religious) truth are not even touched on here: at most I have proposed a new model for thinking about such truth. I have presented no carefully-wrought definition of truth; nor have I suggested criteria for judging what is true or tests which truth-claims must meet. Obviously the question of how emerging 'new insights' are to be evaluated would need to be taken up in any such further elaboration, as well as the pertinence of the pragmatic criterion of 'fruitfulness' (in stimulating further dialogue and new moral and religious reflection, in suggesting new modes of action, etc.). These questions and many others need attention, but they cannot be addressed here.

14

Reflections on the Ambiguity of the World

TERENCE PENELHUM

John Hick devotes a whole Part of *An Interpretation of Religion* to what he calls the religious ambiguity of the universe. He accords due importance to this fundamental feature of our intellectual and religious life in a way that is almost unique among contemporary religious philosophers. This essay is not intended as a detailed examination of his views on it. It consists of some reflections of my own, occasioned by the conclusion of a lengthy teaching career in which the importance of this phenomenon has been brought home to me again and again. My hope is that my own bewilderment about it may prompt useful reflection on the role he assigns to it in those writings of which *An Interpretation of Religion* is such an impressive and magisterial culmination.

I

I begin by quoting from *An Interpretation*:

By the religious ambiguity of the world I do not mean that it has no definite character, but that it is capable from our present human vantage point of being thought and experienced in both religious and naturalistic ways. . . . With the western Enlightenment of the eighteenth century, stimulated by the rapid development of the modern scientific method and outlook, a scepticism that had hitherto hovered in the background as a mere logical possibility now became psychologically present and plausible within the more educated circles of Europe and North America, and the old religious certainties began to crumble. . . . In this post-Enlightenment age of doubt we have realised that the universe is religiously ambiguous. It evokes and sustains non-religious as well as religious responses.

165

Hick continues:

> The culture within which modern science first arose was theistic;
> and accordingly the prevailing form of modern scepticism has
> been atheistic. The sceptics have mostly been secularised Chris-
> tians and Jews or post-Christian and post-Jewish Marxists. Dis-
> tinctively post-Hindu, post-Buddhist and post-Muslim forms of
> scepticism have yet to arise.[1]

Having made this comment, he proceeds to justify and illustrate his
claim about the religious ambiguity of the universe by reference to
the debates between Christians and Jews and their atheistic counter-
parts: that is, to characterise what religious ambiguity is in terms of
the fact that our world is one that can evoke a theistic response, and
an atheistic response. I do not question that scepticism has arisen in
a previously theistic culture, and I am not the one to contest what he
says about the absence of post-Hindu or post-Buddhist or post-
Muslim sceptics. But to confine the characterisation of religious
ambiguity to the debates between theists and atheists is to run the
risk of a kind of parochialism that all of Hick's writings are attempts
to counteract.

II

I can illustrate this from my own case. I am by training and practice
a philosopher, who found himself, by a combination of institutional
circumstances, in the midst of a department of scholars of religion.
This made me aware of problems besetting intellectual positions I
had previously taken up without adequate reflection. It also changed
my teaching milieu: instead of facing audiences for whom religious
commitments were mere grist for the mills of analytical philosophy,
I faced student audiences for whom they were potential life-options.
These audiences were religiously pluralistic, containing both prac-
tising Christians, Muslims, Jews, Hindus, Buddhists and Sikhs, wholly
secularised persons who had hitherto supposed religion to be a mere
repository of pre-scientific fantasies but who were humble enough
to attempt to see whether anything better could be made of it, and
people we would normally classify as receptive and open-minded
seekers.

Before I began to function in this changed environment, I had
perceived the world's ambiguity in much the way Hick describes it.[2]

As I saw the matter, the world can be viewed either theistically or atheistically, and the realisation of this fact is a consequence of the Enlightenment attacks on the enterprise of natural theology, as conceived by Aquinas and his successors. They had thought of natural theology as the enterprise of proving the truth of some key doctrines of Christianity (or Judaism or Islam), such as the reality and unity of God. Even though most believers are unaware of these proofs, the rationality of their belief was thought to be underwritten by their availability; and the alleged revelation in the scriptures or the church was thereby shown to have an authority that a rational enquirer should accept. If natural theology can deliver the proofs it attempts, then we do not live in a religiously ambiguous universe. There may be atheists in it, and even adherents of non-theistic religions in some faraway corners of it; but their position is not a rational position. For if God's being and goodness and providence are demonstrable, it is irrational to deny them if you are aware of the demonstrations, and at best morally excusable to deny them if you are not. For religious ambiguity is not merely a matter of there being people who interpret the world theistically, but also a matter of its being rational to interpret it non-theistically as well.

The Enlightenment has left a legacy of doubt about the possibility of natural theology, and a legacy of doubt about the historical evidences that the church used to connect its revelatory claims with the proofs of God that the philosophers supposedly provided. This doubly-sceptical legacy about theological tradition has been coupled with the ubiquitous recognition in our culture of the autonomy of science, which has made it a tacit criterion of respectability among theologians that one's theology avoid any claims that collide with well-esteemed scientific theories such as Copernican astronomy or evolutionary biology.

My own erstwhile judgement on this cultural situation was the following. While the traditional attempts to show it to be irrational *not* to believe in God were unsuccessful, this failure does not show the programme of natural theology could never be carried through. It does, however, make a negative expectation of this reasonable. Yet this does not show that God does not exist, or that it is unreasonable to believe in God. For that, it would be necessary to show that belief in God entails contradictions, or is inconsistent with known scientific truths; and it did not, and does not, seem to me that anyone has shown this, in spite of notorious difficulties about evil, or grace and freedom, and many other problems. And there are many dimen-

sions and forms of experience in the believer's life that the un-
believer does without, and seem to the believer, reasonably, to be in
themselves reasons for adhering to that life, even though there is not
intellectual compulsion to view them in that light. We are faced with
a situation in which there are two world-views, each with its own
drawbacks, but neither able to refute the other. Each, however, can
subsume the other: that is, each is able to describe the other in ways
that explain why many so apparently rational people are mistaken
enough to embrace it. There are (at least this side of death) no
appeals that show one side or the other to be demonstrably mistaken. We have two groups who share a common world, and share
a common scientific understanding of it, while living in two quite
different worlds. Kierkegaard seems, insufferably, to be right when
he says that a transition from one such world to the other is a leap;
for any reason they may give is a reason that has weight only within
the world-view they arrive at, not in the one they have left.

   This is how I viewed the ambiguity of the universe; and this view
parallels in most respects the account Hick gives us in Part Two of
An Interpretation. I feel now, however, that it is seriously defective.

III

The most obvious way in which this account is defective is that it
is unacceptably parochial and monocultural. It neglects completely
the diversity in the religious traditions of the world. John Hick is, of
course, very prominent among those who have made this clear to
us, and it might be thought that his response to the facts of religious
pluralism offers a theoretically simple way of correcting the post-
Enlightenment perception of the world's ambiguity. He argues that
the post-axial faiths are all to be understood as culturally-relative
responses to one ultimate Reality. So it is tempting to say that the
world's ambiguity is to be defined as a confrontation between a
naturalism that denies the existence of such a Reality, and a plurality of faiths that assert it in ways that differ, but do so, in the
last resort, in ways that are only of secondary importance. I cannot
say that this picture is a demonstrably false one, and am not
arguing such a view here. But I do think we need a close look at
some serious complexities in our intellectual situation before em-
bracing it.

The diversity among the religions of the world (and among competing movements within them) leads to situations in which each judges the others as approximations to itself, and subsumes significant differences under its own doctrines. Indeed, the very likenesses that one finds between religious traditions are sometime assessed as being due to other traditions trying, presumably below the level of explicit consciousness, to attain to the truth of the judge's own tradition: Rahner's notorious concept of anonymous Christianity leaps immediately to mind. We find here an obvious similarity between the way the adherents of different religious traditions confront one another, and the way in which Christian thinkers and atheistic naturalists have confronted one another.

Nor should we underestimate the diversity among the nonreligious perceptions of the world that the religions confront. Hick locates the difference between the post-axial and the pre-axial faiths in the salvific or soteriological character of the former. Each claims to liberate us from the shackles that bind us; or, to use another popular metaphor, each offers a prescription to cure the malady it diagnoses as the ultimate source of anxiety and suffering. Soteriological religions see their first task as that of persuading those they address that their prescription is needed, and this can only be done by persuading them, first, that they suffer from the diagnosed malady. Human beings are wilfully reluctant to accept that they are in as bad a way as the religion teaches, because (or so the religion judges) they resist the troublesome reorientation of the personality that is required to cure it.

It is important to note that this soteriological feature of the great religions is duplicated in some wholly naturalistic systems of thought. The two best-known examples in our time are Freudianism and Marxism.[3] Each has a diagnosis of the human condition that common sense is reluctant to accept, and each interprets that very reluctance as a symptom of the malaise it diagnoses. Each offers liberation from the condition it claims to find, and gives its adherents a release of spiritual energies that enable them to deal with real problems, rather than self-inflicted ones. (As we all know, they have been called religions for this very reason; but this is a patent example of what H. D. Lewis has somewhere called winning converts by definition.) Another secular analogue of post-axial religion that is not quite with us, but has almost arrived, is some form of biologically-based 'green' ideology, which is likely to incorporate a significant degree of hostility toward the major religions (or at least the major Western ones) as species-centred and environmentally indifferent.

Naturalism, then, can take on a saving form. It is true, however, that it more commonly takes on a form that is inimical to demands for self-scrutiny and transformation, amounting to a deliberate secular preference for the unexamined life that dismisses ideology and the demand for transformation as pathological.[4]

I draw attention to these variations in our cultural scene in order to urge that we are not faced with a simple theist–naturalist ambiguity, in which each side can justify itself, at least negatively, in relation to the other; we are faced, rather, by a world that exhibits *multiple* religious and ideological ambiguity. I would now like to comment briefly on the ways in which this fact has come home to me in the practical context of teaching.

IV

To foster fruitful reflection in a mixed audience of the sort I have described earlier, one must try to broaden and deepen the imagination of one's listeners so that each will be able to envision how the world appears through the eyes of adherents of a variety of different faiths and secular outlooks, so that commitments that begin by seeming wholly alien and even preposterous come to seem less so. This enlargement of the imagination requires an enlargement of the intellect, so that one can absorb the *reasons* that can be given from within each of these originally alien outlooks for interpreting the key phases of life, and the crises of society, in the ways these outlooks do interpret them, and for supposing the interpretations one brought ready-made to those situations to be questionable. Enhancing the understanding of other outlooks involves making doubts about one's own intelligible; and this in its turn makes such doubts a real possibility. If it does not generate live doubts about the world-view one begins with, it minimally shows how world-views inconsistent with it can be held with integrity by others possessed of the same range of information as oneself.

It is idle to suppose that the teacher can remain unaffected by his or her assumption of pedagogical reasonableness. It becomes impossible, even if one begins by being assured of some position of one's own, not live it thereafter without some significant degree of *arrière-pensée* derived from highlighting the merits of the competition. The same inner reservations are likely to arise, of course, in the minds of one's students. Then the ambiguity, the *multiple* ambiguity, of one's world becomes a felt reality.

V

This is how I saw the ambiguity of the world, and how I have more lately come to see it. How is one to respond to it? Since each of us who may perceive it will have arrived at that perception from a distinct prior position, there is almost certainly no single right answer to this question. But although the obligations of each person may be unique, I think there is one unqualified obligation for all rational beings, whether they have a prior faith or not: to seek the disambiguation of their world. Before looking at what this could amount to, I must put aside two quite different responses.

The first response can be made equally easily from within a faith, or from within a secular standpoint, although it is more commonly made in the former way. The post-axial faiths demand personal transformation, and say that resistance to their truth-claims is due to wilful reluctance to admit the need for it. Those who try to reflect on the variety of life-options that our culture presents to us must indeed do it in constant awareness of the risk of bad faith. But if I have made a case for the world's ambiguity, I have necessarily made a case for the fact that it is possible to be *conscientiously* unable to decide between two or more world-views or life-options. If the world is ambiguous, it follows that this is possible, even though the motives of any given waverer may be beyond our powers to determine. Those who insist that hesitation in the face of their world-view must be wilful, and not merely that it often is, have the onus of showing that the world is not ambiguous.

In an ambiguous world, conscientious hesitation is not a mere logical possibility. We encounter it continually. It can even happen with regard to several traditions or stances at once: such indecision, in our culture, is not necessarily due to dilettantism, but may be a result of seriousness and of an embarrassment of opportunity. This is a position in which many find themselves, and some of us scholars have put them there. It will not do to judge a recognition of the world's ambiguity as a mere form of resistance to the claims of an unsettling message. This is not merely uncharitable. It is empirically false.

A second response I must reject is that the ambiguity of the world is something we must expect if we are to be truly free agents. Since the post-axial faiths make demands, they require a response that must be given freely; if the truth of such a faith were unambiguously obvious, the argument runs, those it addresses would be deprived of the freedom they require to respond, because they *could not help believing*. I think this is confused. It is true that some of the most famous alleged encounters with the Ultimate appear to have been overwhelming experiences to which the idea of resistance seems absurd. It is interesting that those who feel so much has to be made of the phenomenon of cognitive freedom (to use Hick's name for it) do not seem to find the overwhelmingness of what happened to Isaiah in the Temple or Paul on the Damascus Road as problematic. But there is no reason to suppose a world in which the truth of a faith was unambiguously evident would be one in which it was only evident through experiences like this. To suppose this is to confuse having the truth made clear to one with being shattered into submission. For the former, all that is necessary is the removal of grounds for reasonable doubt, and this does not require being overwhelmed. It could happen when a conclusive argument was produced, or a miracle occurred, or a past life was systematically remembered. Such events would not take away the freedom of those who were aware of them. For they could *refuse to accept* them. This might be an irrational response, indeed; but free beings can be irrational if they choose. Doubts that are thus unreasonable could be censured; but reasonable doubts cannot be. An ambiguous world is one in which doubts are reasonable.

I have said that a rational being in an ambiguous world has a duty to seek disambiguation. While I take this to be self-evident, it can also be supported by a religious reason. If I come to think the tradition I adhere to has rational grounds, but that it is paralleled in this respect by other traditions that can account for it in their own terms as it can account for them, I will be a remarkable adherent indeed if this second-order realisation has no effect on the degree and manner of my participation. By all the normal canons of rationality, I will be a more rational thinker if it does have some effect than if it does not; for it is surely characteristic of the rational thinker that he or she is less deeply committed to one view if there is evidence of comparable weight in favour of alternatives. This will not only reasonably affect the extent to which I will feel obliged to bear public witness to my own tradition, or to proselytise for it, but will affect the way in which

I come to think about the very experiences that have hitherto fed and reinforced the faith I have had. I will have concerns about whether or not they are exactly what they seem, or whether they may not just be what my competitors or my naturalistic detractors say they are. Of course, such inner reservations may be dismissed, once more, as mere resurgences of a blameworthy reluctance to face reality. But I submit that reading them this way is uncharitable and empirically false.[5]

VI

What would disambiguate our world? The answer, I think, is any experience, discovery, or argument that rendered it irrational to hold one world-view rather than another. Disambiguation could well be partial; this would occur when one world-view was undermined by evidence while many alternatives remained unaffected. For an example of this, one might consider the arguments Hick offers in *Death and Eternal Life* against the classical doctrine of *karma*, especially the claim that it is inconsistent with the discoveries of modern genetics.[6] If sound, these serve to undermine any world-view that requires the doctrine of *karma* in its traditional form. A similarly negative result would follow if one accepted Richard Dawkins' case in *The Blind Watchmaker* against the belief in providential guidance of the evolutionary processes.[7] Potentially disambiguating arguments of a positive nature are recent 'design' arguments based on alleged 'fine tuning' in the initial expansion of the cosmos,[8] or Richard Swinburne's contention that biological explanations are incapable of rendering intelligible the existence of consciousness in higher organisms.[9]

I make no comment here on the soundness of these arguments. But in each case we find a plausible case being built upon evidence that exists in the public scientific domain that is common to all religious traditions and to secular persons also. Such a case, positive or negative, is a philosophical case. This fact is enough to persuade some that it could have no religious relevance. I conclude by saying what sort of relevance I think it would have.

For the world to be ambiguous, it must have people in it who could reasonably interpret it in more than one way. It does not follow from this that if all of them interpret it in one way and none in another, it is not ambiguous. The ambiguity of the world is a function of how it is reasonable for an informed person to interpret it at some time, and it can therefore be ambiguous when everyone happens to hold firmly to one reading of it, and sees no merit in the competition. In such a situation, it might well be ambiguous without anyone's recognising this. (If Hume and Kant were right in their criticisms of natural theology, the cultural consensus they undermined was itself an example.) The same is true for some disambiguating truth. People merrily continue to believe in discredited items of received wisdom, or to deny proven facts. So undermining some widely-held world-view, or establishing another, might well eliminate no sect, fill no pew, and send no one off into the quiet to mediate or pray. But what it would do is show that if those who knew this truth did none of these things, failed to respond in the appropriate way, they were being wilful or obstinate, or self-deceiving. It is the core of the claims of the great faiths that those who reject their proffered paths to liberation are indeed being wilful or obstinate or self-deceiving; and it is the core of many naturalistic criticisms of those faiths that it is wilful, obstinate, and self-deceiving affirmation that prevents more allegedly realistic engagement with the actualities of life. In an ambiguous world, these claims are indefensible, even though wilfulness, obstinacy and self-deception are common. But in a disambiguated world one of these claims would indeed be true. And the disambiguation of the world is a philosophical task.

VII

How is an adherent of one of the faiths to respond to the world's ambiguity, and to judge the proper role of philosophical reflection? I suggest there are two parts to the answer. First, such a person should seek a disambiguating argument in favour of the faith he or she lives by. This is of course what the classical natural theologians tried to do, and intellectually responsible believers must continue. (It follows that it is quixotic and irresponsible to *welcome* the fact that their attempts did not succeed.) On the other hand, even though I fail to see any sacrifice of intellectual integrity in seeking for arguments to justify where one already is, there *is* a sacrifice involved in remaining indifferent to the outcome of that quest. If the outcome is merely a prolongation of the ambiguity one begins with, the price is inevitably a prolongation of the dilution of the faith one has.

It therefore appears to me that the world's ambiguity presents the adherent of any of the world's great faiths with a problem. In each case the faith offers reasons why the need it diagnoses, and the way to meet that need, has had to be *revealed* to us by its founder, or in its scriptures. The problem that the ambiguity of the world presents is this: why, when this is revealed, is its truth not unambiguously clear? The question is not why redemption is not easier, but why the need for it, and the path to it, is not more obvious. Human perversity cannot be more than half of the answer. If what enslaves us is ignorance, and what liberates us is an enlightenment that waits within, why is the veil of ignorance so thick? If what enslaves us is rebellion against God, and what redeems us is faith in his forgiveness, why is his very reality rationally questionable? If one of the faiths is true, why is it not more obviously true?[10]

Notes

1. John Hick, *An Interpretation of Religion* (London: Macmillan, 1989), pp. 73–4.
2. I expressed my understanding of it at some length in *Religion and Rationality* (New York: Random House, 1971).
3. I would myself add Stoicism and Spinozism, which is to a large extent an early-modern reinvention of it, to the list of major naturalisms that nevertheless have an obviously salvific aspect.
4. This is the position of the classical sceptics, and is expressed in modern times by David Hume.
5. I cannot forbear commenting that field theory like Hick's, which stresses the cultural relativity of all religious forms, is likely to have the same effect.
6. *Death and Eternal Life* (London: Collins, 1976), pp. 381–9.
7. Richard Dawkins, *The Blind Watchmaker* (Harlow: Longman Sci. Tech., 1986).
8. See John Leslie, *Universes* (London: Routledge, 1989); also John Leslie (ed.), *Physical Cosmology and Philosophy* (New York: Macmillan, 1990).
9. Richard Swinburne, *The Evolution of the Soul* (Oxford: Clarendon, 1986), Chapter 10.
10. A clear demonstration of the urgency of this problem for Christianity is to be found in John Schellenberg's 1990 doctoral dissertation for Oxford University, 'God and the Reasonableness of Non-belief'.

15

A Contemplation of Absolutes

NINIAN SMART

John Hick's well-known doctrine of the Real and its phenomenal manifestations invites us to consider differing ways of conceiving the distinction. More especially, we are drawn to think through the problems posed by the style of language we use for the Real. For, in using Kantian or quasi-Kantian vocabulary (for instance John Hick refers to the Real *an sich*), we are inevitably left exposed to some of the classical critiques of the *ding an sich*. By contemplating these we may stimulate some further thoughts about the ultimate referent or referents of religious language.

It was always, of course, a problem of whether we are right to think of the Real as singular. Again, there is the issue of ontology: should we be thinking at all of some kind of substantive Real? Or would it be better to think of process or energy or some dynamic notion to characterise the ultimate? And again, should not the ultimate be a mere placeholder, with no lineaments at all, but just providing the space, so to speak, to lodge whatever each religious tradition takes as ultimate? Though these are abstract-sounding questions, they have some practical meaning.

For if we take the Real *an sich* to be a substantive entity for which the various religions have differing names, then the moral might be that it does not in the long run matter which faith you adopt, though there might be relatively minor disputes as to which set of values you practically espouse: religions might be critical of each others' practical behaviour up to a point, but beyond this there would be little point in disputation. Most missionary activity could be phased out, with profit, since people would not be misled into thinking that their own Real was not the same as that of others. Undoubtedly such a conclusion would be irenic, and part of the intention of perennial philosophers, including John Hick, is undoubtedly peaceful and ecumenical.

I wish to argue in the first place that a Buddhist notion of an Empty or completely open 'Absolute' may be what is called for. I shall then proceed from there to comment on the variety of shapes of the ultimate.

The first point to note is that a main problem of the language of 'the Real' is that it inevitably suggests that there is a single something which lies in back of all the noumenal deities and so forth, from Śiva to Christ and from the Tao to Brahman, projected by the varied traditions upon it. All these phenomenal deities and the like are so many representations of the one Real. But if we are to continue using Kantian language then it follows that we should not be using either the singular or the plural of that which is noumenal.

But it may be responded that it is natural to think of the Real as singular because the phenomenal ultimates are singular. That is to say, Judaism looks to one God, and Śaivism does too, and there is but one Tao and one Brahman in their respective traditions. It becomes easy to think that somehow Śaivites and Jews are worshipping the same God, and behind that the same Real. Well, it may indeed be that many great religions have a single Focus. But it does not follow that the various Foci refer behind themselves to One Reality. We might put this point in a different way by saying that the abstractness of the idea of the noumenon means that we can infer no resemblance between what lies behind and what is phenomenal. Or we might otherwise say that if the ultimate Focus is plural (perhaps the Trinity is plural or maybe we should think of some plural emanationist theology such as that of Neoplatonism) then, in so far as it refers behind, it refers to a plural entity, and if it is singular then the Real is singular. But strictly the Real should be neither singular nor plural since it lies in an inaccessible realm beyond numbers. It is ineluctably beyond space and time, the framework for applying numbers.

But what about those notions that there is an aspect of the divine known as *nirguṇam* Brahman? Is not this somehow affirming the existence of a Real? But John Hick is clear about this, and I here note from his article in the *Encyclopedia of Religion*:

At this point . . . one might object that in Hindu and Buddhist thought *brahman* and *nirvāṇa* and *śūnyatā* are not forms under which the Real is humanly known but are the Real itself, directly experienced in a unitive awareness in which the distinction be-

tween knower and known has been overcome. The gods may be
forms in which the Real appears to particular human groups; but
brahman, or *śūnyatā*, is reality itself directly apprehended. Nevertheless, this claim is called into question by the plurality of experienced absolutes with their differing characters – for the *brahman*
of Advaita Vedanta is markedly different from the *nirvāṇa* of
Theravada Buddhism and from the *śūnyatā* of the Mahāyāna, and
this very variety suggests a human contribution to these forms of
mystical experience. . . . [1]

So it is clear that the absolutes, however clothed in the negative way,
are themselves phenomenal Foci of aspiration. It is muddled to think
of them as directly being the Real. They are still conceptualised and
experienced as phenomenal, albeit at a very high and interior level of
phenomena. The fact that the subject–object distinction does not
typically apply to this kind of non-dual experience in no way de-
tracts from its experiential character. We may note in passing that
usually the negative path is prominent in those phases of religion
which emphasise the interior, mystical experience (rather than prophetic visions and devotional encounters with the personal Other,
i.e. the world of what Otto calls the numinous).

It would seem, then, that the Real is neither one nor many. It can
by the same token be questioned as to whether it is Real, as we have
already indicated. That is, why should we take it as being a sort of
substance? Some writers, such as Tillich, have perhaps brought out
the point that it is not exactly a thing, because it is not in space and
time or space-time, by using the phrase 'being itself'. But even *being*
as a notion contains something like the ghost of thingness. We could
use the concept *becoming*, for instance, which is equally empty, but
does not suggest substantiality. Or we might turn to such alternatives as *process* or *energy*. Why not?

Indeed, there are philosophical thoughts which might turn one
away from being. They are various. First, some religious philosophies are not substance-bound, such as Theravāda Buddhism,
which does not make out that *nibbāna* is some kind of thing. Second,
there are forms of cosmology which are hooked to the notion of
events or processes rather than substances, such as Whitehead's
metaphysics. Since these event-philosophies can be used to express
religious ideas, they postulate non-substantial religious absolutes.
Third, there are languages such as Chinese where the difference, at

least in classical forms, between substances and processes is fluid. In such languages the sky skies and the tree trees.

So far we conclude that the ultimate is neither singular nor plural and is neither being nor becoming. That is, it is unwise, not to say contradictory, to look on the ultimate as belonging to categories that essentially belong to the world of phenomena. This, of course, poses a problem in relation to the categories used in a religion. For instance, in the Christian tradition, however much it might be affirmed that God is not to be described as this or that, She or He is worshipped as being personal. It is hard or impossible in the last resort to think of God, in that tradition, as non-personal. And so we assume that the properties of the Focus are projected back upon the entity or whatever lying behind. Still, let us pursue the path to that noumenal ultimate which is neither being nor becoming and neither singular nor plural; does this not remind us of Emptiness or *śūnyatā* in the Mahāyāna tradition?

There would be interesting consequences of identifying the noumenal with Emptiness. It would be easy enough, no doubt, to generate a Nāgārjuna-like dialectic which would show that the noumenal is the Empty, or the Open.[3] The argument would go as follows. First, the non-cosmic, not belonging to space–time where entities are identifiable and re-identifiable,[3] is such that it is transcendentally oblivious to numbers and counting. It is, of course, not difficult to conceive the uncountable: for instance, it does not make sense to say that love is one or many, or at least not serious sense. It is true, of course, that there are many lovers and many acts of love: but love is something observable in the world which yet is neither many things nor one thing. It is an aspect of life, I guess, but this hardly means that it is one thing.

Moreover, the notion of being or becoming as lying 'behind' what is presented phenomenally in human experience relies on a metaphor, that of 'behind' (or 'beneath' or 'beyond', etc.). Figuratively it is visualised by us perhaps as lying on the far side of a screen of phenomena. Such a metaphor or analogy happens to be quite common in religion. It is part of the meaning of transcendence which, after all, is simply a latinised extension of the idea of being *beyond* as in *trans*. It is an intelligible notion, but it is not a literal one. Obviously what lies beyond the cosmos, as a Real or *ding an sich*, cannot be literally on the other side of the phenomenal, since the latter is embedded in space-time, and so the conception of what lies on the other side of space has to be a metaphor. 'To be the other side of' means to be in a part of space different from that of which it is on the other side. To be in a different area of space from space makes no literal sense. Consequently the Real or *ding an sich* is only metaphorically beyond or behind what is phenomenal.

So what does the idea amount to that the Focus of worship or mystical experience, or whatever – that is, the presentation of the ultimate in human thought and experience – refers back to the Real behind? Is there some lingering notion left over from Kant's things in themselves that they somehow give rise to phenomena? This, however, does not make sense. Or at least it does not from a strictly Kantian perspective. Causation applies to phenomena: it does not apply to what lies beyond phenomena. So noumena cannot give rise to anything. They are a feeble set of anchors thrown out in order to suggest that phenomena really have something to do with what lies 'out there'. But, strictly speaking, and to extend Gertrude Stein, there is no 'out there out there'.

We would conclude here that if there is going to be room for some ghostly space beyond space into which we project the Foci of religion, that space is best described as Emptiness. This bypasses concepts both of Reality and of Process.

Such a noumenon does not do much, however, towards the thesis that all the representations of the Divine point to the same Real. It leaves that thesis on one side. If you want to hold, after all, that all gods are the same (to speak roughly), then that is your Focus. It is in no way guaranteed by the concept of a space beyond. Emptiness can neither guarantee sameness nor difference, for the simple reason that it is neither singular nor plural. If you want to align yourself with *smārta* thought in India, with Aldous Huxley, with Swami Vivekananda or with John Hick, then you have to devise a phenomenal representation of the Divine which affirms this. This is not at all a bad thing to do, and I almost believe it myself (though I draw back because of *nirvāṇa*), nor do I wish here to be critical of that thesis. It has great plausibility, though probably for epistemological rather than ontological reasons. Its plausibility stems from the fact that you cannot deduce the falsity of one tradition or the non-existence of one Focus simply from the standpoint of another tradition or Focus. On the other hand, the criteria of truth as between religions are soft, to put it no more strongly. Let us put it in a sharper form. Either traditions are hermetically sealed from one another, in which case none can judge any other, and all are relative; or we can rise above traditions as human beings and excogitate criteria for judging different traditions. But, in the latter case, there can be no doubt that the criteria or tests are soft ones. We might judge traditions by fruits, but that is a pretty squashy criterion. Or by religious experience: but here too we have no sharpness. Or by metaphysics but, notoriously, metaphysical judgements differ and allegedly logical arguments move in different directions. And so either we can make no judgements or, if we can, they are soft ones. Now in the light of these epistemological observations, which amount to saying that no point of view or worldview can be proved, it is not implausible to fuse the great traditions together and to see them as so many fingers pointing at the same moon. But even this thesis cannot be proved, and we must have some sympathy for those who, frightened by softness, involve themselves in particularist backlashes. But we cannot preempt discussion by our philosophical apparatus. If we affirm a single Real we have already taken a step inside the cosmos: we have stepped into the Perennial Philosophy thesis. This may well be the truth.

Another thought, however, is a rather differing one, namely the notion that all Foci point to Emptiness, which implies nothing. It is true that this would seem to favour the Focus of that form of Mahāyāna which argues for Emptiness. This is not so: for in an important way the question of the Focus remains. If it is meant to be real Emptiness – that is to say, a kind of conscious blankness as manifested in the higher states of meditation and in the philosophy of Emptiness – then it has no more nor less connection with the transcendental Emptiness than does any other Focus. If the Beyond is, so to say, a blank, then it has no connections at all with anything, however minimally, characterised as lying on the hither side. A blank noumenon represents no phenomenon and is just there, in effect, as a placeholder.

All this, of course, bypasses the argument that we are and should be experiencing a Copernican revolution. It seems less epicyclical to postulate a Real to which all religions point than to wrestle with problems of Christian or Buddhist interpretations of all other religious traditions. I am not here wishing to confront this argument directly. But there is another way of looking at traditions.

This is to hold that the differing traditions point at a placeholder. That is, we can talk of the ultimate as lying beyond them, but that placeholder is a space for alternatives, not the point at which differing paths meet (though it might *par accidens* be that). In other words, the differing religions may overlap somewhat but really have differing, and no doubt complementary, messages. We do not need to suppose that God is really *nirvāna* or that the Tao is *brahman*. Such equations can, of course, be argued for and could be true. But the Focus of Theravāda Buddhism remains very remarkably different from that of the Hebrew Bible. It is not so easy to see them both pointing to the same Real: and even if they do, many of the divergences stay in place. Maybe it is better to think of the various religions as overlapping, and yet being different, and often complementary. Complementarity is probably a better model than that of unity. In the long run, perhaps, not too much difference is generated by the alternative models. The desirable effect of the idea of unity is that different traditions should honour one another and cooperate. On the other hand, the desirable effect of the complementarity model is that differing traditions should not merely honour one another but also provide friendly criticism and advice. Complementary religions can instruct one another and render critiques in a positive and caring manner. So it may turn out that the fruits of the models will resemble one another quite a lot.

Complementarity suggests the possibility, but by no means the certainty, of convergence. Since nothing about world-views and value systems can ever be sure, there can be no way of answering the question as to whether there will be a single world religion or ideology. I doubt it, for several reasons. First, every merger produces a backlash, and every friendship an enmity. So where two religions begin to merge, there are backlashes in both traditions, reacting against what can be seen as a weakening of each tradition. Second, the rather radical distinctions between some theistic traditions and non-theistic faiths, notably Theravāda Buddhism, seems to be unbridgeable. Thus, Theravāda Buddhism believes essentially in no Creator, while Islam and Christianity have faith in a Creator. The Theravāda believes in rebirth or reincarnation; most of Christianity and Judaism do not. And so on. Third, the progress of science and human creativity involves diversity. The critical mind is vital. The human race therefore has a vested interest in pluralism, and so world-views should be somewhat encouraged to differ (no doubt in a friendly way: courtesy is often the oil which lubricates mutual criticism).

Paradoxically, however, there is a feature of Hick's Kantianism which may point in the opposite direction and reinforce his general position. In invoking the categorical structure of the human mind as having input into knowledge as the mind filters the phenomena, he is, in the case of religions, postulating something much weaker than the *a priori*. After all, it is the traditions which mould the minds which experience the Absolute. In the quotation I cited above he obviously thinks of contingent traditions, such as the Theravāda or Advaita Vedānta, as providing the structures which people bring to their meditation. It is because of them that mysticism appears different. I am, of course, highly sympathetic with this account ('of course', because the major conflicts between differing writers on mysticism concern, after all, the question of how many types there are – few go to the extreme of supposing that there are radically different and separately contextualised mysticisms wherever you look – in short radically different forms to the same number as individuals engaged in mystical practices. Such extreme particularism becomes self-defeating since it precludes cross-cultural studies and cross-cultural uses of language).

Now the differing traditions, while they soak into the minds and hearts and social structures of the people and realms over which they hold sway, are contingent. A Chinese does not have to remain Chinese. It is true that once we have been raised in one tradition we may be so heavily influenced by it that we can never fight our way out of it. But it is not an iron paper bag: we can in fact in some degree struggle out of our cultures. Many people come to have two or more cultural milieus. So even if I may think like a Britisher and a Scot in particular, this does not prevent me thinking somewhat like an American, since I have lived much of my life in the United States. I have also been much influenced by the fact that I have an Italian wife, and have been involved a lot in Sri Lankan and Indian cultures. So I am now a bit of a cultural mishmash. I regard that as a good thing, as it happens. But it is clear that the filters through which I experience the world have altered. So it is not as if I possess a fixed *a priori*. Now as traditions influence one another so they may come to converge and generate a more unified view of the ultimate. In other words, because the concepts which different folk bring to bear in interpreting their experience are contingent or accidental they can influence one another. In this way the ground may be prepared for a Perennial Philosophy. It could be, despite the arguments which I used above in the opposite direction, that the developing world civilisation will tend to generate a Perennial Philosophy which is not unlike Hick's. Though this unity might breed boring agreement, it would not in itself be at all disagreeable, for the main trouble in the past has been senseless hostilities between differing traditions.

There might, of course, be aspects of the traditions whose shape is not contingent. For instance, the divergence between the mystical path, culminating in the non-dual experience which abolishes the duality between subject and object, and the numinous encounter with the Other, is something entrenched in religions. There are, in addition, other major forms of religious experience, such as the panenhenic. These three begin to account for Theravāda Buddhism (which emphasises the mystical strand), prophetic Judaism (emphasising the numinous) and early Taoism (emphasising the panenhenic) – and so forth. This is admittedly a crude way of characterising differences, but is not without truth. We could look to deeper structures of religion than the brute particularity of the traditions. So there could be a way of looking at religious patterns which underlies traditionalism. Even so, what we would be revealing by such a phenomenological analysis is patterns of religiosity, and it is a further step to try to establish that these are *a priori*. In brief, the notion advanced by John Hick, quite correctly, that experience is affected and channelled by traditional expectations and background differs from the classical Kantian view. It harbours contingency of traditions. As critical beings we can surely suppose that traditions are neither immutable nor unchallengeable. There is possibly what may be called a 'traditionalist positivism' in his position. This would not be unnatural, since all of us in the field of the study of religion tend to be emerging from a period of (Christian) theological excessivism and so want to accentuate what is positive in 'other' faiths. But even so we should not forget the critical mode. From the standpoint of criticism, the positivist mode of emphasising the actual traditions in filtering experience needs to be sceptically considered. In brief, we do not need to accept any one traditional view of the ultimate. And this already means that our schematism is not truly Kantianism. We might dub it 'contingent Kantianism'. This is, of course, different from the classical notion that certain categories are built into our minds and we filter phenomena through such categories. In short, the way we filter religious experience and so on is culturally contingent.

All this means that we are a long way from Kant. Does this matter? In one way it does not. He was a great philosopher, but he is long dead. Who do these dead men think they are? The upshot is that we cannot pretend that there is anything necessary in the way we interpret religious experience. Given such a critical attitude to religious experience, then we are embarked on a much more broadly-based set of criticisms of religious traditions. We are now in a different age, and we have started to live without authority. 'We' are, of course, those who live in a relatively open society, such as the United States, the United Kingdom, India, and Germany. In the open society we, as individuals, make our choices, as individuals.

It seems inevitable to conclude that we are entering upon an age of eclecticism. This is increasingly true of the democracies of America and Europe, not to mention Australasia and even India. I say 'even India' to exhibit the fact that that great democracy is subject to some of the same forces that operate elsewhere. In short, individualism is spreading. Of course, it encourages individuals to make significant choices in religion (as elsewhere). It is not unnatural that this situation should breed not just individualism, but eclecticism too. This increases the pluralism of modern societies. But so what? How does all this affect the argument about Hick?

It affects it because we can no longer make any assumptions about the stability of traditions. With a certain strength in the continuity of older religions we might suppose that there is less contingency in the way we approach experiences. That is, we might think somehow that there are deep patterns underlying the way we come to see our absolute. But individualism amplifies the contingency of traditions. Eclecticism fragments and dissolves rigid traditions from the ages which we look back to. As traditions crumble, we are more prone to pick and choose. Even where a tradition still retains its appeal, its pattern can be changed and its rigidities can be sapped. Thus, while about 50 per cent or a little under of North Italians are Catholic in behaviour, there is about the lowest birthrate in the world. The people are relatively loyal to the tradition, but they thumb their noses at papal teaching about birth control. They are vigorously displaying an eclectic attitude. Now if all this is so – and if this kind of shift of loyalty be realistic – then it follows that holistic traditions are not as vital as we once may have thought. And all this saps the foundations of what we have taken to be traditions. Those traditions are continuously weakened. Whether this be a good or a bad thing is a question I leave on one side. But we are undoubtedly witnessing great changes in the West concerning world-views. We do not need to suppose that they are much more, in democratic societies, than lobbies and associations, and they are sustained by the loyalty of those who support the activities of church leadership.

In brief, the notion that there are deep categories underlying the church and Sangha, etc., traditions which help to inform and shape our experience, is one which needs to be questioned. Traditions crumble and soften, and we are seeing it happen in front of our eyes as we swivel them across the world. That gaze, sweeping across cultural frontiers, takes in changes across the spiritual horizon. There are no longer genuine fixed points and horizons. Nor are there Crosses and Bodhi Trees and sacred shrines we can easily cling to, as if there were sure means of salvation in today's world or even in yesterday's world, seeing that our world-views are so diverse and uncertain.

So what are we to conclude from all the foregoing argument? First, it may not be necessary to postulate a single Real as though there is a single point towards which the various Foci of the world's religions are supposed to point. As we have argued, there are problems about the noumenal. There is not a single Beyond, nor yet a plural Beyond, for number does not apply outside space–time. This makes the model of Buddhist Emptiness attractive. But it does not mean that Emptiness becomes our absolute. Second, we have noted that the *via negativa* typically arises in connection with the mystical path. Such negative language does not mean that we somehow through it reach beyond experience. Rather it is that minimalist description of experience is registered. The mystic's experience, even if it may be non-dual, that is with no subject–object duality, is still phenomenal. Third, we do not at all resolve the problem of the diversity of Foci by postulating a single Real. One cannot establish the identity of Focus A and Focus B on the basis of their both referring to a single Real: rather the claim that they both refer to the same Real is another way of affirming the identity, which has to be argued on other grounds.

The plausibility of the affirmation of a single Real is high in general, but problematic in particular. For instance, the fact that the Theravāda does not have a substantive Absolute is a stumbling-block in the theory of transcendental unity; but yet the idea is attractive to those who have generous views about other traditions.

There is another way of affirming unity, however, which may not have the problems associated with the notion of a single Real. This is the eschatological way. That is, we notice that differing traditions have evolved quite a lot over time. However much a latter-day liberal Protestant may wish to think that his or her world-view is firmly rooted in that of the New Testament, it is plain that considerable changes have occurred between then and now. For one thing, the major features of our world were absent from the New Testament era. Let me list a few: the industrial revolution and its aftermath; capitalism; modern democracy; birth control; modern psychology and psychotherapy; the global world-order; the abolition of slavery; the feminist revolution; and electronic systems of communication. All these features of our life have large and subtle effects upon faith. Given, then, that of necessity traditions have changed, why should they not continue to be transformed? It is conceivable, therefore, that the great traditions, today in contradiction, may evolve patterns which converge. And so while a single Real here and now may not be easy to establish, we might look towards a future Real. The Empty is also open, as we have remarked earlier.

An advantage of this future convergence theory is that it lets us regard the present traditions as being complementary to one another. They can teach each other lessons. Thus a Christian might wish to hold that the Spirit works in all cultures, and the rivalry of religions is designed by the Divine to keep them honest so far as possible. Universal agreement often breeds corruption, since it certainly engenders complacency. This theory of the complementary roles of religions makes it important, by the way, for education to include learning about the various important spiritual cultures of the world, since they can help to correct one another and at the same time enrich one another. At the same time the theory suggests that we should all take a self-critical stance towards our own traditions. Looking backward in a rigid manner and failing to recognise the transformation of the past are undesirable attitudes. Still, the fluidity of our situation in world society, with its many challenges to traditions, is bound to multiply backlashes against the open and irenic outlooks I am here advocating, and which follow too from John Hick's position. So we would be very foolish to expect agreement. Still, a world-view of world-views which looks to a future convergence will probably become more and more influential as the globe reflects upon its close texture, made dense by instantaneous communications and rapid travel.

Notes

1.   John Hick, 'Religious Pluralism' in Mircea Eliade (ed.), *The Encyclo-pedia of Religion* (New York: Macmillan, 1988), Vol. 12, pp. 332–3.
2.   Nancy McCagney, *Nagarjuna Then and Now* (Santa Barbara: University of California doctoral dissertation, 1991).
3.   Peter F. Strawson, *Individuals: An Essay in Descriptive Metaphysics* (London: Methuen, 1959).

16

Is the Plurality of Faiths Problematic?

NORMAN SOLOMON

Religion involves very much more than formal creeds. In so far as a religion binds people together in a society, purges emotions, teaches morals, comforts the lonely or heals the sick, there is no necessary contradiction between religions, no puzzle as to why God has 'permitted' or even inspired different religions in different societies, no damper or restraint on a relativist view of religion according to which each religion harmonises with a particular time, place, individual or society. Of course, there would still be the possibility of conflict between religious people, because people are quarrelsome; but there would be no logic in the quarrel.

Logic enters when religions make truth-claims. There is often little reason to believe religions are making truth-claims even when they appear to state propositions about the world, for the uses of language are many, and the staking of truth-claims only one, and not the most frequent, use. Even creeds have so many functions – for instance social bonding of the faithful – that they cannot be regarded simply as sets of truth-claims.[1]

Still, if religions really are making truth-claims, even if such claims are neither as clear nor as extensive as believers think, the possibility arises of logical contradiction between those claims. We may then ask, is it reasonable to suppose that God would inspire understandings of the world which contradict each other? Would he not inspire truth only, and in that case is it not evident that no more than one of several mutually contradictory religions can be true (though maybe none is), and therefore that no more than one can have been inspired by God?

Such a question ignores several factors. It is conceivable that each of several religious creeds contains, say, exactly 80 per cent of completely true statements, or 100 per cent of statements which are partly true, for the nature of religious language is such that credal

statements, owing to the indefinability of their meaning, may be
true only in part, or in some way. God may have inspired the total
truth but, accidental inaccuracies apart, it may simply be impossible to convey 'total truth' in human language. God may not himself be constrained by human language in communicating with his
prophets, but the prophets are constrained when they use language
to communicate with the people.

When we consider the use and nature of religious language, including that of creeds, the logical problem of the exclusivity of
religious truth-claims may lose much of its sting. However, it has
greatly troubled modern theologians, and must be addressed, bearing in mind the reservations we have already expressed.

IS THE PLURALITY OF FAITHS A PROBLEM?

Keith Ward, following John Hick, formulates the 'problem' of plurality as follows:

> The problem is this: many religions claim to state truths about the
> nature of the universe and human destiny which are important or
> even necessary for human salvation and ultimate well-being. Many
> of these truths seem to be incompatible; yet there is no agreed
> method for deciding which are to be accepted; and equally intel-
> ligent, informed, virtuous and holy people belong to different
> faiths. It seems, therefore, that a believing member of any one
> tradition is compelled to regard all other traditions as holding
> false beliefs and therefore as not leading to salvation.[2]

Besides the assumption that religious belief involves truth-claims
('claim to state truths about the nature of the universe and human
destiny'), two additional assumptions underlie this formulation. Since
these added assumptions are not the inevitable starting-point for
non-Christians, we must make them explicit.

First, it is assumed that somehow there is a radical disorder, even
malignancy, in the human situation, from which we need to be
'saved'. This malignancy is not simply natural disorder, such as
disease or poverty or accident, which one might hope would eventually be overcome through natural means, including progress in science and economics. Indeed, there is no sort of 'natural' knowledge

which could overcome it, even if people were all of a mind to do so. Of course, varied interpretations of 'original sin' have been adopted by Christians, and the Augustinian interpretation which used to be taken for granted in the Western churches is often questioned; nevertheless, without the premise of radical evil in the world it is difficult to make any sense at all of the Christian 'economy', for the prime function of Christ is said to be the redemption of people from precisely this radical evil.

The second assumption is that some sort of esoteric knowledge, inaccessible other than by initiation (baptism, faith), or by some special revelation or gift of God (grace), constitutes the only path by which we can be 'saved' out of the mess. Of course, this assumption also has been called into question by modern Christians of pluralistic leanings, but it remains the normal Christian starting-point when considering the function of faiths. Moreover, it is entirely dependent on the first assumption for, unless one assumes that there is a radically corrupt predicament from which to be redeemed, the question does not arise as to what special 'mystery' one needs knowledge of in order to achieve redemption.

If these twin assumptions were correct it would indeed be important to each individual to do his or her utmost to acquire this knowledge, especially if people live for a long time after their 'natural' death, let alone if they live for eternity. It is on this basis of these assumptions that 'Christian love' has from time to time led to hideous abominations, such as the methods of torture employed on behalf of the Inquisition to ensure that people would acquire true faith and hence escape eternal damnation.

But is not the problem contrived? Perhaps we should look more closely at what sort of messes people are in and what methods are appropriate to getting them out of ('redeeming' them from) these messes. Writing from a Jewish standpoint, the Israeli scholar Efraim Shmueli, comments:

That dimension of reality which offers a plan for the redemption of man and nation, i.e. the soteriological part of every public ontology, seeks to relieve human anguish in a number of ways. Many and varied are the troubles that afflict mortal humanity . . . Let us list here four main categories:
. . . the finitude of human life
. . . the wearying stress of human conflict

... sin and the sense of guilt
... fear of a world devoid of meaning. ...
The symbols of hope in Israel's culture are multifaceted, and all
express the faith that there is a Master to the City, a watchful,
though not always intrusive, Ruler over men and nations, who
will, by virtue of performed *mitzvot* and good deeds, fulfil His
promise according to the faith of his people.[3]

Is there any justification for the belief that the various messes in
which people find themselves, for instance the four categories in
Shmueli's list, are not in principle amenable to 'natural' solutions, or
at least to solutions which do not depend on precise formulations of
the nature of the Godhead? For people to reconcile themselves to the
finitude and stresses of life, the sense of sin, and the lack of apparent
'meaning' in their existence, they need social structures in which to
find their 'identity', and stories, conceptual structures, arts and games,
sometimes even the skills of the psychiatrist, to cope with their
emotional lives. It does not seem important that they should have
'accurate' knowledge (if indeed the concept is meaningful) of metaphysical propositions about God, or the other matters which are
summed up in creeds or 'mysteries'.

In point of fact, an emphasis on 'religious truth' has all too often
deflected people from the proper solutions to their problems. Certainly, no metaphysical, 'revealed' knowledge has helped the sick as
much as modern, exoteric medical science, even though there have
been many claims of esoteric healing knowledge. Nor has the sort of
information encapsulated in creeds helped create wealth or distrib-
ute it to the needy as well as industry, technological development,
and good economic management. As to the pursuit of peace, it is
precisely the insistence on doctrinal formulations of religion which
has so often diverted nations from their common interests and led
them to squander lives and wealth and engage in repressive and
bellicose endeavours.

So obvious is all this that Christian theologians do not usually
claim that their distinctive piece of knowledge has withheld societies
from conflict and war, or the individual from sinning. The standard
claim for 'faith in Jesus Christ' is that it 'saves from sin', but from all
the preceding reservations it is evident that this 'saving' is itself a
metaphysical process related to radical evil, and with no definite,
observable consequences in the world.

Returning now to Professor Ward's formulation of the 'problem' of the plurality of faiths, we may accept that many religions do indeed 'claim to state truths about the nature of the universe and human destiny'. Certainly, they would claim that such truths are *valuable* for human well-being. But they would not necessarily claim that such truths are 'necessary for human salvation', and indeed they may well not share the concept of 'salvation' which underlies the questions; further, there is no reason why they should be 'compelled to regard all other traditions as holding false beliefs and *therefore* (my italics) as not leading to salvation'.

So far as Judaism is concerned, it is at least plausible that right and attainable behaviour rather than assent to metaphysical propositions constitutes the standard for a 'portion in the world to come', at least for gentiles. Within the terms of the Torah, there is no sharp question as to why God has allowed different belief systems to develop, even if only one is totally true; one is not excluded from 'the world to come' on the grounds of incorrect metaphysical beliefs, hence it is no more surprising that God has refrained from 'informing' everyone about metaphysics than that he has refrained from revealing physics or biology or economics – all useful subjects indeed, but not indispensable to preparation for 'the world to come'.

SCRIPTURE AND MYSTERY

When we look at the Hebrew scriptures and the sort of knowledge revealed through the prophets we find, with small exceptions, that it consists not of deep or mysterious propositions about the nature of the universe, but of exhortations to justice and virtue and compassion, and of down-to-earth legislation. Moses, for instance, tells Israel that the wisdom revealed to them, and for which the nations will esteem them, is a system of wise and just *laws*:

> I have taught you statutes and laws, as the Lord my God commanded me; these you must duly keep when you enter the land and occupy it. You must observe them carefully, and thereby you will display your wisdom and understanding to other peoples (Deuteronomy 4:5–6).

And later in the same book:

What then, O Israel, does the Lord your God ask of you? Only to fear the Lord your God, to conform to all his ways, to love him and to serve him with all your heart and all your soul (Deuteronomy 10:12).

Likewise, it would be crass to suggest that Jeremiah had in mind *esoteric* knowledge when he contended that God wanted people to understand and know him:

These are the words of the Lord:
    Let not the wise man boast of his wisdom
        nor the valiant of his valour;
    let not the rich man boast of his riches;
    but if any man would boast, let him boast of this,
        that he understands and knows me.
For I am the Lord, I show unfailing love
    I do justice and right upon the earth;
        for on these I have set my heart.
        This is the very word of the Lord (Jeremiah 9:23–4).

or that Micah of Moreshet was hinting at secrets and mysteries when he declared:

    and what is it that the Lord asks of you?
    Only to act justly, to love kindness,
    to walk humbly before your God? (Micah 6:8).[4]

Even Wisdom personified, as in Proverbs 8, offers no 'mysteries', but a pattern for the just society:

Pride, presumption, evil courses, subversive talk, all these I hate. I have strength, I also have ability; understanding and power are mine. Through me kings rule and governors make just laws . . . (Proverbs 8:13–15).[5]

Mysteries have been read into Ezekiel 1 and are clearly present in Daniel 12:4. Ezekiel's vision offers inspiration, and Daniel's secret brings reassurance, but there is no suggestion in either book that one needs such knowledge in order to be 'saved'. Apart from Daniel and a few traces in other books apocalyptic literature was excluded from the Jewish canon; this exclusion, probably in the first century, was in part at least a process by which the rabbis attempted to free Judaism from gnostic as well as apocalyptic accretions. Of course, they did not entirely succeed, nor is it clear just what they intended. Recently, scholars have demonstrated the existence of a flourishing Jewish gnosticism at least as early as the first century, and flowing into a mainstream of Jewish mysticism; there are traces in the Talmud itself.[6] The exact nature of this early gnosticism is in dispute; indeed since scholars identify the writings as Jewish on the basis of their strict monotheism and their conformity with *halakhah*, it may be misleading to refer to them as gnostic; perhaps it would be safer to use a more specific term, such as 'merkabah mysticism'.

Whereas some of the writings are concerned with descriptions of the ascent and heavenly peregrinations of the ecstatic, undertaken in holiness and purity, others aim to aid him to acquire a perfect knowledge of Torah, including its mysteries. But is this ecstatic 'journey' merely joyful and enlightening, or is it also salvific? If salvific, is it a necessary or merely a specially privileged path to salvation? One version of the *Lesser Hekhalot* speaks of an angelic figure whose function is 'to arrange the throne . . . and to open the Gates of Salvation',[7] but it would be erroneous to conclude from this one passage that salvation, in some deep sense, was the object of the journey. We are on much surer ground taking the texts at their face value, as being concerned with enlightenment, not salvation. And it is even more certain that the vast majority of people, who could not aspire to the heavenly journey, were not excluded from salvation simply because this privileged enlightenment was beyond their grasp.

KNOWLEDGE AND SALVATION

In its early struggle with the dualist gnostic doctrine of this world as inherently evil, the Church reached a sort of halfway point at which this world is seen not as inherently evil but as redeemably evil. Evil arose not from the nature of the world as created, but from the Fall, however that was explained. Christian 'redemption' differs from gnostic 'escape' for the individual in that it allows for the world itself to be redeemed. Still, the world needs redemption – 'salvation' – and it is the function of the saviour to achieve this cosmic redemption.

But even if, which there is no reason to assume, the world needed 'salvation' in the melodramatic Christian sense, and if esoteric know-ledge really were available about the nature of God and the uni-

verse, why should one assume that salvation depended upon knowledge? *Prima facie* it would be a very strange God indeed – as John
Hick has frequently reminded us – who was unable or unwilling to
accept good and holy people who, in good faith, refused to assent to
some set of metaphysical propositions about His nature and His
created universe. The special knowledge might be interesting, or
marginally useful, or perhaps even inspiring; if that is so, it might
well be regarded by those who believe they possess it as a gracious
and blessed gift. But they should not be surprised if others regard
ethics, psychology, law, technology, economics and other 'natural'
subjects as more relevant to improving the human situation.

In sum, there is little reason to suppose that the difficulty experienced by sensitive Christians in reconciling their traditional teachings on salvation with the conviction that God must surely take
pleasure in good and holy people of all faiths arises within Judaism.
I am far from stating that it cannot or does not arise; indeed, Moses
Mendelssohn raised something very like this point in his correspondence with Jacob Emden in 1773. This correspondence concerned
the nature of the so-called 'seven laws of the sons of Noah', which
rabbis as early as the third century laid down as the basis for gentile
society. These laws were:

Do not worship idols
Do not blaspheme
Do not murder
Do not commit adultery or incest
Do not steal
Do not eat 'a limb torn from a living animal'[8]
Institute courts of justice.[9]

Moses Maimonides (1135–1204) held that a gentile ought to observe the Noahide laws not merely out of reason but through acceptance of the fact that God commanded them in scripture.[10] It may well
be, as Novak argues, that Maimonides' philosophy of law leads him
to this, for there is certainly no talmudic basis for such an opinion.
But then Maimonides, unlike our contemporary philo-sophers and
theologians, had no doubt that the human intellect, used with integrity, would lead one to belief in the authenticity of the biblical text
and tradition, hence to the assumption that correct belief would
accompany moral virtue.

On 26 October 1773 Moses Mendelssohn initiated a correspondence on this theme with Jacob Emden, in terms prescient of Keith Ward's formulation of the 'problem of plurality' cited above:

> And to me these matters are difficult . . . that all the inhabitants of the earth from the rising to the setting of the sun are doomed, except us . . . unless they believe in the Torah which was given to us as inheritance to the congregation of Jacob alone, especially concerning a matter not at all explicit in the Torah . . . what will those nations do upon whom the light of the Torah has not shone at all?[11]

It cannot be said that Emden's reply grasped the epistemological problem that worried Mendelssohn; indeed, the correspondence between the two on this and other problems resembles an abortive attempt at communication between the Middle Ages and modern times.

The point I am making is not whether Jewish theologians have involved themselves with arbitrary belief criteria in saying what God wants of the 'gentiles', or even whether they have developed concepts of radical evil or of esoteric ways of salvation. They have done all these things. What I wish to demonstrate is that (a) there is no inner logic within rabbinic Judaism which leads to such a position and that (b) there are ample resources within Judaism to construct theories of the plurality of religions free from the problems arising from the assumptions I have called into question.

GNOSTICISM?

I was tempted at one stage to argue that the concept of 'salvation through knowledge' presupposed in Hick's question was evidence of a gnostic tendency. This temptation must be resisted for two reasons.

First, to the extent to which the concept is gnostic it is not peculiar to Hick, but Christianity as formulated in its traditional sources. One needs perhaps to adopt a traditional rabbinic (I do not say first-century) Jewish standpoint to appreciate the sheer strangeness of a faith which emphasised the role of 'faith', in the sense of 'assent to belief' (rather than 'trust in God'), as a necessity for salvation. And of course I am well aware that many Christian exegetes today would rightly reject this interpretation of the word *pistis* as it occurs in the New Testament. But unfortunately, the classical creeds such as the Athanasian and Nicene really do seem to have slipped into a 'propositional' understanding of *pistis*, and that has plagued Christianity ever since.

Second, there is an ambiguity in the English term 'knowledge', which covers both information and acquaintance. The gnostics were concerned not with *eidein (wissen, savoir)* but with *gnosis (kennen, connaître)*, that is, attaining mystical experience of God. For instance:

> The proclamation of truth is a joy for those who have received grace from the father of truth, that they might learn to know him through the power of the Word that emanated from the fullness that is in the father's thought and intellect. . . . [12]

Such a 'proclamation' would seem to involve something other than 'propositional' knowledge. In all probability, a gnostic such as the author of the Gospel of Truth would have dismissed propositional knowledge as mere 'error', the product of 'ignorance of the father' causing 'agitation and fear', as he puts it, and belonging to the material rather than the spiritual universe.

John Hick's eventual response to his great question is indeed concerned with more than propositional knowledge, for he conceives of an ultimate reality which all religions recognise. It may well be, as Andrew Kirk has suggested,[13] that this is akin to a gnostic conception, especially as Hick is ready to recognise that all can be saved by this knowledge, without explicit reference to Jesus Christ (a position which would probably be rejected by a Christian gnostic work such as the Gospel of Truth). But it is absurd to accuse Hick of gnosticism, for it is perfectly evident that he nowhere espouses any significant aspect of gnostic cosmogony, nor the characteristic gnostic denigration of the material as opposed to the spiritual world.

Hick's answer to the 'problem' of plurality, to the moral paradox that a believing member of any one tradition is compelled to regard all other traditions as holding false beliefs and therefore as not leading to salvation, is that since there is an ultimate reality to which all religions relate, there is no need to believe that religions other than one's own are entirely false and thus not salvific. The answer I am suggesting here is that there is no 'problem' to begin with, since there is no *a priori* reason to suppose that salvation (whatever that may mean) depends on knowledge, beyond a rather basic knowledge of right and wrong. Though I believe my answer to be in accord with the general tenor of the Hebrew scriptures, I would not claim for it any more than partial support in rabbinic literature.

Notes

1. On the ways that religious people use language see Chapter 8 of my *Judaism and World Religions* (London: Macmillan; New York: St. Martin's Press, 1991). I think it is Frances Young who made the point that some creeds were intended to be sung.
2. Keith Ward, 'Truth and the Diversity of Religions', *Religious Studies*, XXVI (1990), pp. 1–18, in response to John Hick, *An Interpretation of Religion*, (London: Macmillan, 1989).
3. Efraim Shmueli, 'Seven Jewish Cultures', trans. Gila Shmueli (Cambridge and New York: Cambridge University Press, 1990), p. 19, on 'Did you hope for salvation?' (Babylonian Talmud, Shabbat 31a).
4. NEB is wild at this point, translating *hesed* as loyalty and *hatsne'a* as wisely.
5. NEB text, modified.
6. There is a voluminous literature. One of the classics in the field is Gershom G. Scholem, *Jewish Gnosticism, Merkabah Mysticism and Talmudic Tradition*, 2nd edn (New York: Jewish Publication Society of America, 1965). The more recent work of Peter Schaeffer and Moshe Idel should also be consulted.
7. Scholem, ibid., p. 19.
8. Presumably a reference to cruelty to animals.
9. Tosefta Avodah Zara 9:4 is probably the earliest version. For a modern study of the 'Noahide Laws' and their significance see David Novak, *The Image of the Non-Jew in Judaism* (New York and Toronto: Edwin Mellen Press, 1983).
10. Maimonides, *Mishneh Torah Hilkhot Melakhim* 8:11. For a full discussion, see Chapter 10 of Novak's *Image of the Non-Jew.*
11. Moses Mendelssohn, *Gesammelte Schriften*, XVI, pp. 178–80. The translation is Novak's, *Image of the Non-Jew*, p. 370.
12. The Gospel of Truth 16:31, in Bentley Layton, *The Gnostic Scriptures: a New Translation* (London: SCM, 1987) p. 253. The Gospel of Truth is, of course, a work of Christian gnosticism.
13. In a private conversation with the writer. I understand Kirk plans to write on the subject.

17

Acts of God

STEWART SUTHERLAND

I

Christian piety has too long been nurtured largely on those psalms and other biblical materials which portray God as a kind of genie who will extricate the faithful from the difficulties into which they fall; it is this erratic and fickle God who cannot be reconciled with the modern understanding of the order in nature and history. Far better would it be to nourish our piety on the paradigmatic Christian story; a man praying that this cup might pass from him but submitting his will to God's no matter what the consequences.[1]

Ibsen offers a lively caricature of the view which Kaufman describes more soberly, in the second part of *Peer Gynt*. Peer has just been tricked by his business acquaintances who have stolen his gold-laden yacht. He calls petulantly to God:

> Lord God, are you listening? Justice and Truth!
> It's me. Peter Gynt. Can you see me? Down here!
> Take care of me, Lord, as you may see me die.
> Please slacken their speed. Make them lower the boat.
> Arrest them. Make something go wrong with the works.
> Do listen. Ignore other people. Help *me*!
> The world can look out for itself for five minutes.
> No. He's not listening. He's deaf as a post.
> That's brilliant! Our Father, God. Stuck for ideas.[2]

Whether the style is that of Ibsen or Kaufman, the problem of the role of the idea of an act of God looms large in Christian sensibility as much as in the philosophical study of religion. The two perspectives are not unrelated.

Kaufman recognises this point in so far as he argues that if the use that such a central expression as 'an act of God' has, is flawed, then the beliefs and sensibilities which surround it are equally at risk. More pungently, he argues,

> Since the root metaphor that informs the Western notion of God and gives it its special character is that of a supreme Actor or Agent, it is little wonder that the notion of God has become empty for us, that 'God is dead'.[2A]

In this view of the difficulties facing the concept of an act of God, the problem is how to avoid the anthropomorphism without so emptying the concept of all substance that religious sensibility atrophies. Traditionally the discussion has taken the form of a debate between the possibilities of giving either an analogical or metaphorical or (possibly partially)[3] univocal account of the expression. Alternatively, some radical solutions have been proposed which involve wholesale translation of such language into quite different terms. Varied versions of this option have been offered, for example, by Paul Tillich and Charles Hartshorne. Kaufman's own approach in the paper cited is to focus upon a single 'Master' act of God rather than upon 'particularly relatively limited' events.

> This means for a monotheistic theology that it is *the whole course of history*, . . . that should be conceived as God's act in the primary sense.[3A]

In the discussion which follows, I shall adopt a further alternative approach to the questions at issue, but I do not believe that the views which I shall attempt to develop are incompatible with Kaufman's approach, although I am not yet sufficiently persuaded by what he writes to adopt his conclusions. However, I do share with him the diagnosis of some of the problems surrounding the expression 'an act of God', but since I have elaborated my reasons for this diagnosis elsewhere, I shall not repeat them here.[4]

II

In the discussion of what I am calling the 'traditional' view, there have been four main *foci* of exploration. I shall enumerate these briefly in order to clarify, initially negatively, the approach which I wish to develop.

The first two major issues are often regarded as alternative approaches to the questions under discussion, but in fact they are complementary to one another. One may give *initial* weight in one's enquiry either to the issue of the intelligibility of the idea of an act of God, or to the question of whether any justification can be given to the claim that there are acts of God. The relationship between the two may be set out in a number of different ways and some of these will either presuppose or illustrate different theories of meaning. For the record, I do see the questions of intelligibility and justification as interdependent but I give first call on intellectual effort to trying to show whether and, if so, how, the notion of an act of God is an intelligible notion. The general working principle which I adopt is that one cannot specify what justification there could be for claiming that there are acts of God, unless we can give an account of what it means to say that there are acts of God. Thus the questions of whether there are miracles or answers to prayer which can structure philosophical discussion of acts of God, should and can only be asked helpfully if one has at least an outline of what it would mean to claim that God acts, whether in this way or that. This approach is quite compatible so far with the Kaufman paper referred to earlier.

If one does focus upon the notion of intelligibility as a first step then two other central issues arise immediately: What do we mean by 'an act' – whether human or divine – and what do we mean by 'an agent' – again, whether human or divine? Alston, for example, spells out the connection between these two questions and *ipso facto* indicates some of the difficulties which they raise.[5] It could be argued that our paradigm case of an action (if such there be) is human action and that if we cannot give a sensible account of that, then it will certainly be more difficult to give an account of what we mean by 'an act of God'. Alston offers some help here by arguing that it is only a contingent fact about 'human beings' that the changes which they bring about in the world by their acts are brought about *via* bodily movements. Clearly if he is correct, then this should ease at least some of the difficulties raised by the notion of 'an act of God'. However, two point arise from this.

The first is the clear reminder that we must have some account of what it means to be an 'agent' (or 'person who acts' and therefore 'person'), whether human or divine. Again, the difficulties are not insignificant as the volume of philosophical discussion over two millennia and more indicates. This account ought to include an account of how we individuate between persons.

The second point is that there is parallel disputed philosophical terrain about what counts as 'an act' and about how we individuate between actions. Acts are not like physical objects and for the most part cannot be, or be reduced to, segments of the space–time continuum which can be individuated by reference to spatio-temporal coordinates quite independently of the description given to the action. Physical objects can be individuated in this way, e.g. we can refer without ambiguity to the object standing on the furthest corner of the room at 2.18 p.m. on 15 August 1990 and individuate it from all other objects, without using any of the many descriptions which may truly apply to it – 'my favourite chair' or 'a late Victorian chair made of oak' or 'the item which Aunt Agatha left to me in her Will', etc.

The difference between the case of a physical object and the case of an action in respect of individuation can be brought out by asking how one would individuate the act of writing this chapter. Is it one act or many? Is it sitting putting pen to paper or digits to keys at a specific time? Surely not, for there were many such occasions which played a part in writing the paper. Equally from one point of view, that is the least significant part of the act. Is the act then two acts – thinking and writing? But does that include the jotting of notes, the preliminary reading (and how preliminary is preliminary?), the pacing of the floor, the tearing up of the draft sheets, the ruminating over cups of coffee, the flashes of insight (illusory or real), in the moments when one should be and is doing something else? The point of asking these questions is not to receive and debate answers: it is to suggest that identifying and individuating an action is much different from identifying and individuating a physical object where, in the latter case, the individuation of the object can be distinguished from its description.

To identify something as an act is, I suggest, to identify it under a single description. However, the weight of the description is not wholly independent of context. Thus for some purposes it might be appropriate to refer to the act in question as the single act of writing a chapter in the month of August in a particular year! For other purposes, however, it may be more appropriate to talk about the chapter 'really' being written on the date in mid-August when the structure of it was clarified. Equally, it would be true, but in some contexts pedantic, to note that minor editing took place in September, or that preliminary notes were made in April. A less trivial example is explained in some detail in Camus's short novel *The*

Outsider[6] where the question of whether Meursault did what he is accused of doing is in the first instance one of trying to identify an individuating description of an act for which he stood trial.[7] When does the act of which Meursault is accused begin? Is it the flexing of a finger on the trigger? Is it being dazzled by the sun on the sea? Is it the first sight of his 'victim'? . . .

The point here is not to explore further either these examples, or in general an account of the nature of action. For our purposes it is sufficient to remark upon the depth of the philosophical waters into which we are led by focusing upon the traditional picture of an act of God, implying as it does individual (and therefore surely individuated) acts by an agent in the sense of a person who acts.

Negatively, I do not propose to follow that route of enquiry into the intelligibility of a divine act. Rather I wish to follow a pattern of discussion loosely comparable to a method developed in a related context by Peter Strawson.[8] In this discussion of the issues which surround the philosophical concept of determinism, Strawson does not engage directly with the debate between those who disagree about whether the truth or falsehood of determinism will radically affect our view of whether such concepts as moral obligation and responsibility have application. Rather he focuses upon a range of other related concepts such as resentment, gratitude, forgiveness, love and hurt feelings which he identifies reasonably as illustrating and giving content to reactive participant relations to other people.

> The question we have to ask is: What effect would or should, the acceptance of the truth of a general thesis of determinism have upon these reactive attitudes? More specifically, would or should the acceptance of the truth of the thesis lead to the decay or the repudiation of all such attitudes?[8A]

In so far as there is a loosely comparable question to fit the theme of this chapter, I shall be focusing upon those attitudes of both belief and unbelief which imply a reactive relationship or set of relationships which go beyond interpersonal human relationships. Thus there are those who feel guilt or seek a forgiveness which is at a different order from the definition of those attitudes implied in the relationship of one human being to another. Equally, there are those who rebel against, in high-flown terms, the 'Universe' or 'the order of things', whose rebellion is, in Camus's terms, 'metaphysical'.[9] Some would claim to be variously judged or blessed, or quite differently angered (cf. Ivan Karamazov).

These attitudes can certainly be either shallow or perhaps pathological. My question is whether they can take other forms than these, forms which might give shape to our discussion of the intelligibility of the notion of an act of God. More plainly, if the sentiment of guilt which seeks a forgiveness which is not simply the forgiveness given by one human being to another, is neither shallow nor pathological, then that is significant for the theme of this chapter in two ways: the first is that it presupposes the possibility and therefore intelligibility of a non-human action – the act of forgiving; and the second is that if the sentiment is non-pathological, it may provide the basis of an account of what believers mean when they talk about 'an act of God'. *Mutatis mutandis* a comparable claim could be made for the sentiments of hate, or anger, which underlie so-called 'metaphysical' rebellion (cf. Camus and Ivan Karamazov).

III

As we have noted, Strawson asks of the thesis of determinism:

> What effect would, or should, the acceptance of the truth of a general thesis of determinism have upon these reactive attitudes (i.e. resentment, gratitude, etc.)?[10]

In my final reference of tribute, or possibly distorted plagiarism, I shall use Strawsonian terms to phrase the questions which will constitute the content of the rest of this chapter.

> What effect would the rejection of the truth of the claim that there is a God who is active in his creation have upon reactive attitudes such as a sense of deep guilt, and need for forgiveness as 'metaphysical' rebellion and rage? More specifically would or should the rejection of the truth of this claim lead to the decay or the repudiation of all such attitudes?

Is the story of Prometheus and his struggle with the Gods to be considered only as a suitable subject for scholarly analysis? Are the accusations of Ivan Karamazov only an over-dramatic way of pointing out that all is not for the best in the best of all possible worlds? Is the pursuit of Orestes by the Furies simply the sign of a young man who could not come to terms with the fact that he had killed his mother in revenge for her murder of his father? Is the final agony of

Faust really rather misplaced because we all have to die sometime and all in all, he had had a rather more exciting life than most of us? Would Oedipus have been better advised in the moment of self-knowledge to take two Valium tablets rather than to gouge out his eyes?

Of course, to put the question in these terms is to be both tendentious and dramatic. The issues, however, can be approached through calmer waters.

Someone whose sense of guilt is such that there is a perceived need for forgiveness of this order implicitly, or perhaps even explicitly, assents to three different claims:

F(i)   there is a moral order against the claims of which they judge themselves to be guilty

F(ii)   their guilt is such that neither forgiveness by self, nor by other human beings, will set it aside

F(iiia) *sub-specie aeternitatis* there must be an alternative source or form of forgiveness with which to neutralise the acids of such a guilt.

In such a context, the need for forgiveness is the need for an *act* of forgiveness which transcends all human acts. These reactive attitudes presuppose the possibility of such an act of forgiveness. If there is no such possibility then such attitudes are at best misguided but more likely based on delusion.

I have, for the sake of argument, ruled out the possibility that a concern of this order for guilt and forgiveness is inevitably pathological. Suffice it to say for present purposes that the testimony of the poets is against such a radical conclusion and that to proceed beyond this would not be possible within the confines of one chapter. If that hypothesis is at least temporarily ruled out, then those whose reaction to aspects of their lives is defined by guilt and the need for forgiveness have before them only two possibilities: either (iiia) above which postulates the possibility of an act of forgiveness which transcends the possibilities of forgiveness of one human being by another, or

F(iiib) one lives in a moral world defined by, and solely defined by, one's actions and the empirical consequences of those actions.

Faust, Orestes, Oedipus and Judas Iscariot each help us define such a world. I shall return to this point.

Let us, however, consider the case of the very different reactive attitudes of rage and rebellion, personified most acutely in the figure of Ivan Karamazov, and explored in some detail in Camus's *L'Homme Revolté*. Again, for the sake of argument, and allowing that separate discussion is necessary, I shall rule out the interpretation of all such attitudes as inevitably pathological. In parallel with those driven by the realities of guilt and the possibilities of forgiveness, those for whom rebellion and rage are primary forms of engagement with the cosmos may be construed to give implicit or even explicit assent to a number of claims.

R(i)   there is a moral order against which the injustices of the empirical world may be clearly defined

R(ii)   the injustices are such that there is no human scale in terms of which compensation or reconciliation can be adequately contemplated, let alone achieved

R(iiia) Someone whose creation this is, is to blame, unless there is the possibility, *sub specie aeternitatis* of justice[11] which would of course require the possibility of an *act* of reconciliation which transcends the possibilities ruled out in R(ii).

The possibilities open to the rebel are, on the one hand, persistence in the reactive attitude of rage or the hope for reconciliation *sub specie aeternitatis*, both of which imply at least the possibility of acts of God; or, on the other hand,

R(iiib) one lives in a moral world defined by and solely defined by the actions of other human beings and their empirical consequences.

The world is defined in what we may too easily or lazily come to see as a characteristically Beckettian fashion by the emptiness to which Beckett with a grim smile consigns his audience. It is as if he had added a final line to *Waiting for Godot*:

The Bastard doesn't exist.

My argument is that in a world in which there is a place for the reactive attitudes of guilt and the need for forgiveness on the one

hand and rage and rebellion on the other, assumptions are made
about the possibility of certain acts which are mutually dependent
for their intelligibility upon the intelligibility of such reactive attitudes. Either way, if we eliminate the one we eliminate the other. If
the demand for forgiveness or the cry of rage is not focused upon the
possibilities or realities of human action, then the attitudes are, to
that extent, different in character, and the possibility of action to
which they are addressed has equally to be seen *sub specie aeternitatis*.
No human acts can give sense to such attitudes and equally in the
absence of the possibility of such transcendent acts, these attitudes
themselves are at best based on delusion or misunderstandings.

From such an absence, there seem to me to be only two possibilities which remain. Either the attitudes are pathological and those
who hold them should be treated rather than discussed and exam-
ined; or, the attitudes will decay or be repudiated leaving those who
hold them to be content with a view of the world which amounts to
learning to live with and only with one's own acts, the acts of other
human beings and the empirical consequences which follow from
them, as defining the moral possibilities. If such possibilities do not
include the possibilities of forgiveness, or legitimate accusation, or a
just reconciliation, then so be it; the world does not exhibit such a
moral order and the alternative to such preoccupation *sub specie
aeternitatis* may well be a this-worldly form of stoicism.

To suggest this, however, is not to come to a conclusion about
whether there are acts of God; or whether such guilt or rage is
pathological; or alternatively that such reactive attitudes must be
metamorphosed into something else. The points which I want to
make are rather more modest than that. They are as follows:

(a) A primary focus of the religious sensibility on the notion of an
    act of God has its roots in moral sensibilities.
(b) In such a context, the primary focus is on such moral acts as
    those of forgiveness and just reconciliation rather than on,
    say, miracle-working.
(c) The issues at stake between atheism and belief are issues
    about the intelligibility of, say, forgiveness by God and the
    reactive attitude to the world which perceives the need for
    such forgiveness. The intelligibility of each is dependent mu-
    tually on the possibility that the other is not illusory.

These points are a long way from Ibsen's caricature of the interest of piety in such acts and perhaps help reframe the issues for discussion. What I am proposing has a long and distinguished, albeit somewhat heretical, history in philosophical discussion: it sometimes helps to consider questions of a theological nature afresh if we start from the implications which they have for moral beliefs as much as for strictly defined metaphysical beliefs.

Notes

1. Gordon D. Kaufman, 'On the Meaning of "Act of God"', in Owen C. Thomas (ed.), *God's Activity in the World*, AAR Studies in Religion 31 (Georgia: Scholars Press, 1983). See p. 157.
2. Henrik Ibsen, *Peer Gynt*. Translated and adapted by Kenneth McLeish, published jointly by The Royal National Theatre and Nick Hern Books, 1990. See pp. 58–9.
2A. Gordon D. Kaufman, op. cit., p. 141.
3. See, for example, W. Alston, 'Divine and Human Action', in T. V. Morris (ed.), *Divine and Human Action* (Ithaca, NY: Cornell University Press, 1988).
3A. Ibid., p. 149.
4. See S. R. Sutherland, *God, Jesus and Belief* (Oxford: Basil Blackwell, 1984), Chapter 4.
5. See W. Alston, op. cit.
6. Albert Camus, *L'Etranger*, translated by Stuart Gilbert as *The Outsider* (Harmondsworth: Penguin, 1961).
7. I have discussed this case in greater detail in 'Philosophy, Literature and Imagination', *British Journal of Aesthetics*, 1971.
8. See his British Academy lecture 'Freedom and Resentment', reprinted in his book of that title (London: Methuen, 1974). It should be added, however, that in the lecture in question Strawson provides no validation, nor has he any responsibility for the stimulus which it gave to the next section of this chapter.
8A. Ibid., p. 10.
9. See Albert Camus, *L'Homme Révolté* trans. Anthony Bower, as *The Rebel* (Hamish Hamilton, 1953). See Chapter 2.
10. See above p. 204 and note 8.
11. Ivan, of course, rules out the latter possibility with what Camus characterises as his 'even if' (see *The Rebel*, footnote 9). Kant, on the other hand, at least in the *Critique of Practical Reason*, uses the gap between virtue and happiness to postulate the act which will reconcile these into the *Summum Bonum*.

18
Divine Ineffability
KEITH WARD

'We know our God from his operations (*energeia*), but do not undertake to approach near to his essence (*ousia*)' (Basil, Epistle 234). There is a strong tradition in Christianity of the ineffability of God, the utter transcendence of the Divine nature to any human thought. John Hick, in his recent work, uses what seems to be a similar doctrine of the distinction between the noumenal nature of the Real and the phenomenal appearances which are known to human beings. He uses it, however, to suggest that the noumenal reality may appear in many different ways to different observers, depending upon their conceptual equipment, culture and temperament. Thus many of the great world faiths may be responding to the same Real, as it appears to them in various ways. We might indeed put this by saying that we know the Real from its appearances (phenomena), but do not undertake to approach near to its noumenal essence. It could be, then, that Professor Hick's use of the noumenal/phenomenal distinction simply restates the classical Christian doctrine of Divine ineffability. I want to explore the extent to which this may be the case.

It is difficult to know exactly what the Cappadocian Fathers had in mind when they distinguished the nature from the operations of God. But since a question about the *ousia* of something is often a request to be told the sort of thing it is, one may take the Divine essence to be that which is definitive of God as God really is, that which makes this entity God and not something else. When one asks about the operations of God, however, one is asking about the things God does, or about how God relates to the world, about the actions in the world of a being of a certain nature.

Obviously, the actions of a being express its nature to some extent. Some philosophers would hold that it is my actions which define my nature, what I am. But it is quite conceivable that a being might conceal its nature or act in ways which reveal, at best, only a small part of what it is. Suppose, for example, we meet a being from another galaxy which appears to us only as a blob of light. It causes systematic changes in its environment, which we conceive as actions, since they seem to exhibit purpose and design. Yet we may have no idea of what is going on in its 'mind'; whether it has thoughts and feelings like ours, or how much about it there is that is invisible to us and that we cannot understand. All we see are the apparently purposive changes in the world around it. We might say that these changes do show how that being wishes to relate to us. In one sense, then, they do show something of the nature of the being; they show that the being can and wishes to relate to us in these ways. But they may not show what that being is like 'from the inside', or when it is not relating to us. Its inner processes may remain quite mysterious to us.

It does not seem to be an absurd supposition that there may be something which human concepts simply cannot describe at all, if it is so different from anything we know that we are at a loss to know how to describe it. However, even in saying, if we do, that it is a 'thing' and that it is different from all other things, we are saying something about it. Basil was not supposing that the essence of God was unknowable, in the sense that it might be blind energy or a malevolent committee of demons for all we know. If God is indescribable by us, it is because God is a reality of greater, not lesser, intelligibility, beauty and bliss than any we can imagine.

We get to the notion of Divine ineffability by starting with the power and wisdom of a personal creator, as seen in the world; or by starting with personal experience of a presence which seems to be both awe-inspiring and mysterious. Only when we qualify these initial concepts by successively denying all limitations on the creator and denying the adequacy of all specific descriptive terms to characterise the object of our experience do we come to say that God is ineffable. In other words, the idea of 'the ineffable God' is not simply the idea of something totally unknowable. Since it is necessarily true that whatever is unknowable is unknown, this would entail that such a God is quite unknown. But it is essential to theism to claim that one *knows* the ineffable God; one is acquainted with what is beyond understanding. One can put this by stressing that this idea of the ineffable is not just of some ineffable thing or other; it is the idea of an ineffable *God*; that is, of a creator truly known to us in experience, yet whose essential nature transcends our understanding. Certain statements, for Basil and for all orthodox Christians, are unequivocally true of God – that God is more perfect than human beings; that God is one; and that God is Trinitarian in being. It is just that we cannot comprehend what such a being is really like, in the fullness of its reality. It is wholly misleading, therefore, to say that, according to Basil the Great, we have a purely negative knowledge of God.

Immanuel Kant perhaps came closest to having such a doctrine of negative knowledge in the *Critique of Pure Reason*, when he argued that, because of the Antinomies of Reason, we can know that the real world is not as we suppose it to be; but we can be certain that there is a real world. The 'proof', repeated in various forms by many later Idealist philosophers, shows that this world is contradictory (that we can prove contradictory propositions to be true of it); therefore we can know it is not real. In Kant's case, one can resolve the antinomies of space and time by positing that they are not objective realities, but forms of intuition; from which it follows that reality must be positively unlike them – but, of course, we cannot know in what way.

It is rather unsatisfactory to say merely that reality is completely indescribable, since it seems to get one no further towards knowing what reality is. At that point, the antinomies of freedom and necessity, and of contingency and necessity, suggested to Kant that, though one could *know* nothing of the real world, one was forced to think of it in a specific way, as a necessary demand of Reason. One had to postulate God, freedom and immortality for practical purposes to do with the regulative employment of the Understanding in respect of the phenomenal world. So Reason compels one to think the unknowable in a specific manner. One has no knowledge of it, theoretically speaking; but one has a thought of it, which one must adopt for practical purposes. The justification for thinking of the unknowable in a specific way is that Reason compels us to do so as a condition of the possibility of scientific investigation into and moral action in the world.

For this argument to succeed, one must show both that phenomenal reality, as ordinarily conceived, is contradictory; and that some urgently practical and totally unavoidable necessity compels one to think of reality in a specific way. It has to be said that few have been convinced that Kant succeeded in either of these tasks; and it seems likely that his concept of a noumenal or intelligible world, as the very name implies, is a hangover from the pre-Critical philosophy which permitted real and indeed certain knowledge of the intelligible realm, which was in no doubt that reality was 'intelligible' or noumenal, and saw the phenomenal world as a sort of confused appearance of what only pure Reason could truly discern. Divorced from that full-blooded metaphysic, Kant's demythologising of the noumenal is likely to seem rather like the Cheshire Cat's smile – no longer fully appealing once the cat itself has gone.

Professor Hick has a rather similar two-stage argument, which may seem rather more convincing than Kant's. For the first stage, religious experience is seen to be contradictory, in the sense that various religions, all with a *prima facie* claim to truth, present contradictory views of the nature of reality. This suggests either that all are false, which just has too many wise and saintly people suffering from delusions; or that one is correct and all the rest are false, which is not much better; or that all are genuine encounters with reality, not with reality as it is but with phenomenal appearances of reality. As with Kant, the implication is that in fact none of our knowledge is of the Real as it really is; it is largely if not entirely a product of our minds. In the second stage of the argument, what compels us to think of reality in a specific way is not some universal demand of Reason, but the claim of religious experience to objective validity. The idea of a noumenal Real is a postulate for asserting that such experiences can be both contradictory and veridical – for they are of appearances only, and not of the Real in itself; yet they are appearances *of* the Real.

The problem that is at once glaringly apparent is to decide how anyone can be sure that appearances are of the Real, that they are 'authentic manifestations' of the Real, rather than pure inventions of the mind. I think Professor Hick simply wants us to *postulate* that they are, to accept that all widely-accepted experiences that seem to be of the Real are what they seem to be. But there is a major paradox in this position, which can be briefly set out as follows:

1. When it seems to me that X, then probably X. (This 'principle of credulity' is one that Hick applies to religious experiences.)
2. It seems to some that X, to some that Y, to some that Z. . . .
3. So probably X, Y and Z (from 1, 2).
4. X, Y and Z are inconsistent.
5. Reality cannot be inconsistent.
6. So X, Y and Z are not true of Reality (from 4, 5).
7. What is true of appearances need not be true of Reality.
8. So X, Y and Z are true of appearances, not of Reality (from 3, 6, 7).

This is all satisfactory, until it seems to someone, *P*, that *X* is true of Reality in itself, but it seems to *Q* that it is not. Then, it is probably true that *X* is true of Reality in itself (by 1); but *X* cannot be true of Reality (by 6). Therefore if *P*'s belief that *X* is true of Reality is probably true, it can only be so if it is true of appearance, not of Reality (by 8). In other words, it can only be true if it is false. *X* is both true of Reality and not, at the same time. Since a contradiction is unacceptable (as 5 states), some of the premises of this argument must be modified.

The obvious premise to modify is 1, which is highly dubious in any case, and to admit that many people are mistaken in claims as to what they apprehend. Professor Hick himself does not hesitate to do this in the case of the dispute between realism and non-realism in religion. Here, while he insists on the epistemic right of differing individuals to hold conflicting beliefs, he also insists that one of them must be mistaken (*An Interpretation of Religion* (Macmillan, 1989), p. 13). I am simply pointing out that the same must be true of many religious disputes, when I must admit that someone is mistaken, and I am clearly not going to think it is me! But, of course, this is not a matter of 'all or nothing'. I need not say that all my truth-claims are valid and none of anyone else's is. I can easily say that some of my claims will be false (though I do not now know which); and many of your claims may be true (though I doubt all of them are). So I do not have to say that either all experience claims in religion are false, or only my claims are true. Nor need I get into the self-refuting position that all claims about objects of worship or devotion are veridical. If there is an ineffable God (not a wholly unknowable noumenon), there will plainly be many truths about God I have not perceived, and I may well have misconstrued some of the things I think are true about God. Yet I do at least claim that there is a being whose nature is ineffable, but some of whose causal manifestations in the world I take myself to have true beliefs about.

I therefore doubt whether a Kantian philosophy can provide an adequate construal of Divine ineffability. According to Kant's way of resolving the contradictions of experience, the transcendental ideality of space and time means that space and time are not objectively real at all; they are forms of human perception, contributed by the perceiving mind. But it would not satisfy many religious believers to be told that their gods are not objectively real; that they are contributed by human imagination; and whatever it is that underlies them is totally unknowable. One does not wish to discard the experiences of others and claim sole validity for one's own; that does seem arbitrary and arrogant. An obvious move is then to see all such experiences as subject to conceptual interpretation, which may qualify the character of the experience. The validity of the experience will then depend on the accuracy of the interpretation. And it may be true that no interpretation is adequate to the richness and complexity of the religious object. What one will have is a range of more or less adequate interpretations, caused in part by an object which probably transcends any of them.

This, I think, is the situation Professor Hick has well illuminated by his writings. But does the introduction of a noumenal/phenomenal distinction help, or does it introduce needless confusion? What seems wrong with it is, first, that it leads us to regard all objects of religious experience as illusory or subjective in some sense; whereas believers want to make claims to objectivity, however inadequate. Second, it leads us to renounce all claims to knowledge of noumenal reality; whereas most believers wish to claim some knowledge of ultimate reality – again, even if inadequately conceived. In other words, the Kantian distinction turns disputes about the relative adequacy of interpretations of reality into wholly unresolvable claims about a completely unknowable reality. In fact, if reality is completely unknowable, no cognitive claims can be made about it at all; so religion inevitably becomes a wholly subjective matter of personal attitudes.

Kant was not speaking of a diverse set of inadequate and partial interpretations of an experienced, very complex reality. He was speaking of a universal and necessary phenomenal reality which left noumenal reality both unexperienced and unknowable. But Professor Hick does claim to know some things about the Real – that it is a supremely valuable reality; that it is one cause of everything other than itself; that it manifests to human experience in a number of ways which are not wholly misleading. And he does wish to rule out some experiences as inadequate – experiences of the Real as malevolent, as having no causal effects on the future, or as entailing no ontological claims about how the world is. So he does work with a criterion of adequacy, embodying ideas of moral demand and promise for the future; and with a concept of the Real as one supreme cause. Bluntly, he is a theist who is concerned to show how God may be experienced in many traditions, which partially show aspects of the Divine being. Some of these ways are more adequate than others, though one might be unwise to claim that one was wholly adequate and all the others quite inadequate by comparison. It is, however, quite clear that Professor Hick believes there is one supremely valuable reality which can bring us into conscious relationship with itself, a relationship which will realise human hopes for a fulfilled and happy existence. His complete rejection of non-realism in religion in favour of some form of 'cosmic optimism' shows his commitment to ontological realism, and against the view that we can know nothing of what is truly real.

Since Professor Hick is a religious realist, he does not really believe in a noumenal reality at all, as something of which one can say absolutely nothing. He rather believes that there is a reality of supreme value, love and power (for it can and will bring us all to final happiness by knowing and loving it in the end). This is a definite claim to knowledge of the Real. It is quite consistent to go on to say that our knowledge of the Real is very inadequate and may well be mistaken in many details. It will be affected by our culture, our background knowledge and temperament. Now we see in a glass darkly; though we hope to see face to face; and we claim to know there is a face, however dimly discerned, to be seen.

Consequently, we do not need Kant's complex doctrine of a regulative use of concepts, in accordance with which we think of a reality which is theoretically completely unknown to us. That is just as well, since the reasons Kant gave for thinking that the regulative idea of God was practically necessary are generally adjudged to be almost wholly unconvincing. He thought we needed to postulate a God in order to view the natural world as an ordered systematic whole; but physicists can apparently dispense with God without too much regret. He thought we needed to postulate God in order to reinforce our moral commitment; but moralists tend to think of such an appeal to God as an abandonment of morality for the sake of long-term prudence. We do not need to postulate God to back up any of our independent practical commitments. We do not even need God to be happy, altruistic and psychologically well-balanced, as any Freudian analyst will testify. Once a claim to the objective truth of theism is given up, any attempted pragmatic justification for a religious way of life will be shattered by the hatred, violence and bigotry of its adherents. Only if one believed it to be true could one possibly accept a form of belief which is so often and so clearly destructive of human good.

Professor Hick's underlying argument is that, if there is a reality of supreme power, love and value, it will not confine its saving activity (its efforts to bring humans to fulfilment in conscious loving relation to it) to one part of the human race or one culture. Thus one will expect to find traces of its actions everywhere and at all times. This seems to me a most persuasive point. The moral world we are moving in here is very different from, say, the fifth-century Augustinian view that all humans are born in sin and deserve eternal damnation; so that it is unmerited grace if God saves anyone at all; and who he saves is entirely up to him. On the contrary, humans should not be damned unless they really knowingly choose to be; and such a conscious choice is almost unthinkable; so that God is seen more as a universal persuader towards love and away from selfishness, than as the Judge who will be merciful to whom he wills. And if God is such a universal persuader, his persuasion must naturally be seen universally; that is, presumably, in most religious traditions, and even, in however hidden a form, in non-religious traditions too.

In contrasting the Augustinian view with Professor Hick's, it is immediately clear that there are real religious conflicts, and that no one can regard Augustine and Hick as having an equally adequate view of the Real. One gives a more adequate view than the other, because it has reflected more deeply on the nature of Divine love and human freedom. It does not follow that Augustine had no veridical experiences of God. All that follows is that some interpretations of some of his experiences were inadequate to the reality of God. By parity of reasoning, one might expect that all of us will be prey to some inadequacy of interpretation; but we cannot accept that our view is no more adequate than that of others. At points of conflict we must claim the exclusive correctness of our perception. If one believes as Professor Hick does, in the universal persuasiveness of the Divine love, one must accept that this is just one view of religion and of the Real among others; and that it would be rejected by those who do not believe there is a Divine love (e.g. Buddhists) or that, if there is, it is universally persuasive (e.g. Calvinists).

How pluralistic is this view, in fact? It is not pluralist in the sense that all competing views are in some sense correct. It claims exclusive truth for the propositions that the Divine love is universally persuasive. We must look at all religions, then, to see in them the persuasive self-disclosure of the love of God. Such love will be active and finally effective in all religions; and that is a form of pluralism (it might be called 'soft pluralism'). However, it does not follow that all religions will present God in equally adequate ways. If that were so, it would not matter which religion one adopted, or which form of which religion. Yet there are both moral and rational choices to be made in religion; and Professor Hick himself is clear that some religious beliefs are immoral (substitutionary atonement, for example), and that some are irrational (seven-day creation, perhaps). One must seek the most intellectually, morally and spiritually adequate view one can find (one that is consistent with well-established scientific and historical knowledge; that enshrines a sensitive concern for the good of all human lives; and that contains a sustainable concept of individual human perfection).

Now as one looks at the religious traditions of humanity, one can discern a development from pre-scientific cosmologies, restricted tribal moralities and ritualistic concepts of piety towards a more experimental attitude to the world, a more universal approach to morality and a more inward idea of faith. Christianity itself shows a development from early apocalyptic expectations of the end of the world to a vision of a God of universal self-giving love, discerned in the Christ-event. Once one treats the Christian tradition in this way, not as a preservation of literal and definitive truths about the life and status of Jesus but as a matrix for developing theological reflection, it is possible or even obligatory to treat other traditions in a similar way. The pluralistic hypothesis now becomes the view that virtually all serious religious traditions will contain matrices of myth which implicitly contain a disclosure of a reality of compassion and bliss which calls human beings to union with itself. This is not the view that all traditions are true or even compatible; rather, they contain the possibility of evoking more adequate insights into the Real as time goes by. The committed pluralist will now call members of all traditions to explore their own paradigm myths and develop them to find a more adequate disclosure of the Real in them. In so far as such an exploration is expected to disclose one supremely valuable reality calling humans to union with itself, it may be termed 'convergent pluralism'.

But the essential presupposition of this form of pluralism is that religious traditions contain myths which manifest a supreme reality of value, love and power, perceived in many names and forms. This is an exclusive truth-claim, though it does not belong to only one tradition. It entails that any traditions which explicitly make this claim are, in that respect, more adequate than traditions which do not (though they may make many false claims in other respects –

about life after death, for example; so that one may hesitate to call them 'more adequate' traditions *per se*). The full truth of religion does not lie in the past, in some completed and final revelation. It lies ahead, in the continuing exploration of that infinite Divine nature which requires a dialectic of conflict and convergence between many traditions to disclose the richness of its being more adequately.

This is not most helpfully put by saying that there is a noumenal reality the nature of which is wholly unknowable. That entails that no one will ever know it or have any idea of its true nature; and that therefore no one can be in any position to see whether or not it is being truly expressed to any extent at all in human concepts. Nor is it helpful to say that all religions are, as they stand, authentic expressions of this reality. For certain views are plain wrong, and truth would be a casualty on any such view. What needs to be said, to capture the position most adequately, is that there is a spiritual reality of supreme power and value; but we are unlikely to have a very adequate conception of it. However, there are many ways in which it may be disclosed to human beings; and all of them are likely to exhibit defects of human conception and limitation of vision. In particular, the claims of any tradition to have an exclusively true grasp of it must be denied. This is one possible interpretation of the pluralistic hypothesis. It says that religious truth is not confined to one tradition (exclusivism); nor does one tradition contain in a more adequate form all the truths that others contain (inclusivism).

However, it does not suppose that all traditions are equally adequate expressions of the Real or that they will lead with approximately equal efficacy to one common goal or salvation. Nor does it imply any noumenal/phenomenal distinction. On the contrary, it requires that there are genuine experiences of the Real, however difficult it is for us to distinguish the real from the illusory; and thus that the Real is truly expressed in the phenomenal, even if its nature far transcends what we can grasp. We can still truly say that it is one, perfect, the cause of all. We can agree with Basil that its operations are truly known, but that its essential being lies beyond our complete comprehension, even though we know some true facts about it. One can agree with John Hick that God is partially known in many traditions and that God can be expected to operate in all. It then does seem plausible to think that one cannot claim a complete and final apprehension of God in any tradition, and thus that the interaction of many traditions is desirable to attain a more adequate grasp of its reality. In face of this degree of agreement, it may seem a small cavil to protest at the terminology of noumenon and phenomenon.

Its importance, however, is this: once all knowledge of the noumenal is renounced, all criteria of the adequacy of religious beliefs must operate simply on a pragmatic basis, of what best suits our human needs and purposes. Truth then becomes a means to an end, whether of happiness, morality or human perfection. It seems to me that religion must continue to make claims to truth, and indeed only define what salvation is in terms of its perception of the truth about what is ultimately the case about the world, human nature and destiny. Religion must be fundamentally realist; and realists can have nothing to do with the noumenal. In the end, Basil the Great has little in common with Immanuel Kant. Orthodox theists can, however, coherently claim that God's essence is ineffable; meaning, not that they know nothing at all about it, but that they admit that in its perfection, its value and its power it transcends our understanding. Professor Hick's exciting and visionary theology takes this insight, adds the Christian belief that God is a God of universal love, and presses home the implications of this for a global view of revelation and salvation. Where he leads I am happy to follow – until he begins to walk towards the unknown country of the noumenal, at which point I feel constrained to tell him that there is simply nothing there.

19

The Meaning of Christ
MAURICE WILES

This essay is being written as a tribute to John. John is a common name. If the context did not show immediately which John is intended, I would have needed to have given some additional indication. That would be done most simply by a further naming, by saying that it is for John Hick. But the same task could be achieved with the aid of a title or some distinguishing achievement of his. I could say it is for the Danforth Professor of the Philosophy of Religion at Claremont Graduate School or for the outstanding pioneer of a pluralist approach to religion among Christian theologians from the United Kingdom.

The essay is about Jesus. Jesus too was a common name. Again, if the context did not answer the question, which Jesus is intended, even more decisively, some further indication would have been called for. While we might say it is about Jesus-bar-Joseph, we would be more likely in this instance to make the needed clarification by way of a title or allusion to his distinguishing achievement. We might say it is about Jesus, the prophet from Nazareth, or about Jesus, the focal figure of Christianity. A vast number of titles have been given to Jesus. Origen lists over thirty of them, distinguishing between those like Wisdom and Truth, which indicate his fundamental nature, and those, like Good Shepherd or Lamb of God, which relate to more specific functions for the good of humankind.[1] Origen describes them at the outset as 'titles of Jesus', but more often in the course of his discussion refers to them as titles given to Christ. Yet Christ, the anointed one, figures also within the list of titles. Indeed, Origen not only puts it in his secondary, less fundamental category, but also argues that it is one that relates specifically to the human aspect of Jesus, since to be anointed implies entry into the office of king or high-priest, a process of becoming which in Origen's eyes is in-applicable to the unchanging eternal character of Jesus's divine nature. Thinking in more historical terms, we might be more inclined to represent it as embodying the affirmation that Jesus is the fulfilment of God's promises and purposes in relation to the people of Israel. But however we define its particular significance as a title, it stands out from all the other titles in that it alone came, quite early, to function not only as a title but also as a name, as we have already seen it doing in Origen's case. Although the particular Messianic significance of the term 'Christ' has not simply been forgotten or fallen wholly into abeyance, 'Jesus Christ' can be used as a name without any intended reference to it. This transition from title to name is a well-known phenomenon. In the days of smaller, more static communities 'Johns' were distinguished as 'John the smith' or 'John the baker'; today we have simply our 'John Smiths' and our 'John Bakers'. They now function purely as names; both may turn out to be politicians or bishops rather than shoers of horses or makers of bread. 'Christ' is peculiar in that it has continued over a long period of time to function in both capacities, as a name and also as a title indicating a particular role. This ambivalence of connotation is not to be regarded as necessarily a negative factor. The play between differing senses over the range of possible meanings that can be given to a single term is a fundamental and creative usage in the writing of poetry; but it can cause misunderstanding in the development of a logical argument. Christian discourse incorporates both the poetry of immediate religious utterance and the prose of theological reasoning. In the latter case it is important to keep an eye open to see if variable uses of the word 'Christ' have given rise to confusion. One context in which the ambivalence of meaning attaching to the term 'Christ' has been much exploited, partly consciously, partly unconsciously, is the discussion of a Christian interpretation of other religions. My aim in this chapter is to look at this usage and to ask whether it is, in this case, a source of creativity or of confusion.

As a kind of prologue to the main issue I propose to discuss, it is worth recalling briefly the appeal to Christ characteristic of neo-orthodox rejection of any divine revelation outside the Christian sphere. For Hendrik Kraemer, Jesus Christ was the revelation of God and the one authority in whose light every religion, including Christianity, was to be judged. Kraemer recognises that people might be in some doubt as to how he intends 'Jesus Christ' to be understood in the context of that claim. To remove any doubt he states explicitly:

> By Jesus Christ I mean that Jesus whom we know from the total witness of apostles and evangelists in the New Testament: the Jesus who says . . . 'I am the Truth'.[2]

The problem of reference in this case is whether there is a single Jesus who says 'I am the Truth' to whom the New Testament as a whole bears a united witness. But even if that problem can be overcome there is a further question whether that Jesus Christ can be known in such independence of Christianity that he can serve equally as a judge of all religions, including Christianity itself. Kraemer has rightly indicated the need for a principle of criticism within Christianity, as well as within all other religions. But in identifying that principle with the Jesus Christ witnessed to in Christianity's canonical scriptures, he has not succeeded in avoiding the problematic claim of Christianity's assumed superiority over all other religions.

But the more enigmatic problem, towards which this chapter is directed, concerns the use of the terms 'Christ' by many of those who do want to affirm a revelation of God in and through non-Christian religions but who do not want to espouse as full-blooded a religious pluralism as John Hick advocates. Other religions are uninhibitedly acclaimed to be the medium of divine revelation or salvation, but that revelation and that salvation are said to be the work of Christ. Thus D'Costa notes that

> Rahner does not concede a true pluralism in that he always affirms that all salvation is salvation, implicitly or explicitly, through the grace of God in Christ.[3]

Many other examples could be given from a wider variety of writers, using essentially the same language. Two examples will suffice. John Taylor declares:

> We do not have to deny the reality of grace and salvation that are found, because of Christ, in all the faiths of mankind.[4]

And Julius Lipner expresses his conviction that we can say of 'most non-Christian religions of the world' that 'God through Christ operates from within their traditions and draws all men to himself'.[5]

What is the intended significance of the words 'in Christ', 'because of Christ', and 'through Christ' in the context of these affirmations? What is the relation of the use of the term 'Christ' here to its use as a name for Jesus of Nazareth? One answer, given by Raimundo Panikkar, is to see this way of speaking as deriving from the fundamental dogmatic principle that 'whatever God does *ad extra* happens through Christ'.[6] Those words come from the final paragraph of the Epilogue to Panikkar's book, *The Unknown Christ of Hinduism*, and he rather surprisingly describes them as 'a theological conclusion which is directly consequent upon [the] Christological approach' he has followed. To me they appear more like a theological premise on which the Christological approach is directly consequent rather than the other way round. But his way of putting it is perhaps a not-too-surprising feature of his discursive and imaginative rather than sequentially ordered style of reasoning. If it were simply a matter of faithfulness to the old dogmatic principle, which Panikkar's wording alludes to, it would be more natural to speak in terms of a work of the Father through the Son. Some further explanation is needed for the use of the term 'Christ' instead. Moreover, one might then expect the words to reappear in every statement about God's activity in the world, rather like some people's use of 'D. V.' in any statement of future plans. Something more needs to be said about the specific preference for the term 'Christ' in this context and the particular emphasis given to this universal principle of God's activity being through the Son or through Christ in relation to revelation in non-Christian religions. Panikkar's answer is to emphasise not merely the *ambi*valence of 'Christ', to which I have already referred and which he also acknowledges,[7] but the *poly*valence of its use as a symbol.[8] With ample grounding in New Testament usage, it has taken on a rich range of meaning in the course of Christian history, where 'Christ' has come to serve 'as that symbol which "recapitulates" in itself the Real in its totality'.[9] 'Christ' is, therefore, for Panikkar the natural and appropriate term to use in speaking of the cosmic or world-wide nature of God's activity.

Another form of basically the same answer relates specifically to the issue of salvation through the medium of other religions. In this case Panikkar does express himself in the deductive form that more accurately represents the structure of his argument.

> Christ is the universal redeemer. There is no redemption apart from him. Where there is no redemption there is no salvation. *Therefore*, any person who is saved – and we know by reason and by faith that God provides everybody with the necessary means of salvation – is saved by Christ the only redeemer.[10]

Here the logic of the argument is explicit. We know that Christ is the only and universal saviour. Salvation is to be found in and through non-Christian religions. Therefore Christ must be at work there and the salvation received there be salvation through Christ. But the clear logical structure of the argument requires us to ask questions about the consistency of the way the term 'Christ' is used. We have noted the ambivalence, or indeed polyvalence of its use. Is that ambivalence involved here in a way that might undermine the force of the argument? Is there an intended reference to the crucified Jesus of Nazareth in the major premise? And if so, is there an intended reference to him of the same order in the conclusion of the syllogism?

It is not easy to be clear about Panikkar's position on that question. It would seem that while he does not want to deny the link, he has chosen increasingly, as time has gone on, to play it down. In a further reference to redemption, a little after the one I have just quoted, he wrote in 1964: 'The Christian way is always one of co-redemption and there is no other redemption but in the cross.' In the revised edition of 1981, however, the last ten words with their reference to the cross are omitted.[11] Paul Knitter has drawn attention to a general move of this kind in Panikkar's thought over the period between the two editions in a helpful discussion, based on a much wider range of Panikkar's writings than has been available to me.[12] But on this crucial issue, Knitter appears to have overstated his case. In 1964 Panikkar wrote

> The stumbling-block appears when Christianity further identifies, with the necessary qualification, Christ with Jesus, the Son of Mary. A full Christian faith is required to accept this identity.

Knitter cites this concern with the 'identity' of Christ with Jesus, Son of Mary, as something that Panikkar has moved away from since the 1970s. But the words are still there in the revised edition of 1981. Indeed the 'identity' is spoken of in the later revision as not merely required by a 'full Christian faith' but, if anything, more basically as that which 'characterizes the Christian belief'.[13] Panikkar's sense of what constitutes Christianity's self-identity does not allow him, it would seem, to abandon an identity between the Christ at work in Hinduism and the historical figure of Jesus, but his positive attitude to the underlying, and less historical, conceptions of Hinduism makes him keen to maintain at the same time a clear separation between them. The ambivalence of the term 'Christ' serves his purpose. But if the way it does so can be claimed to contribute to creativity, it seems liable to contribute to confusion also.

Panikkar is exceptional in the degree to which he seeks to loosen the ties between Jesus and the Christ who is the medium of God's

revelation and salvation in other religions. The three writers whom
I quoted earlier as representative examples of an insistence that
God's revealing and saving work in non-Christian religions is
'through Christ' – Karl Rahner, John Taylor, and Julius Lipner – all
want to insist on closer links than Panikkar implies. For the Catholic
Rahner and the Evangelical Anglican Taylor the heart of the argument is the same. However universal the working of God's grace
may be, it can only be so on the basis of its having one perfect and
complete instantiation in the contingency of the historical order.
D'Costa explains Rahner's use of the controversial term 'anonymous
Christian' (rather than, for example, anonymous theist) as a description of anyone who responds to the grace of God, wherever and
however it comes to him, as justified by the fact that 'all grace is
teleologically directed to its explicit expression of the definitive self-
revelation of God in *Christ'*.[14] And Rahner himself describes the
Incarnation as 'the end and the goal of this world's reality', 'the point
of climax in the development of the world towards which the whole
world is directed' and 'a condition for the universal bestowal of
grace to spiritual creatures'.[15] John Taylor makes essentially the same
point in terms of his different theological background:

> What God did through Jesus Christ is the one act which it was
> always necessary that he should accomplish in time and at the
> right time if he were to be the God who throughout time is
> accessible and present to every human being in judgment and
> mercy, grace and truth.[16]

Once again there is a dogmatic principle at work in both writers, but
one to which the role of the one, definitive and unrepeatable, historical act of God in the incarnation and crucifixion of Jesus Christ is
integral in a way that it is not for Panikkar. How this dogmatic
principle, with its talk of the necessity of a once-for-all divine action
in Christ, can be known to be true, in advance of a deeper dialogue
with those other religions in which the grace of God is also acknowledged to be operative, is beyond the scope of this essay.[17] For our
present purpose it is sufficient to notice that it is this principle, which
lies behind and gives substance to the use of the words 'in Christ' or
'because of Christ' in relation to the grace of God operative in non-
Christian religions. Both aspects of the ambivalence in the meaning
of 'Christ' have a significant role to play. Its function as a name for
Jesus is an intended part of its reference, because there is a necessary

link between his historical life and every other occasion of divine grace at work.

Lipner is even more explicit in making the traditional Catholic doctrine that Christ and his Church are 'the necessary channel of grace for all mankind' the determining factor in his position. The basic understanding of that traditional doctrine is not changed, he says, by the recognition of its operation in major non-Christian religions like Hinduism; it is only the implications of its scope and range that are affected. How then does he see the relation of the 'unknown Christ of Hinduism' (a phrase which he himself explicitly allows)[18] to the historical person of Jesus? In an earlier article he states that 'except where another sense is clear, I use 'Jesus' and 'Christ' throughout as they are commonly used, viz. as proper names referring to one and the same person'.[19] Although in that article he sees 'major non-Christian religions like Hinduism' as 'salvific structures within the confines of their own development', he does not describe that salvific work directly as a work of Christ. They 'display the workings amid personal encounter of a wise and loving Deity' and we are free to acknowledge 'the stirrings of his [Christ's] spirit in alien traditions'.[20] So there the salvific activity present in and through other religions is ascribed in less specific terms to 'Deity' or 'Christ's spirit'. But when in the later article he ascribes it more specifically to 'Christ', it is natural to ask whether the term is still being used as a proper name for the person who is also named Jesus or whether this is a case 'where another sense is clear'. It appears that the naming role of the term 'Christ' is still intended, though its title role is designed to accentuate one aspect of the person named. Lipner makes use of 'a dichotomy between Jesus as a human, culture-bound figure and his transcendent and unrepeatable relationship to the Father as the Logos'. It is, in fact, the old two-nature Christology in its Alexandrian form to which he appeals, though it is its use by contemporary theologians rather than its historical pedigree to which he draws explicit attention. John Hick's acknowledgement of the Logos as active in other cultures and other religions is good as far as it goes, but is not enough. The affirmation, in Lipner's view, needs to be related not merely to the Logos, but also explicitly to 'the Logos (in so far as this name refers to the historical figure of Jesus)'.[21] Lipner speaks here in terms of Logos rather than of Christ, because Logos is the terminology used by Hick whose views he is seeking to criticise. To make this point, he has to speak rather oddly of 'Logos' as a name. One can see, therefore, why he prefers to speak himself (with Rahner and so many others) of the wider operation of grace as work done 'through Christ'. The ambivalence of name and title is more naturally conveyed by the term 'Christ'. It will more readily suggest both the historical figure of Jesus as such while at the same time pushing 'the human culture-bound' part of the dichotomy away from our attention.

One writer who has reflected more explicitly and at greater length on the meaning of 'Christ' in such discussions is John Cobb. He begins by distinguishing between words which 'designate particular things or persons' and those which 'stand for concepts'. But many words have a vast range of meanings which may unite entities and concepts. These words are said to name images, and 'Christ' is one of them.[22] 'Christ' can therefore be said to name the process of creative transformation and the hope to which that process leads.[23] But '"Christ" names also, and more certainly, the singular figure of a Nazarene carpenter.'[24] For Cobb 'the identity of Jesus with Christ' is 'a matter of literal truth'.[25] It is so because the principle of creative transformation is not just a force from outside that influences Jesus from time to time; it is constitutive of his very selfhood. The fact that the identity is complete does not mean that it is exhaustive or exclusive. There is no question, as with Rahnner and Taylor, of any logical necessity inherent in the operation of divine grace which requires that it should be true only of Jesus. The selfhood of others could have been constituted in the same way. It is only 'so far as we know' that Jesus is unique.[26] So the polyvalence of the image named by 'Christ' encourages a mutually illuminating interplay between what we know of Jesus and what we experience as creative transformation, whenever it occurs. And experience certainly suggests that it occurs in and through other religions than Christianity. Where it occurs, for example in Buddhism, Christians will naturally name it as Christ at work. But they will not expect Buddhists to name it that way.[27] Their own use of the name of Christ is a true and appropriate use. But it is not necessarily the only valid or final way in which such creative transformation may be named.

Of all the writers we have considered so far, John Cobb is the freest in attaching a broader range of meaning to the word 'Christ'. Neither Rahner nor Taylor would quarrel with his understanding of it as creative transformation and as hope. And they would applaud his affirmation of its literal identity with Jesus. But because that identity is not exhaustive, it allows for a more flexible understanding of the forms that creative transformation or hope may take. When the Christian sees such creative transformation at work in other religions, he or she naturally speaks of it in terms of Christ. But that is his or her way of interpreting something which members of other religions will name differently. Yet it is not just a matter of alternative names. The Christian's understanding of creative transformation, implicit in the use of the name 'Christ', may properly challenge the understanding of such transformation that is implicit in those other religions. But the Christian's is not a necessarily superior understanding that has in the end to be imposed upon the other. For since Jesus, though a perfect embodiment of Christ, is not a definitively unique embodiment, the understanding that grows out of the union of the two in Jesus is not automatically decisive for all spheres where Christ is understood to be at work.

In the discussion so far I have been trying to tease out what is implied by the widespread tendency to describe the work of divine revelation and salvation in other religions as work done 'through Christ'. In conclusion I want to draw out those implications more systematically and give them some kind of evaluation. In the first place it is clear that such language is primarily addressed to a Christian audience or readership. D'Costa defends Rahner's use of the terms 'anonymous Christian' and 'anonymous Christianity' against the charge that it is offensive to the non-Christian by claiming that 'the reflection is not meant to gain approval by the Hindu or the Buddhist but is addressed by the Christian to his, and the Church's, own self-understanding'.[28] And Panikkar gives as one of the reasons for his choice of 'Christ' in *The Unknown Christ of Hinduism* the fact that the book is 'intended principally though not solely for a Christian readership'.[29] Certainly the intended readership of a book is an important factor in determining an author's choice of words and images. So we might describe the use of the term 'Christ' in the context of the discussion of a Christian understanding of religions as an appropriate form of Christian rhetoric. It can serve as a way of reassuring a hesitant Church and reluctant Christians that the acknowledgement of God's grace at work in other religions need not be seen as in opposition to the experience of revelation and salvation that has come to them within the Christian church. The ambivalence of the term 'Christ' can well serve that creative purpose.

But these writings, as Panikkar acknowledges, are not 'solely' for a Christian readership. And Rahner explicitly discusses the response of the Zen Buddhist, Nishitani, to his conception of 'anonymous Christians'.[30] The Christian authors can, of course, underline the fact that it is their way of speaking about the divine grace, and there is no expectation that adherents of other religions should do the same. If Christians 'find themselves obliged to call this mysteric aspect "Christ"', says Panikkar, that is a mark of their recognition of Hinduism as a genuine religion. But a Hindu may speak of Rāma, Krishṇa, Īśvara or Purusha.[31] And Rahner can acknowledge the appropriateness of his Zen Buddhist interlocutor describing him as an 'anonymous Zen Buddhist' and express himself honoured to be the recipient of such a title.[32]

But once we recognise that the language has a role to play not only in intra-Christian discourse but also in interreligious dialogue, the question inevitably arises whether the 'through Christ' language is the most helpful to employ. It is not the only term that Christians have traditionally employed to refer to God's activity outside the sphere of special revelation or of the Church. And even if no term, when transplanted from the internal discourse of one religion to play a part in interreligious discourse, will be altogether free of hidden assumptions or misleading associations, some terms carry a lot more negative baggage from the past than others. The term 'Christ' (however useful as part of an intra-Christian rhetoric) seems to have two serious disadvantages in the interreligious context. First there is the linguistic link between Christ and Christianity. It is very difficult for interreligious dialogue to take place without either the reality, or at least the suspicion, of an assumed superiority of one party over the other. The history of the attitude and behaviour of Christianity as an institution to other religious bodies in the past provides ample ground for such suspicion. And despite Kraemer's attempt to drive a firm wedge between Christ and Christianity, the initial assertion by Christians that the grace of God acknowledged to be at work in the other religious traditions involved in the dialogue is 'through Christ', can hardly avoid being heard as subordinating that religion to the institutional phenomenon of Christianity. Thus while the choice of 'Christ' language in this context may be seen as fulfilling a constructive rule in the context of an intra-Christian rhetoric, it has also to be seen as fulfilling a negative role in the context of interreligious dialogue. Secondly, the fact that Christ (alone among the many titles of Jesus) is also a name for the historical figure of Jesus, adds to its problematic character in this context. Panikkar goes so far as to issue a warning against presupposing 'the Christian concept of Christ' with its emphasis on the historical particularity of Jesus.[33] We have already seen from Lipner's discussion that, when using the term 'Christ' in this wider context, Christians themselves have to appeal to a dichotomy in its application to the historical figure of Jesus, if their claim is to make coherent sense. Yet just because 'Christ' functions also as a name for Jesus, it conceals that dichotomy in a way that other titles which also relate to Jesus, such as Logos, do not. That would seem to make them less misleading titles to use in this particular context of interreligious dialogue.

The most obvious alternatives to speaking of divine grace in non-Christian religions as 'through Christ' would be to ascribe it to the Logos, as suggested above, or to the Spirit, or simply to describe it without further specification as the work of God. In distinguishing between these alternatives, it is not, of course, a question of determining which is the true account. It is a question rather of which fits better with the ways in which those differing terms are normally understood with respect to the activity of God, and which carry the more helpful associations for readers or for participants in dialogue with their diverse backgrounds.

The various writers with whom I have been concerned in this chapter do reflect occasionally on the grounds for their preference for the use of the term 'Christ' over the other three suggestions that I have put forward. Lipner, as we have seen, accepts the validity of the use of the term 'Logos' but prefers the term 'Christ' precisely because of its more obvious naming of the historical Jesus and its continuation of the dogmatic principle which affirms Christ to be the universally necessary channel for divine grace. It goes hand in hand with a desire (which he shares with several other Catholic writers) to maintain the claim that there is no salvation outside the Church, in a way which extends the meaning of 'church' beyond the institutional church while at the same time keeping the links between the two as close as is consistent with that extension of meaning. In both cases, in respect both of 'Christ' and of 'Church', the extended range of meaning makes, as it seems to me, for lack of clarity and confusion in understanding. The ambivalence inherent in the term 'Christ' is being stretched to the point of incoherence.

Cobb's preference for Christ over Logos is based on very different but also unsatisfactory grounds. Although he recognises that in Christian history Logos has served as a bridge between divine transcendence and divine immanence, he sees 'Logos' as suggesting primarily a transcendent possibility and 'Christ' as designating that Logos incarnate throughout nature and history.[34] It is questionable whether that distinction represents either the main historical tradition or the most natural contemporary understanding of the terms. Cobb gives less consideration to the possible use of the term 'Spirit'. His suggested distinction of meaning between the terms 'Christ' and 'Spirit' is the priority of the link with Jesus in the former and with the goal of the Kingdom and of Resurrection in the latter.[35] Yet his own substantial discussion of Kingdom and Resurrection is entirely in terms of Christ as hope without reference to the Spirit.[36] He does not seem himself to use the pattern of differentiation he proposes. Without a more consistent distinction in the usage of the two terms, his own vigorous espousal of the term 'Christ' cannot carry great weight in the deliberations of others about the most appropriate term to use.

Panikkar's discussion of the relative merits of the terms 'Christ' and 'Spirit' in relation to other religions evidences an indecision in his own mind. He expresses a preference for 'Christ' over 'God' or 'Spirit' on the ground that the latter are not such living symbols.[37] But Christ's 'necessary identity with Jesus' is not for him the positive recommendation that it is for Lipner. He sees it rather as an inhibition on fruitful dialogue and at that point goes on to set out the advantages inherent in the use of 'Spirit'.[38] But they are evidently not strong enough in his eyes to become the determining factor in his own usage.

It is Rahner, with his more comprehensive and precisely articulated theological scheme, who provides us with the fullest and firmest grounding for an emphasis on Christ as the medium of God's salvation in other religions. We have already referred to D' Costa's explanation of why 'anonymous Christian' is more appropriate than 'anonymous theist': the incarnation is the indispensable condition of all God's gracious dealing with the world.[39] Rahner himself, in an article entitled 'Jesus Christ in the non-Christian Religions', lays great stress on the Spirit as the medium of his presence there. But he lays still greater stress on the fact that it is the Spirit of Jesus Christ. The historical event of the incarnation is the goal of all the work of the Spirit in our human world, so that Rahner can even affirm that 'Jesus is the "cause" of the Spirit'.[40]

It is that unqualifiedly determinative link between the historical figure of Jesus and the whole gracious outreach of God to the world that lies behind and justifies Rahner's insistence on Christ as the medium of God's self-communication to the non-Christian world. With him the ambivalence of Christ as name and title makes precisely the bridge he desires between the historical particular and the divine universal which faith apprehends but which human conceptuality finds it so difficult to provide. But not all Christians can tie the two together in so absolute a manner. Even John Cobb, as we have seen, despite his affirmation of an identity of Christ with Jesus, does not see that identity as a necessarily unique phenomenon, decisive for the whole process of God's gracious self-giving. And John Hick has argued on many occasions against any suggestion that such a view is a necessary corollary of finding salvation through Jesus Christ.

Christian recognition of God's revelation and saving presence in other religious traditions is a development to be warmly welcomed. To describe that work as work 'through Christ' can serve as a reassurance to Christians that there is no ultimate conflict between that revelation and saving presence and those experienced within the Christian Church. But it also has, as I have tried to show, some serious disadvantages. It is likely to prove a source of intellectual confusion and of added difficulty to the already difficult venture of interreligious dialogue. And there are other ways in which that reassurance can be effected. The essential point seems to me to be more simply and more clearly made in language proposed by Wilfred Smith, with which I will bring this chapter to close:

> A Buddhist who is saved, or a Hindu or a Muslim or whoever, is saved, and is saved only, because God is the kind of God whom Jesus Christ has revealed him to be. . . . Because God is what he is, because he is what Christ has shown him to be, *therefore* other men *do* live in his presence.[41]

Notes

1. Origen, *Commentary on John* 1, 22–42.
2. H. Kraemer, *Why Christianity of all Religions?* (London: Butterworth, 1962), pp. 15–16.
3. G. D'Costa, 'Karl Rahner's Anonymous Christian – A Reappraisal' *Modern Theology* 1:2 (January 1985), p. 139.
4. John Taylor, 'The Theological Basis of Interfaith Dialogue' in ed. J. Hick and B. Hebblethwaite, *Christianity and Other Religions* (London: Collins, 1980), p. 224.
5. J. J. Lipner, 'Does Copernicus Help? Reflections for a Christian Theology of Religions', *Religious Studies* 13:2 (June 1977), p. 258.
6. R. Panikkar, *The Unknown Christ of Hinduism* (London: Darton, Longman and Todd, 1964) (rev. edn. 1981), p. 138 (p. 169). The revised

edition of 1981 incorporates significant changes to the earlier edition some of which are discussed later in the essay. Where the two editions overlap, page references are given to the 1964 edition, with the 1981 page nos. given in brackets. The wording of the quotations is from the 1981 edition.

7. Ibid. (1981), pp. 26–7.
8. Ibid. (1981), pp. 37–8.
9. Ibid. (1981), p. 28.
10. Ibid. p. 33 (pp. 67–8) (italics added).
11. Ibid. p. 42 (p. 76). For a similar omission of an earlier reference to the cross, cf. p. 18 (1964) with p. 50 (1981).
12. P. Knitter, *No Other Name?* (London: SCM, 1985), pp. 152–7.
13. R. Panikkar, op. cit., p. 24 (pp. 56–7). Knitter, op. cit., p. 155.
14. G. D'Costa, art. cit. p. 135 (italics original).
15. K. Rahner, *Foundations of Christian Faith* (London: Darton, Longman and Todd, 1978) p. 199 (= 'Christology within an Evolutionary View', *Theological Investigations*, 5 (London: Darton, Longman and Todd, 1966), p. 180).
16. J. Taylor, art. cit., p. 223.
17. I have discussed this question more fully in my *Christian Theology and Interreligious Dialogue* (London: SCM, 1992), with special reference to Karl Rahner in Chapter 3.
18. J. J. Lipner, art. cit., p. 257.
19. J. J. Lipner, 'Christians and the Uniqueness of Christ', *Scottish Journal of Theology*, 28 (1975), p. 359.
20. Ibid., p. 365.
21. J. J. Lipner, 'Does Copernicus Help?', pp. 256–8, 251.
22. J. B. Cobb, *Christ in a Pluralistic Age* (Philadelphia: Westminster Press, 1975), pp. 64–5.
23. Op. cit., pp. 24–5. Cf. also pp. 43, 45, 57–9, 183, 186.
24. Op. cit., p. 97.
25. Op. cit., p. 142.
26. Ibid.
27. John B. Cobb, 'Response II' in Leonard Swidler, John B. Cobb, Paul F. Knitter and Monika K. Hellwig, *Death or Dialogue?* (London: SCM, 1990), p. 118.
28. G. D'Costa, art. cit., p. 133.
29. R. Panikkar, op. cit. (1981), p. 27.
30. K. Rahner, 'The One Christ and the Universality of Salvation', *TI*, Vol. 16, p. 219.
31. R. Panikkar, op. cit. (1981), pp. 26–7.
32. K. Rahner, ibid.
33. R. Panikkar, op. cit., p. 133 (pp. 164–5).
34. J. Cobb, op. cit., pp. 72, 76–7.
35. Op. cit., pp. 261–2.
36. Op. cit., Part 3, pp. 177–258.
37. R. Panikkar, op. cit. (1981), p. 27.
38. Op. cit. (1981), pp. 57–8.

39. See n. 14 above.
40. K. Rahner, 'Jesus Christ in the non-Christian Religions' *TI*, Vol. 17, pp. 43–6.
41. W. C. Smith, 'The Christian in a Religiously Plural World', in ed. J. Hick and B. Hebblethwaite, op. cit., pp. 105–6 (italics original).

20

How to speak of God:
A Meditation
YAGI, SEIICHI

First we will examine an example, our text being the well-known parable of the good Samaritan. (Lk 10:30–37)

(Jesus, replying to the question of a lawyer, told a parable:)

A man was on his way from Jerusalem down to Jericho when he fell in with robbers, who stripped him, beat him, and went off leaving him half dead. It so happened that a priest was going down by the same road; but when he saw him, he went past on the other side. So too a Levite came to the place, and when he saw him, he went past on the other side. But a Samaritan who was making the journey came upon him, and when he saw him, he was moved to pity. He went up and bandaged his wounds, bathing them with oil and wine. Then he lifted him onto his own beast, brought him to an inn, and looked after him there. Next day he produced two silver pieces and gave them to the innkeeper, and said, 'Look after him; and if you spend any more, I will repay you on my way back.'

(Then Jesus asked the lawyer) 'Which of these three do you think was neighbour to the man, who fell into the hands of the robbers?' He answered, 'The one who showed him kindness.' Jesus said, 'Go and do as he did.' (NEB)

In the Lucan text the parable is combined with the preceding dialogue between Jesus and a lawyer on how to inherit eternal life (Lk 10:25–28). But as the dialogue is also found in other contexts in varying versions (Mt 22:35–40) and Mk 12:28–34), it must have been an isolated tradition. It is also presumably the third evangelist who combined it with the following parable of the good Samaritan, which

236

is perhaps the case as well with Mt 18:21–2 and verses 23–5, where we may see the redaction of the first evangelist. If so, we can treat our parable apart from the context of the Gospels.

Now it is interesting to see that not a single person of our parable symbolises or allegorises God as is the case with other parables (e.g. landowner, Mt 20:1ff; father, Lk 15:11ff), that not a single word of it refers to God, the Kingdom of God or even to religion directly – except the negative depiction of the religious figures, a priest and a Levite – so that we can ask legitimately, 'Is this word of Jesus religious? If it is, how can we assert that? Under what conditions can we interpret it as a religious discourse? If it is religious language, in what way does it refer to God?' and so on. Akaiwa Sakae (1903–66), after he had left his former Barthian standpoint, wrote *Exodus from Christianity* (1963) where the historical Jesus was a 'humanist', and Akaiwa, still a follower of Jesus according to his own assertion, no longer spoke about God and Jesus became to him the symbol of 'Śūnyatā'[2].

Indeed, the actors of our parable are all human and the drama is completed without any reference to the transcendent. We may assume that not only humanists, but also Buddhists and even 'atheists' would sympathise with our parable. If so, where does their sympathy come from? It is clear that human behaviours, in so far as they are seen from outside or observed objectively, have nothing to do with God. It is not the case that God is invisible to objective observation though at work in objective reality. It is the case that God is not there in our historical reality or in nature as far as they are observed objectively. To put it another way, it is impossible for the language of objective information to refer to God. The language of objective information is by nature 'non-realist'. One could use a mythological language and say that to objective observation there would be no God at all, even in the Kingdom of God when it reveals itself at the end of our history.

Does our parable, then, have no religious value? Is it a merely 'humanistic' or even 'atheistic' language, to understand which we need no sense of religion? In a sense we should affirm that not all would find it religious, that there would be some who, rejecting the religious interpretation of the parable, think it to be a model of human love to the oppressed.[3] But at the same time there are surely those who find it religious because they sense in the behaviour of the good Samaritan something at work that transcends the merely human. But how does the religious interpretation of the parable occur? How is it possible? For, to repeat it once more, there is no single word which refers to religious reality positively.

On the other hand, one could argue that, even though we can cut the parable off from the preceding dialogue which Luke has combined with it and treat it separately, we must ultimately put it into the framework of the words of Jesus as a whole which make up a synchronic system of meaning. It is then clear that our parable should be read as a religious text because Jesus spoke surely about God and the Reign of God. Even given this, the problem is still how we can interpret it in the context of the words of Jesus on God or the Reign of God. Our text should not be read, at least directly, in the light of the preceding dialogue on how to inherit eternal life, nor in the light of discussions on what is the most important commandment (Mt 22:34ff.), or on which commandment has priority (Mk 12:28ff.). For our parable is not concerned with these problems, and the theoretical question of the lawyer, 'Who is my neighbour?' (Lk 10:29) which evoked from Jesus our parable, Jesus does not answer directly. He refuses to give a definition of the neighbour to the lawyer. Apart from the possible assumption that the lawyer's question was formed by the third evangelist, who thus threw a bridge between the dialogue and the parable, the point of our parable does not lie, at least directly, in showing who our neighbour is. It gives an example of love to the neighbour, as verse 37 shows ('Go and do as he did!').

The motivation of the saving act of the Samaritan is noteworthy: he was moved to pity (v.33). This word also may have been added by the third evangelist but it does not bring something alien into the text. Rather it interprets the text in a proper way. The Samaritan did not think of the commandment. He did save the half-dead Jew (the text implies that he was a Jew, cf.v.30a), not in obedience to the commandment as his ultimate concern or reality, but simply in answering directly his voiceless cry. At that moment he forgot the law, reward or punishment of God – in short, all except the fallen Jew – just as the one who forgot ninety-nine sheep for the sake of one lost sheep (Lk 15:4). And it should be noted again that because of certain historical backgrounds the Jews were at that time inimical to the Samaritans (cf. John 4:9). In spite of the circumstances the Samaritan had natural pity for the Jew. How is it possible for us to have *natural* love for the suffering enemy?

We find then the word of Jesus which illuminates our parable, e.g. Mt 5:44: 'Love your enemies!' Both sayings of Jesus, we can say,

interpret each other. 'Love your enemies!' is no 'ethical' commandment. We cannot observe it as an ethical norm. It is either impossible
or we fall into hypocrisy if we endeavour to keep the 'commandment' in a 'ethical' way. We should become such, or we are by nature
such that can have natural pity on our 'enemies'. It is what Jesus
means and what Jesus showed in the figure of the good Samaritan.
But, even if we affirm that, we can still ask: 'What has that to do with
God? Why is such an idea religious?'

I am not intending here to give an interpretation of the text which
all are bound to follow. Such an interpretation is by nature impossible. There is a way in which our text is held to be religious for it
bears testimony to the act of God. Now such a paradoxical matter as
'natural' love for the enemy cannot come from our ego, in the sense
of ego-centredness or egoism. It is totally impossible for the ego to
love enemies. If, nevertheless, one has natural love for one's enemy,
this love must originate from somewhere other than one's ego.[4]

> Dear friends, let us love one another, because love is from God.
> Everyone who loves is a child of God and knows God, but the
> unloving know nothing of God. For God is love; . . . Though God
> has never been seen as any man, God himself dwells in us if we
> love one another: his love is brought to perfection within us.
> (1 John 4:7–12 (NEB))

The text interprets the kerygmas of primitive Christianity from
the standpoint of, so to speak, a theology of love (vv. 9–10). But we
are interested here in the way that God is known. The text asserts
that everyone who loves knows God. Here we are not merely the
object of love of God. Rather we are the subjects of love: based on the
fact that God loves us, we love one another and when we love one
another we know that our love originates in God, that it is divine–
human, so that we know God who has never been seen by any of us.
What is the mode of this cognition? It is by no means the cognition
of objective facts. It is nonsense if one would like to observe objectively how divine love comes from God and enters humans to make
them love each other. If the one who loves knows God, the cognition
is the matter of Self-awareness which we find in such sayings as
'Christ lives in me' (Gal. 2:20), 'Christ accomplished his work through
me' (Rom. 15:18), 'To me to live is Christ' (Phil. 1:21), and so on.

Love is genuinely human and still is of divine origin so that it is
at the same time divine and human. The cognition of God in this

way – for in this awareness the cognition of God is included – is a matter of Self-awareness and is, one may say, intuitive, or by 'inner sense'. But it is important to emphasise here that God is not the 'object' of intuition or inner sense. If God were the object of intuition or inner sense, we would have to understand God as something eternal in our temporal body, or as something substantial in our transient being, as was the case with classical Greek thinking which understood psyche (soul) as something divine–eternal in the temporal human body. In other words, we should not apply the subject–object scheme to this mode of cognition. It is an error caused by our daily thinking in the subject–object scheme if we grasp the relation between God and humans as if there were God on the one hand and humans on the other apart from God, as if God came afterwards into humans to dwell in them.

No, there is a simple fact that we love each other and as love breaks through the ego-centredness we become aware that love is of deeper origin. We articulate the simple fact of love into two aspects, divinity and humanity, so that we 'experience' the work of God in us. Is divine love then merely subjective? This is a bias of those who absolutise the subject–object scheme and hold the objective for the real. Divine love enables us to break through the ego-centeredness and love even the suffering 'enemy'. Why is it not real?

This mode of cognition is said to be 'mystical' in contrast to the 'prophetical' in which 'prophets' experience God as personal and opposite. In reality both modes complement each other.[5] No one can 'encounter' God directly as humans do each other because we always 'experience' God through certain mediums. If one hears God address through the medium of a historical situation, one 'encounters' God in a 'prophetical' way and if one becomes aware of the work of God in oneself through the medium of one's own heart–bodily existence, one 'experiences' the work of God in a 'mystical' way (cf. Phil. 2:13). Here we come back to our parable of the good Samaritan. As he saw the fallen Jew, he saved him, forgetting all other cares. But, if he should narrate what he had done, he would say that he had heard God address him personally through the situation of his encounter with the wounded Jew, thus experiencing God in a prophetical way, and that he had become aware of the love of deeper origin in himself which overcame his inimity to the Jew, thus experiencing God in a 'mystical' way. The one cannot be separated from the other and we should note that hearing the address of God is a matter of 'inner', rather than objective and physical, experience.

We come to our conclusion: seen from outside (i.e. to the objective observer) we find nothing especially religious in the parable of the good Samaritan. The parable can be read and interpreted in a 'humanistic–atheistic' way. That means: the language of objective information and the objective world are correlatives. They posit each other.[6] As there is no God at all in the objective world, it follows that we cannot speak of God with the language of objective information, just as we cannot speak of artistic beauty with physical or physiological language. But, seen from inside, i.e. as far as events or language are understood as the expression of Self-awareness, they bear witness to the work of God in our historical reality. To name one more instance, the very event of nature: 'The ground produces a crop by itself.' (Mk 4:28). The expression 'by itself' is remarkable, as if it were a natural event which take place without any divine intervention. It can be seen 'from inside' as the activity of the Reign of God, so that it bears witness to Him. That means: here we witness the qualified language of religion.[7]

Here we must mention that the language of religion is understood only by those who already know the words and grammar of it; i.e. by those who have become aware of religious reality in them. It is not understandable to all, as is the case with the verifiable or falsifiable language of objective information. Religious reality is real only to those who have become aware of it. Otherwise it is virtually non-existent. We find an example of this state of affairs in the case of St Paul. Though he had been set under the grace of God from his birth, he persecuted primitive Christianity until 'God revealed His Son in' him (Gal. 1:15–16). The grace of God which determined his whole career as the apostle to the 'Gentiles' had been virtually non-existent in and to him before he became aware of the reality of 'Christ' who lived in him. Thenceforth he could see the presence of Christ not only in him but also in the Christian Church as the Body of Christ (1 Cor. 12).

But, by so saying I am not exalting the religious to a race of special rank. No, religious language is by no means the secret language of a closed society. The language of religion has the task of addressing everyone, breaking through the ego-centredness of everyone and evoking Self-awareness in everyone. Because the language of religion is based on one's Self-awareness and not on the historical event of salvation or of revelation once and for all – language of Jesus is understandable to all who are awakened to themselves, irrespective of who they are and whether they are Christians or not – it is free from self-absolutisation.

This view surely demands the transformation of traditional Christianity, or at least the re-examination of it. If so, we must ask many questions, such as: what does Christian theology look like if one holds this position consistently? We cannot answer this question here. But to address it quite briefly, we cannot speak of creation or the coming Kingdom of God in terms of objective language. Christology and the Trinity are interpreted from the standpoint of Self-awareness as the teachings which bring to light the nature and ground of human existence. Then the Christian church will be *communio sanctorum*: the community of those who have become aware of 'Christ who lives in me', or 'the Formless Self', or, to put it another way, the community of those who do not reject *a priori* other religions or religion as such as false.

Notes

1. The following literature gave me direct occasion to write this meditation: John Hick, 'Religious Realism and Non-Realism: Defining the Issue', CGS Philosophy of Religion Conference, 1988 (manuscript); Mase Hiromasa, 'John Hick's View of the Language of Religion', in *Philosophy*, Keio University Tetugaku Kai, Vol. 86 (December 1989); idem, 'Philosophy of Religion Today – The Formation of Analytical Philosophy of Religions'; idem, 'The Language of Religion and its Meaning – a Wittgensteinian Approach', in Koyama Chumaru, Tamaru Tokuzen and Mineshima Akio (eds), *Philosophy of Religion* (Tokyo: Hokuju Shuppann, 1989), pp. 143–57 and pp. 218–31.

2. One of Mahāyāna-Buddhism's key words which means 'openness' or 'vacancy' as the basic condition of mutual dwelling or mutual dependence of beings, i.e. of dependent origination (*pratītya–samutpāda*).

3. Tagawa Kenzo in *A Man called Jesus* (Tokyo: Keiso Shobo, 1980) interprets Jesus consistently *in a non-realist way* as a man who, standing on the side of the oppressed, rebelled against the *status quo*, his love being a paradoxical–cynical expression of his anger.

4. To make the matter clearer we must make a distinction between ego and Self. We see 'Self' in distinction to and in unity with 'ego' most clearly in Gal. 2:19f: 'For through the law I died to the law – to live to God. I have been crucified with Christ. It is no more I who live. Christ lives in me.' Here 'Christ in me' is 'Self' and 'I' the 'ego' of Paul. It is noteworthy that 'Self' is something divine–human; that is to say,

something which has essentially to do with Christology. Cf. Seiichi Yagi and Leonard Swidler, *A Bridge to Buddhist–Christian Dialogue* (New York, Mahwah: Paulist Press, 1990), pp. 114–24. See also note 6 of this essay. As a matter of fact, love in the following quotation comes from God through the medium of 'Self'.

5. Peter L. Berger (ed.), *The Other Side of God: A Polarity in World Religions* (New York: Anchor Press, 1981) examines the typology of religious experience proposed by Peter Berger (confrontation model and interiority model) and finds that many religious personages – for example, Paul, Francis of Assisi, Shinran – evince both a confrontation model and an interiority model in their understanding of the person's relationship with God. We can see the reason why. See below.

6. It is not the case that there is an objective reality apart from our cognition and that the latter reflects the former. Rather, our objective cognition with the unequivocal language of information posits the reality which is adequately cognised by this mode of cognition. Reality presents to the objective cognition its 'objective' aspect and other aspects conceal themselves from it.

7. That the central matter of both Zen-Buddhism and the religion of the New Testament lies in the awakening of the ego to the Self (the Formless Self, or 'Christ in me', Gal. 2:20), which reveals itself to the ego so that the latter awakens to the former and reflects the latter in itself) and that the language of religion is the language of the ego which reflects the Self in itself is the common conclusion of a long dialogue between Akizuki Ryomin (Zen-Master) and Yagi. See Yagi-Akizuki, *When Dharma reveals itself, Philosophical Dialogue between a Buddhist and a Christian* (Tokyo: Seidosha, 1990). It is a matter of consensus that 'the Formless Self' of Zen-Buddhism and the 'Christ in me' of St Paul are different names of the same reality, and that the claim of religions to absoluteness must therefore be forsaken.

Part IV
Bibliography

John Hick: A Bibliography

PRIMARY BOOKS, ARTICLES AND REVIEWS

1952

'The Will to Believe: William James's Theory of Faith', *The London Quarterly & Holborn Review* (October), pp. 290–5.

1953

'The Nature of Religious Faith', in *Proceedings of the XIth International Congress of Philosophy*, Vol. XI (Amsterdam: North-Holland Publishing Company), pp. 57–62.

1954

'The Structure of the War Problem', in *Studies in Christian Social Commitment*, ed. John Ferguson (London: Independent Press), pp. 19–36.

1956

Review of *A Modern Philosophy of Religion* by Samuel M. Thompson, *The Philosophical Review*, Vol. LXV, no. 3, whole number 375 (July), pp. 427–9.

1957

Faith and Knowledge: A Modern Introduction to the Problem of Religious Knowledge (Ithaca: Cornell University Press), pp. xix + 221.
'The Engineer: His Need for Education As Well As Training', *The Cornell Engineer*, Vol. 22, no. 6 (March), pp. 29–36.
'Love', *The Inner Disciplines* (series of sermons preached in the Sage Chapel, Cornell University), pp. 16–18.
Review of *The Modern Predicament: A Study in the Philosophy of Religion* by H. J. Paton, *The Philosophical Review*, Vol. LXVI, no. 2, whole number 378 (April), pp. 271–4.

1958

'The Christology of D. M. Baillie', *Scottish Journal of Theology*, Vol. 11, no. 1 (March), pp. 1–12.

Review of *Words and Images: A Study in Theological Discourse* by E. L. Mascall, *Scottish Journal of Theology*, Vol. 11, no. 1 (March), pp. 83–6.

1959

'A Non-Substance Christology?', *Colgate-Rochester Divinity School Bulletin* (May), pp. 41–54.

'Belief and Life: The Fundamental Nature of the Christian Ethic', *Encounter*, Vol. 20, no. 4 (Fall), pp. 494–516.

Article review on *Systematic Theology*, Vols I and II by Paul Tillich, *Scottish Journal of Theology*, Vol. 12, no. 2 (June), pp. 193–5.

Review of *The Self as Agent* by John Macmurray, *Scottish Journal of Theology*, Vol. 12, no. 2 (June), pp. 193–5.

Review of *An Analytical Philosophy of Religion* by Willem F. Zurdeeg, *Ethics*, Vol. LXIX, No. 4 (July), pp. 297–9.

Review of *The Reality of Faith* by Friedrich Gogarten, *Theology Today*, Vol. XVI, No. 3 (October), pp. 412–14.

Review of *Christ and the Christian* by Nels Ferré, *Scottish Journal of Theology*, Vol. 12, no. 4 (December), pp. 414–17.

1960

'Theology and Verification', *Theology Today*, Vol. XVII, no. 2 (April), pp. 12–31.

'God as Necessary Being', *The Journal of Philosophy*, Vol. 57, nos 22 and 23 (November), pp. 725–34.

'The Idea of Necessary Being', *Princeton Seminary Bulletin*, Vol. LIV, no. 3 (November), pp. 11–21.

Review of *The Role of Knowledge in Western Religion* by J. H. Randall, *Theology Today*, Vol. XVI, no. 4 (January), pp. 543–5.

Review of *Revelation Through Reason* by Errol E. Harris, *Theology Today*, Vol. XVI, no. 4 (January), pp. 554–5.

Review of *Religion and Culture* edited by Walter Leibrecht, *Scottish Journal of Theology*, Vol. 13, no. 1 (March), pp. 83–5.

Review of *The Gospel of the Incarnation* by George Hendry, *Scottish Journal of Theology*, Vol. 13, no. 1 (March), pp. 86–9.

Review of *The Freedom of the Will* by Austin Farrer, *Theology Today*, Vol. XVII, no. 2 (July), pp. 268–70.

Review of *The Word Incarnate* by Norman Pittenger, *Princeton Seminary Bulletin*, Vol. 54 (July), pp. 76–7.

Review of *Introduction to Religious Philosophy* by Geddes MacGregor, *Princeton Seminary Bulletin*, Vol. 54 (July), pp. 77–8.

Review of *An Analytical Philosophy of Religion* by Willem F. Zurdeeg, *Scottish Journal of Theology*, Vol. 13, no. 3 (September), pp. 312–15.

1961

Introduction to *Grace and Personality* by John Oman (New York: Association Press), pp. 5–10.

'Meaning and Truth in Theology', in *Religious Experience and Truth* ed. Sidney Hook (New York: New York University Press), pp. 203–10.

'Is Religion an American Heresy?', *Theology Today*, Vol. XVIII, no. 1 (April), pp. 1–9.

'Necessary Being', *Scottish Journal of Theology*, Vol. 14, no. 4 (December), pp. 353–69.

Review of *Ethical Naturalism and the Modern World-View* by E. M. Adams, *Theology Today*, Vol. XVIII, no. 2 (July), pp. 242–4.

Review of *Language, Logic and God* by Frederick Ferré, *Theology Today*, Vol. XVIII, no. 2 (July), pp. 247–50.

Review of *Relativism, Knowledge and Faith* by Gordon D. Kaufman, *Interpretation*, Vol. XV, no. 3 (July), p. 368.

Review of *The Transcendence of God: A Study in Contemporary Philosophical Theology* by Edward Farley, *Religion in Life*, Vol. XXX, no. 4 (Autumn), pp. 630–1.

Review of *Religious Knowledge* by Paul F. Schmidt, *Religious Education*, Vol. LVI, no. 6 (November–December), p. 464.

1962

'Courteous Query for Bennet and Ramsey', *Theology Today*, Vol. XVIII, no. 4 (January), pp. 503–5.

'A Philosopher Criticises Theology', *The London Quarterly*, Vol. 187 (April), pp. 103–10.

'What Does It Mean to Believe in God?', *Princeton Seminary Bulletin*, Vol. LV, no. 3 (April), pp. 53–7.

'Theological Table-Talk', *Theology Today*, Vol. XIX, no. 3 (October), pp. 402–11.

'What Characterises Religious Language? A Comment', *Journal for the Scientific Study of Religion*, Vol. II, no. 1 (Fall), pp. 22–4.

Review of *Philosophy and Religion* by John Wilson, *The Christian Century*, Vol. LXXIX, no. 6 (February 7), p. 166.

Review of *The Teachings of the Mystics; Being Selections from the Great Mystics and Mystical Writings of the World*, ed. Walter Stace, *The Journal of Philosophy*, Vol. LIX, no. 5 (March 1), pp. 135–6.

Review of *The Faith of a Heretic* by Walter Kaufmann, *Theology Today*, Vol. XIX, no. 1 (April), pp. 120–2.

Review of *Prospect for Metaphysics*, ed. Ian Ramsey, *Theology Today*, Vol. XIX, no. 3 (October), pp. 451–53.

1963

Philosophy of Religion (Englewood Cliffs, NJ: Prentice-Hall), pp. xii + 111.

'A Comment on Professor Binkley's Reply', *Journal for the Scientific Study of Religion*, Vol. II, no. 2 (Spring), pp. 231–2.

Review of *Exploring the Logic of Faith* by Frederick Ferré and Kent Bendall, *Princeton Seminary Bulletin*, Vol. LVI, no. 2 (February), pp. 61–2.

Review of *The Logic of Perfection* by Charles Hartshorne, *Theology Today*, Vol. XX, no. 2 (July), pp. 295–8.

1964

Classical and Contemporary Readings in the Philosophy of Religion, ed. John Hick (Englewood Cliffs, NJ: Prentice-Hall), pp. xv + 494.

'Preface' (pp. v–vii), 'Religious Faith as Interpretation' (pp. 490–506), 'The Irenaean Theodicy' (pp. 506–21), 'Appendix I: The Ontological Argument' (pp. 523–6), 'Appendix II: The Cosmological Argument' (pp. 526–8), 'Appendix III: The Design Argument' (pp. 528–30), 'Appendix IV: The Moral Argument' (pp. 530–3), 'Appendix V: The Religious Rejection of Theistic Proofs' (pp. 533–5), 'Appendix VI: Miracles' (pp. 535–7), 'Appendix VII: Religious Experience and Knowledge' (pp. 537–40), 'Appendix VIII: The Problem of Evil' (pp 540–2), 'Appendix IX: Immortality' (pp. 543–6), 'Appendix X: The Rejection of Theism and New Forms of

Religious Naturalism' (pp. 546–9), and 'Appendix XI: Religious Language' (pp. 549–52), in *Classical and Contemporary Readings in the Philosophy of Religion*, ed. John Hick (Englewood Cliffs, NJ: Prentice-Hall). Page numbers taken from the 2nd edition.

Faith and the Philosophers, ed. John Hick (London: Macmillan, and New York: St. Martin's Press), pp. vii + 256.

'Preface' (pp. v–vi), and 'Chairman's Retrospect: Sceptics and Believers' (pp. 235–50), in *Faith and the Philosophers*, ed. John Hick (London: Macmillan, and New York: St. Martin's Press).

The Existence of God, ed. John Hick (New York: Macmillan), pp. xiv + 305.

'Preface' (pp. xiii–xiv), 'Introductory Essay' (pp. 1–20), and 'Religious Statements as Factually Significant' (p. 252–74), in *The Existence of God*, ed. John Hick (New York: Macmillan).

Review of *Reason in Religion* by Nels Ferré, *Religion in Life*, Vol. XXXIII, no. 4 (Autumn), pp. 632–4.

Review of *Meaning and Truth in Religion* by William A. Christian, *Religious Education* Vol. LIX, no. 6 (November–December), pp. 519–20.

1965

'The Purpose of Evil', *The Listener*, 12 August, pp. 231–2.

'Evil and the God of Love', *John O' Gaunt* (Independent Newspaper of the University of Lancaster), No. 5, May.

Review of *Metaphysics and Religious Language* by Frank B. Dilley, *Theology Today*, Vol. XXII, no. 2 (July), pp. 285–6.

1966

Evil and the God of Love (London: Macmillan, and New York: Harper & Row), pp. xvi + 404.

Faith and Knowledge, 2nd edition (Ithaca: Cornell University Press, and London: Macmillan), pp. x + 267.

'Vapor Theologicum – Reply to R. P. Scharleman', *Theology Today*, Vol. XXII, no. 4 (January), pp. 528–9.

Review of *Christian Ethics and Contemporary Philosophy*, ed. Ian Ramsey, *Theology*, Vol. LXIX, no. 555 (September), pp. 417–18.

1967

The Many-Faced Argument: Recent Studies on the Ontological Argument for the Existence of God, ed. John Hick and Arthur C. McGill (New York: Macmillan), pp. vii + 375.

'Introduction' to 'Part II: The Argument in Recent Philosophy' (pp. 209–18), and 'A Critique of the "Second Argument"' (pp. 341–56), in *The Many-Faced Argument: Recent Studies on the Ontological Argument for the Existence of God*, ed. John Hick and Arthur C. McGill (New York: Macmillan).

Articles in *The Encyclopedia of Philosophy*, ed. Paul Edwards (New York: Macmillan and the Free Press).

'Christianity', Vol. 2, pp. 104–9.

'Evil, the problem of', Vol. 3, pp. 136–41.

'Oman, John', Vol. 5, pp. 537–8.

'Ontological Argument for the Existence of God', Vol. 5, pp. 538–42.

'Revelation', Vol. 7, pp. 189–91.

'Tennant, Frederick Robert', Vol. 8, pp. 93–4.

'Christology at the Crossroads', in *Prospect for Theology*, ed. F. G. Healey (London: James Nisbet & Co.), pp. 137–66.

'Faith and Coercion', *Philosophy*, Vol. XLII, no. 161 (July), pp. 272–3.

Review of *God, Pain and Evil* by George Buttrick, *Theology Today*, Vol. XXIII, no. 4 (January), pp. 583–4.

Review of *God and Philosophy* by Antony Flew, *Theology Today*, Vol. XXIV, no. 1 (April), pp. 85–7.

Review of *The Concept of Prayer* by D. Z. Phillips, *Journal of Ecumenical Studies*, Vol. 4, no. 2 (Spring), pp. 320–1.

Review of *Signs and Wonders* by Louis Mondan, *Journal of Ecumenical Studies*, Vol. 4, no. 1 (Winter), pp. 157–8.

Review of *New Studies in Berkeley's Philosophy*, ed. Warren E. Steinkraus, *Journal of Theological Studies*, NS Vol. XVIII, Part 2, no. 570 (October), pp. 535–7.

Review of *Faith and Philosophy* by James Richmond, *Journal of Theological Studies*, NS Vol. XVIII, Part 2, no. 570 (October), pp. 550–2.

Review of *Faith and Speculation* by Austin Farrer, *Theology*, Vol. LXX, no. 570 (December), pp. 557–8.

1968

Christianity at the Centre (London: Macmillan, and New York: Herder & Herder, and London: SCM Press), pp. 124.

'Theology's Central Problem', Inaugural lecture, University of Birmingham, pp. 16.

'On Being Mortal', in *Sermons from Great St Mary's*, ed. H. Montefiore (London: Collins–Fontana), pp. 146–52.

'The Justification of Religious Belief', *Theology*, Vol. LXXI, No. 573 (March), pp. 100–7.

'God, Evil and Mystery', *Religious Studies*, Vol. 3, no. 2 (April), pp. 539–46.

'The Problem of Evil in the First and Last Things – Reply to I. Trethowan', *Journal of Theological Studies*, NS, Vol. XIX, Part 2 (October), pp. 591–602.

Review of *War and the New Morality* by Dewey Hoitenga, *The Reformed Journal*, Vol. XVIII, no. 2 (February), pp. 24–5.

Review of *The Symbolism of Evil* by Paul Ricoeur, *Theology Today*, Vol. XXIV, no. 4 (January), pp. 521–2.

Review of *God-Talk* by John Macquarrie, *Journal of Theological Studies*, NS, Vol. XIX, Part I (April), pp. 395–6.

Review of *A Question of Conscience* by Charles Davis, *Outlook* (Journal of the Presbyterian Church of England), May, p. 18.

Review of *Theological Ethics*, Vol. I, by Helmut Thielicke, *The Expository Times*, Vol. LXXX, no. 1 (October), p. 23.

Review of *Man's Concern With Death* by Arnold Toynbee (and others), *Birmingham Post*, 30 November.

1969

'Religious Faith as Experiencing-As', in *Talk of God*, ed. G. N. A. Vesey (London: Macmillan, and New York: St. Martin's Press), pp. 20–35.

'Theology's Central Problem' (abbreviated version of inaugural lecture), *The Expository Times*, Vol. LXXX, no. 8 (May), pp. 228–32.

'A Plea for Systematic Theology', *Regina* (the magazine of the Queen's College, Birmingham), no. 3, pp. 172–3.

Review of *Origins of Pragmatism* by A. J. Ayer, *The Expository Times*, Vol. LXXX, no. 6 (March), pp. 172–3.

Review of *Adam* by Adrian Cunningham, *The Church Quarterly*, Vol. 1, no. 4 (April), p. 344.

Review of *Evil and the Concept of God* by E. H. Madden and P. H. Hare, *Philosophy*, Vol. XLIV, no. 168 (April), pp. 160–1.

Review of *Theological Science* by T. F. Torrance, *The Expository Times* Vol. LXXXI, no. 2 (November), pp. 57–8.

Review of *Death and Immortality* by Josef Peiper, *Birmingham Post*, 15 November.

1970

Classical and Contemporary Readings in the Philosophy of Religion, 2nd edition, ed. John Hick (Englewood Cliffs, NJ: Prentice-Hall), pp. vii + 558.

'Towards a Christian Theology of Death', *Dying, Death and Disposal* ed. Gilbert Cope (London: SPCK), pp. 8–25.

'A New Form of Theistic Argument', in *Proceedings of the XIVth International Congress of Philosophy*, Vol. V, Vienna, pp. 336–41.

'The Reconstruction of Christian Belief for Today and Tomorrow: 1', *Theology*, Vol. LXXIII, no. 602 (August), pp. 339–45.

'The Reconstruction of Christian Belief for Today and Tomorrow: II', *Theology*, Vol. LXXIII, no. 603 (September), pp. 399–405.

'Freedom and the Irenaean Theodicy Again (Reply to K. Ward)', *The Journal of Theological Studies*, Vol. XXI, Part 2 (October), pp. 419–22.

Review of *Experience and God* by John E. Smith, *Philosophy*, Vol. XLV, no. 171 (January), p. 74.

Review of *The Moment of Truth* by Ladislaus Boros, *Scottish Journal of Theological Studies*, Vol. 23, no. 1 (February), pp. 107–8.

Review of *The Foundations of Belief* by Leslie Dewart, *Theology Today*, Vol. XXVII, no. 1 (April), pp. 111–13.

Review of *Do Religious Claims Make Sense?* by S. C. Brown, *Philosophical Books*, Vol. XI, no. 2 (May), pp. 3–4.

Review of *The Five Ways* by Anthony Kenny, *Mind*, Vol. LXXIX, no. 315 (July), pp. 467–9.

Review of *The Elusive Mind* by H. D. Lewis, *The Expository Times*, Vol. LXXXI, No. 11 (August), p. 335.

Review of *The Mind/Brain Identity Theory*, edited by C. B. Borsch, *The Expository Times*, Vol. LXXXII, no. 2 (November), p. 56.

Review of *The Theology of Death* by Karl Rahner, *The Journal of Religious Studies* (Punjabi University, Patiala), Vol. II, no. 1 (Autumn), pp. 161–3.

1971

Arguments for the Existence of God (London: Macmillan, and New York: Herder and Herder), pp. xiii + 148.

'Some Recapitulation Theories of Immortality', *The Visvabharati Journal of Philosophy*, Vol. VII, no. 2 (February), pp. 60–7.

'Faith, Evidence, Coercion Again', *Australasian Journal of Philosophy*, Vol. 49, no. 1 (May), pp. 78–81.

'Reincarnation: A Critical Examination of One Form of Reincarnation Theory', *The Journal of Religious Studies* (Punjabi University), Vol. III, no. 1 (Spring), pp. 56–9.

'Religious Language – Cognitive or Non-cognitive?', *Anviksiki* (Banaras Hindu University), Vol. III, nos. 3 & 4 (July and October), pp. 131–46.

'The Idea of Rebirth – a Western Approach', *Indian Philosophical Annual* (University of Madras), 1970, pp. 89–101.

Review of *Theism and Empiricism* by A. Boyce Gibson, *Philosophy*, Vol. XLVI, no. 178 (October), p. 365.

Review of *Grace and Common Life* by David Harned, *The Journal of Religious Studies*, (October), pp. 186–8.

1972

Biology and the Soul, Eddington Memorial Lecture, (Cambridge: Cambridge University Press), pp. 29.

Foreword to *Reflective Faith* by Austin Farrer (London: SPCK), pp. xiii–xv.

'Mr Clarke's Resurrection Also', *Sophia*, Vol. XI, no. 3 (October), pp. 1–3.

'The Christian View of Other Faiths', *The Expository Times*, Vol. LXXXIV, no. 2 (November), pp. 36–9.

Comment on 'Hick, Necessary Being, and the Cosmological Argument' by D. R. Duff-Forbes, *Canadian Journal of Philosophy*, Vol. 1, no. 4 (June), pp. 485–7.

Review of *Clement of Alexandria's Treatment of the Problem of Evil* by W. E. G. Floyd, *Religious Studies*, Vol. VIII, no. 2 (June), pp. 175–6.

Review of *Meaning and Method in Philosophy and Religion* by Anders Nygren, translated by P. S. Watson, *The Times Literary Supplement*, 24 November, p. 1434.

1973

God and the Universe of Faiths (London: Macmillan, and New York: St. Martin's Press), pp. xii + 201.

Philosophy of Religion, 2nd edition (Englewood Cliffs, N. J.: Prentice–Hall), pp. ix + 133.

'Christianity and Reincarnation', in *Sri Aurobindo: A Garland of Tributes*, edited by Arabinda Basu (Pondicherry: Sri Aurobindo Research Academy), pp. 65–9.

'Christians and Colour', *New Initiative Papers*, No. 1 (Birmingham Council of Christian Churches).

'Resurrection Worlds and Bodies', *Mind*, Vol. LXXXII, no. 327 (July), pp. 409–12.

'Coherence and the God of Love Again', *Journal of Theological Studies*, Vol. XXIV, Part 2 (October), pp. 522–8.

Review of *Science and Sentiment in America* by Morton White, *Theology Today*, Vol. 30, no. 1 (April), pp. 88–92.

Review of *Essays in the Philosophy of Religion* by H. H. Price, *Religious Studies*, Vol. 9, no. 2 (June), pp. 238–41.

Review of *The Edges of Language* by Paul van Buren, *Journal of Theological Studies*, Vol. XXIV, Part 2 (October), pp. 633–5.

Review of *Value and Reality: The Philosophical Case for Theism* by A. C. Ewing, *The Times Literary Supplement*, 28 December, p. 1594.

1974

Truth and Dialogue in World Religions: Conflicting Truth-Claims, ed. John Hick, (London: Sheldon Press, and Philadelphia: The Westminster Press), pp. vii + 164.

'Editor's Preface' (p. vii), and 'The Outcome: Dialogue into Truth' (pp. 140–55), in *Truth and Dialogue in World Religions: Conflicting Truth-Claims*, ed. John Hick (London: Sheldon Press, and Philadelphia: The Westminster Press).

Preface to the Collins–Fontana edition of *Faith and Knowledge*.

'Christ's Uniqueness', *Reform*, October, pp. 18–19.

1975

'John Hick Replies', *Reform*, January, p. 5.

'The Lordship of Christ', *Carrs Lane Journal*, April, pp. 8–17.

'On Multi-Religious Birmingham', *One World*, no. 6 (June), pp. 7–9.

'Whatever Path Men Choose is Mine', *The Modern Churchman*, Vol. XVIII, nos. 1 & 2 (Winter), pp. 8–17.

'The Christian Church and People of Other Religions', *The Times*, 4 October.

'Changing Views of the Uniqueness of Christ', *The Times*, 11 October.
'Seeing the Pattern in a Puzzle Picture', *The Times Educational Supplement*, 12 December, p. 30.
'Philosophy, Religions, and Human Unity', in *Philosophy – Theory and Practice* (University of Madras), pp. 462–71, and 'Comments', pp. 19–21, 162–3, and 344–6.
'Christians and Other Faiths', *New Initiative Papers*, no. 3 (Birmingham Council of Christian Churches).
Review of *Positivism and Christianity* by Kenneth Klein, *Philosophical Books*, Vol. XVI, no. 3 (October), pp. 27–9.
Review of *Evil, Karma, and Reincarnation* by G. C. Nayak, *Religion*, Vol. 5 (Autumn), pp. 175–6.
Review of *Why Does Evil Exist?* by Colm Connellan, *Religious Studies*, Vol. XI, no. 4 (December), p. 494–5.

1976

Death and Eternal Life, (London: Collins, and New York: Harper & Row), pp. 495.
'Is There a God?', *Radio Times*, 17–23 April, p. 17
'Education and the Law in Birmingham – A Comment', *Learning for Living*, Summer, pp. 135–6.
Review of *The Forgotten Dream* by Peter Baelz, *Reconciliation Quarterly*, June, pp. 53–4.
Review of *The Resurrection of Man* by Michael Perry, *The Christian Parapyschologist*, Vol. I, No. 4 (June), p. 59.
Review of *The Transcendental Unity of Religions* by Frithjof Schuon, *The Ecumenical Review*, Vol. XXVIII, no. 3 (July), pp. 369–70.
Review of *Reason and Belief* by Brand Blanshard, *The Journal of Religion*, Vol. LVI, no. 4 (October), pp. 400–3.

1977

Evil and the God of Love, 2nd edition (London: Macmillan, and New York: Harper & Row), pp. xiv + 359.
The Centre of Christianity, revised edition of *Christianity at the Centre* (London: SCM Press, and San Francisco: Harper & Row), pp. 128.
The Myth of God Incarnate, ed. John Hick (London: SCM Press, and Philadelphia: The Westminster Press), pp. 211.
'Preface' (pp. ix–xi), and 'Jesus and the World Religions' (pp.

167–85), in *The Myth of God Incarnate*, ed. by John Hick (London: SCM Press, and Philadelphia: The Westminster Press).

Preface to the Collins–Fontana edition of *God and the Universe of Faiths*.

'Mystical Experience as Cognition', in *Mystics and Scholars*, ed. Harold Coward and Terence Penelhum (Waterloo: Wilfred Laurier University Press), pp. 41–56, and p. 61.

'Remarks on the Problem of Evil', in *Reason and Religion*, ed. Stuart C. Brown (Ithaca: Cornell University Press), pp. 122–8.

'Incarnation' (Reply to Brian Hebblethwaite), *Theology*, Vol. LXXX, May, pp. 204–6.

'Eschatological Verification Reconsidered', in *Religious Studies*, Vol. XIII, no. 2 (June), pp. 189–202.

'Christian Theology and Inter-Religious Dialogue', *World Faiths*, No. 103 (Autumn), pp. 2–19.

'The New Nazism of the National Front and National Party' (pamphlet) (Birmingham: All Faiths for One Race), pp. 11.

Review of *Evil, Suffering and Religion* by Brian Hebblethwaite, *Learning for Living*, Summer pp. 187–8.

Review of *The Truth of God Incarnate*, ed. Michael Green, *Reform*, November.

Review of *Believe it or Not* by Garth Moore, *Faith and Unity*, Vol. XXI, no. 3, pp. 60–1.

1978

Foreword to *The Meaning and End of Religion* by W. Cantwell Smith (New York: Harper & Row, and London: SPCK), pp. ix–xviii.

'Christian Theology and Interfaith Dialogue', in *The Frontiers of Human Knowledge*, ed. T. T. Segerstedt (Stockholm: Almquist & Wicksell), pp. 1–14.

'The Challenge to the Churches', in *The Chosen Race: Christians and the Rise of the New Fascism* (London: SCM Press), pp. 22–4.

'Present and Future Life' (The Ingersoll Lecture), *Harvard Theological Review*, Vol. 71, nos. 1 & 2 (January–April), pp. 1–15.

'Living in a Multi-Cultural Society: Practical Reflections of a Theologian', *Expository Times*, Vol. LXXXIX, no. 4, pp. 100–4.

'Racism – The Church's Responsibility', *Regina*, pp. 8–9.

'Not Troubled by More Orthodox', *Religion and Freedom*, July, p. 16.

'The Bible and Race', *All Faiths for One Race*.

Chairman's Report, *AFFOR News*, October.

'Christ in a Universe of Faiths', *The Seeker*, Autumn, pp. 14–23.
Review of *God, Freedom and Evil* by Alvin Plantinga, *Religious Studies*, Vol. 14, no. 3, pp. 407–9.

1979

Foreword to *An Introduction to Buddhist Psychology* by Padmasiri de Silva (London: Macmillan, and New York: Barnes & Noble), pp. ix–x.
Foreword to *The Problem of the Self in Buddhism and Christianity* by Lynn de Silva (London: Macmillan, and New York: Barnes & Noble), pp. ix–x.
'Christianity and Race in Britain Today' (pamphlet) (Birmingham: All Faiths for One Race), pp. 15.
'Is There a Doctrine of the Incarnation?' (pp. 47–50), 'Evil and Incarnation' (pp. 77–84), and 'A Response to Hebblethwaite' (pp. 192–4), in *Incarnation and Myth: The Debate Continued*, ed. Michael Goulder (London: SCM Press).
'Pilgrimage in Theology', *Epworth Review*, Vol. VI, no. 2 (May), pp. 73–8.
'Black and White as Well as Green and Pleasant', *Reform*, July/August.
New Year Messages, No. 9, in *Reconciliation Quarterly*, December, pp. 23–4.
Review of *Religious Encounters with Death: Insights from the History and Anthropology of Religions*, edited by Frank Reynolds and Earle Waugh, *The Journal of Religion*, Vol. LIX, no. 4 (October), pp. 495–6.

1980

God Has Many Names: Britain's New Religious Pluralism (London: Macmillan), pp. viii + 108.
Christianity and Other Religions: Selected Readings, eds John Hick and Brian Hebblethwaite (Glasgow: William Collins Sons, and Philadelphia: Fortress Press), pp. 253.
'Life After Death', *Epworth Review*, Vol. VII, no. 1 (January), pp. 58–63.
'Towards a Philosophy of Religious Pluralism', *Neue Zeitschrift fur systematische Theologie und Religionsphilosophie*, Vol. XXII, Part 2, pp. 131–49.

'Apartheid Observed' (pamphlet) (Birmingham: All Faiths for One Race), pp. 16.

1981

'An Irenaean Theodicy' (pp. 39–52), 'Response' (pp. 63–8), and 'Critiques' (pp. 29–30, 86–7, 122–3, and 151–2) in *Encountering Evil*, ed. Stephen Davis (Atlanta: John Knox Press).

'Sketch for A Global Epistemology of Religion', in *Vardag och Evighet* (Karlshamm: Doxa), pp. 101–7.

'Pluralism and the Reality of the Transcendent', *The Christian Century*, Vol. XCVIII, no. 2 (21 January), pp. 45–8.

'John Hick on Religion, Philosophy and Related Issues', *Religion in Southern Africa*, Vol. II, no. 1 (January), pp. 3–9.

'Tension and Fear: John Hick Reports from South Africa', *AFFOR Newsletter*, Spring, p. 1.

'Christology in an Age of Religious Pluralism', *Journal of Theology for South Africa*, no. 35 (June), pp. 4–9.

'Response to James Moulder', *Journal of Theology for South Africa*, no. 35 (June), pp. 24–6.

'Jewish–Christian–Muslim Conference', *University of Birmingham Bulletin*, no. 411 (November).

Review of *The Expansion of God* by Leslie Howard, *Reform*, April, p. 26.

1982

God Has Many Names (Philadelphia: Westminster Press), pp. 140.

Foreword to *Bhagat Kabir: His Life and Teaching* by Kushdeva Singh (Patiala: Guru Nanak Mission), pp. 44.

'Is God Personal?', in *God: The Contemporary Discussion*, eds Frederick Sontag and M. Darrol Bryant (New York: The Rose of Sharon Press), pp. 169–79.

'A Recent Development within Christian Monotheism', in *The Concept of Monotheism in Islam and Christianity* ed. Hans Kochler (Vienna: Wilhelm Braunmuller), pp. 60–70.

1983

Philosophy of Religion, Third edition (Englewood Cliffs, NJ: Prentice-Hall, Inc.) pp. xii + 148.

The Second Christianity (revised edition of *The Centre of Christianity*), (London: SCM Press), pp. 140.

Why Believe in God? (with Michael Goulder) (London: SCM Press), pp. vii + 117.

Foreword to *Mahatma Gandhi: The Significance of His Teachings Today* by Kushdeva Singh (Patiala: Rotary Club).

Foreword to *The Uniqueness of Guru Granth Sahib* by Khushdeva Singh (Patiala: Guru Nanak Foundation Committee).

Preface to 'Blind Leaders for the Blind: Theological Training in Today's Plural Society', AFFOR pamphlet by Kenneth Cracknell, David Jennings, and Christine Trethowan.

'Only One Way to God?', letter in *Theology*, Vol. LXXXVI, no. 710 (March), pp. 128–9.

'The Theology of Pluralism', *Theology*, Vol. LXXXVI, no. 713 (September), pp. 335–40.

Articles in *The Westminster Dictionary of Christian Theology*, eds Alan Richardson and John Bowden (Philadelphia: Westminster Press, and London: SCM Press): 'Arguments for the Existence of God', pp. 37–40; 'Life after Death', pp. 331–4; 'Reincarnation', p. 491; 'Theocentricity', pp. 563–4.

1984

Foreword to *Gandhi's Religious Thought* by Margaret Chatterjee (London: Macmillan, and Notre Dame: University of Notre Dame Press).

'Seeing-As and Religious Experience', in *Proceedings of the 8th International Wittgenstein Symposium, 15th to 21st August, 1983*, Part 2 (Wien: Holder-Pichler-Tempsky), pp. 46–52.

'A Recent Development within Christian Monotheism', in *Christians, Muslims and Jews*, eds David Kerr and Dan Cohn-Sherbok (Birmingham: Centre for the Study of Islam and of Christian–Muslim Relations), pp. 1–20.

'Jesus and Mohammed', ibid., pp. 222–8.

'Religious Pluralism and Absolute Claims', in *Religious Pluralism*, ed. Leroy S. Rouner (Notre Dame: University of Notre Dame Press), pp. 193–213.

'The Foundation of Christianity: Jesus or the Apostolic Message?', a review article of *The Point of Christology* by Schubert Ogden, *The Journal of Religion*, Vol. 64, no. 3 (July), pp. 363–9.

'The Philosophy of World Religions', *Scottish Journal of Theology*, Vol. 37, pp. 229–36.

Review of *Immortality or Extinction?* by Paul Badham and Linda Badham, *The Journal of Religion*, Vol. 64, no. 3 (July), p. 410.

Review of *A History of the Future: A Study of the Four Major Eschatologies* by Christopher C. Hong, *Journal of Ecumenical Studies*, Vol. 21, no. 2 (Spring), p. 369.

'A Note on Pannenberg's Eschatology', *Harvard Theological Review*, Vol. 78, no. 4, pp. 421–3.

1985

The Experience of Religious Diversity, eds John Hick and Hasan Askari (Hants, England and Brookfield, Vermont: Gower Publishing Company), pp. vi + 236.

'Religious Diversity as Challenge and Promise' in *The Experience of Religious Diversity*, pp. 3–24.

Problems of Religious Pluralism (London: Macmillan, and New York: St. Martin's Press), pp. x + 148.

Preface in reissue of *Evil and the God of Love* (London: Macmillan), pp. xiii–xiv.

Preface in reissue of *Death and Eternal Life* (London: Macmillan), pp. 9–10.

1986

Review of *God and Skepticism: A Study in Skepticism and Fideism*, by Terence Penelhum, *Canadian Philosophical Review*, Vol. vi, no. 4 (April), pp. 171–2.

Foreword to *Into Every Life a Little Zen Must Fall*, by Alan Keightley (London: Wisdom Publications), pp. 9–10.

Review of Alvin Plantinga and Nicholas Wolterstorff (eds), *Faith and Rationality* (Notre Dame University Press, 1983), *The Journal of Religion*, Vol. 66, no. 1, January 1986, pp. 84–5.

'A Remonstrance in Concluding', *Jesus in History and Myth*, eds R. Joseph Hoffman and Gerald A. Larue (Buffalo, New York: Prometheus Books), pp. 211–17.

1987

'A Possible Conception of Life after Death', in *Proceedings of the*

Symposium on Consciousness and Survival, ed. John S. Spong (Sausalito, Calif.: the Institute of Noetic Sciences), pp. 91–104.

The Myth of Christian Uniqueness, eds John Hick and Paul Knitter (New York: Orbis, and London: SCM Press), pp. xii + 227.

'The Non-Absoluteness of Christianity', in *The Myth of Christian Uniqueness*, eds. John Hick and Paul F. Knitter, pp. 16–36.

'Theology and Mind–Brain Identity', *The Oxford Companion to the Mind*, edited by Richard L. Gregory (Oxford: Oxford University Press), pp. 770–2.

'Religious Pluralism', *Encyclopedia of Religion* (New York: Macmillan, and London: Collier Macmillan), Vol. 12, pp. 331–3.

'Keynote Speech', *The Second Asian–Pacific Cultural Symposium of the Cultural and Social Centre for Asian and Pacific Region*, Seoul, Korea and Tenri Yamato Cultural Congress, Tenri, Nara, Japan; 23–6 May, pp. 16–21.

1988

'An Inspiration Christology for a Religiously Plural World', in *Encountering Jesus*, ed. Stephen T. Davis (Atlanta: John Knox Press, 1987), pp. 5–22, 'Hick's Response to Critiques [by Stephen T. Davis, James M. Robinson, John B. Cobb, Jr, Rebecca D. Pentz]', pp. 32–8.

'Religious Pluralism and Salvation' and 'A Concluding Comment', *Faith and Philosophy*, Vol 5, no. 4 (October), pp. 365–77 and 449–55.

Critique of 'Jesus Christ: Savior or Guru?', by Stephen T. Davis in *Encountering Jesus*, ed. Stephen T. Davis, pp. 66–9.

Critique of 'Can Jesus Save Women?' by Rebecca D. Pentz in *Encountering Jesus*, ed. Stephen T. Davis, pp. 93–6.

Critique of 'Very Goddess and Very Man: Jesus' Better Self', by James M. Robinson in *Encountering Jesus*, ed. Stephen T. Davis, pp. 127–9.

Critique of 'Christ Beyond Creative Transformation' by John Cobb, in *Encountering Jesus*, ed. Stephen T. Davis, pp. 158–61.

1989

Three Faiths – One God, eds John Hick and Edmund Meltzer (London: Macmillan, and New York: SUNY Press), pp. xiv + 240.

'Trinity and Incarnation in the Light of Religious Pluralism', in *Three Faiths – One God*, pp. 197–210.

An Interpretation of Religion (London: Macmillan, and New York: Yale University Press), pp. xv + 412.

'The Lord's Prayer', *Carrs Lane Church Journal* (Birmingham), February, pp. 6–7.

'Comment on "Jesus'" Unsurpassable Uniqueness', *Horizons,* Vol. 16 no. 1 (Spring), pp. 121–4.

'Letter to the Editor', *Theology*, Vol. XCII, no. 748 (July), p. 297.

'Christian Philosophy', *The New Encyclopedia Britannica*, 15th edn, 1989 revision, Vol. 16, pp. 323–30.

'The Christian Church and non-Christian Religions: Modern Views', *The New Encyclopedia Britannica*, 15th edn, 1989 revision, Vol. 16, p. 363.

'The Proper Limits of Christian Arrogance', *The Independent.*

'The Buddha's "Undetermined Questions" ' and 'The Conflicting Truth Claims of Different Religions' in *Hermeneutics, Religious Pluralism and Truth* (Winston-Salem: Wake Forest University), pp. 1–17, and 55–61.

'Dunelm Disease', Letter to the Editor, *Clarity*, Vol. 21, no. 5, pp. 99–101.

'The Real and Its Personae and Impersonae' (pp. 143–58), 'Response' (pp. 171–6), 'Comment on Stephen Davis' (pp. 32–3), 'Comment on Francis Cook' (pp. 136–7), in *Concepts of the Ultimate*, ed. Linda Tessier (London: Macmillan and New York: St. Martin's Press).

'A Possible Conception of Life After Death' (pp. 183–96), 'Response to Nielsen' (pp. 31–5), 'Response to Cook' (pp. 177–9), in *Death and Afterlife*, ed. Stephen T. Davis (London: Macmillan and New York: St. Martin's Press).

'The Logic of God Incarnate', *Religious Studies*, Vol. 25, no. 4, pp. 409–23.

'Response' in David L. Edwards, *Tradition and Truth* (London: Hodder & Stoughton), pp. 306–10.

Gandhi's Significance for Today, edited with Lamont Hempel (London: Macmillan).

1990

Classical and Contemporary Readings in the Philosophy of Religion, Third edn. Edited. (Englewood Cliffs: Prentice Hall), pp. xv + 540.

Philosophy of Religion, Fourth edn (Englewood Cliffs: Prentice Hall), pp. ix + 148.

'Straightening the Record', *Modern Theology*, Vol. 6, no. 2, pp. 187–95.
'For Future Religious Leaders who Guide our Planet', translated by
Osamu Ichikawa into Japanese, *Religion and Parapsychology*, no. 37
(January, 1990), pp. 15–50.
'A Response To Gerard Loughlin', *Modern Theology*, Vol. 7, no. 1,
pp. 57–66.

1991

'Response' in C. Robert Mesle, *John Hick's Theodicy: A Process Human-
ist Critique* (London: Macmillan, and New York: St. Martin's Press),
pp. 115–34.
'Responses' in Harold Hewitt (ed.), *Problems in the Philosophy of
Religion: Critical Studies of the Work of John Hick* (London: Macmillan,
and New York: St. Martin's Press), pp. 24–7, 51–3, 82–5, 104–7,
134–7, 160–1, 176–7, 206–9, 242–3.
'Religion as "skilful means": A Hint From Buddhism', *International
Journal for Philosophy of Religion*, Vol. 30, pp. 141–58.
Review of Peter Byrne, *Natural Religion and the Nature of Religion*,
Religious Studies, Vol. 27, pp. 425–6.
Review of Hendrik Vroom, *Religions and the Truth*, *Religious Studies*,
Vol. 28, pp. 118–20.

Name and Title Index

Geertz, Clifford, 147
Gerrish, B. A., 135, 137
Gifford Lectures. See: An
  Interpretation of Religion
God and the Reasonableness of Non-
  belief, 175n.10
God and the Universe of Faiths,
  162n.2
God Incarnate: Story and Belief,
  142n.14
God in History: Shapes of Freedom,
  163n.11
Grace and Reason, A Study in the
  Theology of Luther, 135

Habermas, J., 163n.11
Hägglund, Bengt, 141n.1
Hartshorne, Charles, 106, 110, 201
Hazelton, Hugh, 86
Hedenius, Ingemar, 141n.1
Hegel, Georg Wilhelm Friedrich,
  45n.13
Heidegger, Martin, 45n.13
Hick, John H., 3–5, 9, 11, 12, 13, 14,
  15, 16, 18–23, 24–30, 62, 66,
  67–8, 70, 86, 87, 92, 93, 94, 95,
  96, 97, 99–110, 124–34, 135, 138,
  139, 143, 162n.2, 165, 166, 168,
  172, 173, 175n.5, 176, 177, 180,
  182, 183, 184, 185, 187, 190,
  196, 197, 198, 210, 213, 214,
  215, 216, 217, 218, 219, 220,
  221, 223, 227, 233, 242n.1
Hick, Hazel, 3
Hindu Perspective on the Philosophy
  of Religion, A, 12
Hiromasa, Mase, 242n.1
Hitler, Adolf, 54, 99
Hodgson, P., 163n.11
Holkot, Robert, 137
Holmer, Paul, 24
Howe, Daniel, 71n.1
Hume, David, 174, 175n.4
Hussein, Saddam, 74, 78, 84
Huxley, Aldous, 180

Ibsen, Henrick, 200, 208
Idel, Moshe, 199n.6

Image of the Non-Jew in Judaism, The,
  199n.9
Irenaeus, 19
Isaiah, 172

James, William, 143
Jaspers, Karl, 67
Jeremiah, 194
Jesus/Christ, 4, 15, 35, 36, 37, 40,
  56, 57, 61n.20, 88, 90, 91, 92, 95,
  97, 119, 120, 127, 129, 137, 138,
  139, 140, 141, 150, 177, 191,
  192, 198, 218, 221, 223, 225,
  226, 227, 228, 229, 230, 231,
  232, 233, 236, 237, 238, 239, 242
Jewish Gnosticism, Merkabah
  Mysticism and Talmudic
  Tradition, 199n.6
Josephus, 89
Judaism and World Religions, 199n.1
Judas, 57, 206

Kant, Immanuel, 22, 28, 29, 124,
  125, 126, 127, 128, 130, 132,
  133, 174, 176, 177, 180, 182,
  184, 209n.11, 212, 213, 214, 215,
  216, 220
Karamazov, Ivan, 47, 205, 207
Kaufman, Gordon D., 200, 201, 202
Keiji, Nishitani. See Nishitani
Kenzo, Tagawa, 242n.3
Khomeini (Ayatollah), 73, 74
Kirk, Andrew, 198, 199n.13
Knitter, Paul, 225
Kraemer, Hendrik, 222, 223, 230
Küng, Hans, 38, 39

L'Homme Révolté, 207
Langan, John, 71n.1
Leibniz, Gottfried Wilhelm, Baron
  von, 46, 48, 50
Lewis, H. D., 169
Lipner, Julius, 223, 226, 227, 230,
  231, 232
Logic of Religion, The, 142n.15
Lohse, Berhand, 138, 141n.1
Luke, 238
Luther, Martin, 135–41